# Dictatorship and
Armed Struggle in Brazil

# Dictatorship and Armed Struggle in Brazil

## João Quartim

TRANSLATED BY DAVID FERNBACH

Monthly Review Press
New York and London

Copyright © 1971 by New Left Books
All Rights Reserved

Library of Congress Catalog Card Number: 71–178711
First Printing

Manufactured in the United States of America

To Norberto Nehring
who died for the liberation of the Brazilian people
'Ta seule oraison camarade
vengeance, vengeance pour toi'

For Silvia, Cecilia and Laércio

Publisher's note 9
Map and Demographic note 10–11
Chronology 13
Historical Introduction 1930–64: The Legacy of Vargas 17

1. The Ruling Class and its Transformations 57
    Towards 'Guided Democracy' 57
    Costa e Silva: Castelo Branco's Legacy
    and Permanent Coup d'état 64
    From the Fifth Institutional Act
    to the Garrastazu Dictatorship 79
    The Balance of Economic Power within the Ruling Class
    and the Nature of the Present Regime 85

2. The Exploited Classes under the Dictatorship 114
    The Working Class and its Organizations 114
    Workers' Struggles in 1968 117
    The Countryside and the Peasantry 127
    Peasant Struggles 135
    Students: A Leading Role in the New Vanguard 139
    The Marginal Sector 150

3. The Passage to Revolutionary War   155
    The Crisis of the Left
    and Reorganization for Armed Action   155
    The First Armed Actions   162
    Rural Guerrilla Warfare   167
    Urban Guerrilla Warfare   180
    Terrorism and Armed Propaganda   191

4. The Perspectives for Revolutionary Struggle   201
    The First Two Years of Urban Partisan Warfare   201
    The Most Recent Developments   213
    Regroupment around Armed Struggle:
    The Question of a National Organization   217
    The Minimum Programme   225
    Perspectives for the Revolution   236

Appendix: Parties and Organizations   239

Index   245

# Publisher's note

The kidnapping of the United States Ambassador, Burke Elbrick, from Rio de Janeiro in September 1969 drew the attention of the world to Brazil's urban guerrilla fighters. Since then many similar actions have been given prominence in the media. This book explains the military tactics and political strategy on which these actions were based. It is a balance sheet of the first three years of armed struggle in Brazil. To draw up such an account, however, it was necessary not only to explain the different class forces at work in Brazil and of the different tendencies within the Left, but also to give a political analysis of the military government and the new state which it has created. In order for this to be accessible to those unfamiliar with the recent history of Brazil, a historical introduction, 'The Legacy of Vargas', was written in co-operation with NLB to accompany the main text. The book was written originally in French for NLB and translated by David Fernbach.

Brazil: *Areas* and States

*North East*
1. Maranhão
2. Piauí
3. Ceará
4. Rio Grande do Norte
5. Paraíba
6. Pernambuco
7. Alagoas
8. Sergipe
9. Bahia

*South East*
10. Minas Gerais
11. Espírito Santo
12. Rio de Janeiro
13. Guanabara
14. São Paulo

*South*
15. Paraná
16. Santa Catarina
17. Rio Grande do Sul

*Central West*
18. Mato Grosso
19. Goiás

*North*
20. Territory of Rondônia
21. Acre
22. Amazonas
23. Territory of Roraima
24. Pará
25. Territory of Amapá

# Demographic note

The distribution of Brazil's estimated population of one hundred million into regions is as follows: North East 32%; North 3%; Central West 4%; South East 44%; South 17%.

More than 90% of the population is concentrated on the eastern seaboard. The population density is highest in the industrialized South East and South. The infant mortality rate is 17% but in certain regions in the North East it reaches as much as 30%. The rate of growth of population during the early sixties was slightly more than 3% per annum. The largest cities (1968 figures) are São Paulo (5·6 million), Rio de Janeiro (4·2 million), Belo Horizonte (1·1 million), Recife (1·1 million), Pôrto Alegre (0·9 million) and Salvador (0·9 million).

(Figures based on the 1960 census and data for 1968 taken from the *Anuário Estatístico do Brasil*, Rio de Janeiro, 1969.)

# Chronology

1870: Republican party formed. 1889: Republicans forced Emperor Pedro II's resignation. Republic of Brazil proclaimed.

1922: July: Tenente revolts began. 1924: The 'Prestes Column' began its guerrilla campaign in the interior. 1926: Washington Luiz elected President. 1927: Strikes outlawed. 1928: Overproduction of coffee made US stop buying. 1929: Price of coffee dropped by a fourth.

1930: May–October: Government presidential candidate Julio Prestes narrowly defeated Vargas who headed Liberal Alliance. Large sections of the army refused to accept result; the southern states revolted. Vargas marched on Rio de Janeiro and assumed the Presidency. 1932: July: Vargas crushed 'Constitutionalist' rebellion in São Paulo led by Democratic Party (PDP)\* and Paulist Republican Party (PRP). 1933: October: Vargas's supporters won majority in congressional elections. 1934: July: New Constitution drafted centralizing power and making Presidential election indirect. Vargas elected to four year term. 1935: May: Brazilian Communist Party (PCB) organized mass rallies against regime. Its leader Luís Carlos Prestes called for 'all power to the ANL' (Alliance for National Liberation) and it was disbanded. October: PCB militants staged barracks revolt in Recife-and Natal but were crushed. The Left mercilessly persecuted. PCB outlawed. 1936: May: Prestes caught and jailed. 1937: November: On pretext of restoring order Vargas solved

\* For check list of acronyms see Appendix.

problem of succession by overthrowing 1934 Constitution with connivance of higher military. Took decree powers and named himself President for six years. Established 'Estado Nôvo'. Political parties banned. **1938: May:** Vargas put down the abortive fascist coup mounted by *Integralista* leader Plinio Salgado.

**1942:** Brazil broke off relations with Germany and established joint defence board with USA. **1943–45:** Vargas worked to preempt Left with welfare legislation and formation of Labour Party (PTB). **1945:** Vargas prepared for reintroduction of party system and set date for election. **May:** Protests mounted against Vargas's candidacy. In attempt to win Left, Vargas legalized PCB which in return organized huge pro-Vargas demonstrations. **October:** Vargas deposed in military coup, led by General Góes Monteiro. **December:** General Dutra, candidate of the PSD-PTB, defeated Gomes of the National Democratic Union (UDN). PCB won 9% of congressional vote: 15 seats. **1946: September:** New constitution introduced on democratic lines. President to be elected every five years. Suffrage still restricted to literates. **1947: May:** PCB outlawed and relations with USSR broken off.

**1950: October:** Vargas re-elected president. **1954: February:** Vargas sacked Goulart, his minister of Labour, but refused to retrench to check growing inflation. **August:** Military served Vargas with ultimatum. Vargas shot himself, provoking huge pro-Vargas riots. Café Filho sworn in as President. **1955: October:** Kubitschek won Presidency, Goulart Vice-Presidency. Rightist alliance of generals and UDN planned coup to prevent them taking office. **1956: January:** General Lott intervened to ensure their inauguration. **1956–60:** Kubitschek's Presidency marked by rapid industrial growth, massive foreign aid and investment. Brasilia project conceived and executed. SUDENE (North East Development Scheme) established. **1959: June:** Kubitschek broke off negotiations with IMF while negotiating £300m. loan. **August:** Nationalist economics ministers appointed by Kubitschek.

**1960: October:** Jãnio Quadros, Governor of São Paulo won Presidency on independent anti-corruption ticket with support from UDN defeating PTB-PSD General Lott. Goulart won Vice-

Presidency. 1961: June: Quadros adopted stabilizing policy to halt inflation. August: Quadros resigned in face of pressure from Right. After attempted 'preventive' coup by Right, Goulart succeeded him in modified presidential system. Tancredo Neves appointed Prime Minister. 1962: May: Goulart proposed agrarian reform, nationalization measures. June: Tancredo Neves resigned. CNTI organized strikes in support of Goulart who marshalled further support in crisis by forming CGT. 1963: January: Return to presidential system adopted in plebiscite by huge margin. June: Faced with growing inflation Goulart scrapped Celso Furtado's Triennial Plan. September: Sergeants' revolt in Brasilia. October: Goulart asked Congress to declare state of siege. Fearing a leftist putsch it refused. Goulart began to look to the Left for his support. 1964: March: Goulart appealed to masses in rallies organized by CGT. Proposed rent control, suffrage for all, and signed oil nationalization and land reform decrees. The Right counter-attacked with its own mass rallies. Goulart refused to suppress sailors' revolt. Military seized power. April: Goulart fled Brasilia for Uruguay. Supreme Revolutionary Command promulgated First Institutional Act. Castelo Branco elected President by Congress. 1965: July: Small parties disbanded. October: Opposition won large victory in Congressional elections after Presidential elections postponed for a year. Second Institutional Act was passed further strengthening powers of President. 1966: September: Government swept twelve gubernatorial elections. October: Costa e Silva elected President designate by Congress. November: Congress closed after refusal to make further expulsions. In Congressional elections Government ARENA won huge majority against MDB. 1967: January: New Constitution promulgated. March: Costa e Silva took office planning 'redemocratization'. December: Bourgeois opposition *Frente Ampla* banned. 1968: March: First armed actions of urban guerrilla war began in São Paulo. Police shooting of Rio student sparked upsurge of student opposition to regime. June: Student protests against dictatorship reached height. July: Engineering workers struck in Osasco. October: UNE Congress surrounded by army, 800 students arrested.

**December:** Fifth Institutional Act promulgated proroguing Congress and suspending basic legal guarantees. Massive police operation against urban guerrilla mounted. **1969: August:** Costa e Silva stricken with heart attack. **September:** US Ambassador Burke Elbrick kidnapped and ransomed. Fifteen militants released in exchange. **October:** Garrastazu Medici 'elected' President by military high command. **1970: June:** German Ambassador Von Holleben kidnapped and exchanged for forty prisoners. **December:** Swiss Ambassador Bucher kidnapped and exchanged for seventy prisoners.

# Historical Introduction 1930-64: The Legacy of Vargas

The sheer size and diversity of Brazil has always been a major problem for its rulers. In land area it is the world's fourth largest country – larger than the sub-continent of India – and in population the world's seventh largest country with a population approaching one hundred million. Admittedly some ninety-eight per cent of the Brazilian people speak Portuguese as their first language and since the Portuguese colonization of the sixteenth century Brazil has had in theory at least a continuous history as a single political entity. But almost every economic and historical circumstance has conspired to weaken the central power, usually to the disadvantage of one section or another of the possessing classes.

Three main zones have emerged since Brazil's earliest days as a Portuguese colony. During the first two centuries the economy was dominated by the sugar planters of the North East. By the early nineteenth century, however, growing competition from West Indian sugar and the boom in mining in the South East had reduced the production of sugar to a backward sector in Brazilian agriculture. The final blow was struck by the abolition of the slave trade in 1850. The 'hot Siberia' of the North East, devastated by frequent droughts, remains today an area of appalling poverty in which live a third of Brazil's population, mostly poor or landless peasants and underemployed *favelados* who scrape a marginal existence in the large cities like Recife and Salvador.

The agricultural South was for a long time isolated and underdeveloped. Its rolling grasslands were used as pasture for scattered herds and its rich farm land remained unexploited, until the first of a series of immigrations – the Germans in the mid-nineteenth century – opened up a flourishing agriculture. Though the large cattle ranches still predominate in terms of size, particularly in Rio Grande do Sul, the small farmers – the descendants of immigrants from Germany, Italy, Russia, Poland and Japan – now enjoy a third of Brazil's agricultural income, out of proportion to their numbers. A major producer of cattle, the South provides most of the country's wool and wheat as well as a quarter of the dietary staples like rice and cassava. The region is in almost total contrast to the North East: its land and climate are good, and its smallholders comparatively prosperous.

By far the richest and politically most powerful region of Brazil is the South East. Its industrial triangle links the three major cities, Rio de Janeiro, São Paulo, and Belo Horizonte. The region accounts for almost half the whole population and more than two thirds of the national product. Its middle class is as large as that to be found in Western Europe and is at least as rich. It should be borne in mind that São Paulo with its skyscrapers in the centre, its large and prosperous suburbs, its industrial estates and a population approaching six million, is one of the world's major cities. Brazil's urban population as a whole is growing at more than three times the rate of the population in the countryside and now stands at more than fifty million. The South East accounts by itself for half of this.

Late in the seventeenth century the discovery of gold and

diamond mines in the South East converted Minas Gerais and São Paulo into the country's economic and political centre. Although the mineral deposits were exhausted by the beginning of the nineteenth century, the region continued to dominate the economy as the major producer of coffee. This grew into Brazil's largest export and by 1900 accounted for four-fifths of the world supply.

The development of industry in the South East was impeded by the smallness of the internal market and the dominance of coffee. Manufacturing was on a tiny scale in scattered businesses employing on average four workers or less. It was only after the First World War that industrial production particularly in textiles began to provide the necessary surplus for infra-structural investment. Though the coffee crisis and the Wall Street Crash in 1929 finally broke the Minas – São Paulo axis and displaced the coffee-planters of the old Republic as the major force within the ruling bloc, the region itself has continued as the motor of Brazilian 'development'.

During the period from 1930 to 1964 the masses were for the first time brought into the arena of national politics. This historical introduction outlines the attempts made by the ruling classes to integrate these new political forces into an enduring framework. The revolution of 1930 led, under Vargas, to the establishment of a new state – the *Estado Nôvo* – based on European fascist models, but the institutions necessary for a corporate state were never strengthened enough in Brazil and the new regime did not survive the Second World War.

In the post-war period, first under Vargas and then under Kubitschek, Quadros and Goulart, an attempt was made to give political expression to the new middle class and the growing working class within the framework of a bourgeois democracy. Mass organizations such as parties, unions and even peasant organizations were created from above which, while appearing to express the aspirations of the oppressed and the exploited, in fact consolidated the power of their oppressors and exploiters. The failure of this populist – or rather pseudo-populist experiment – led to the 'March revolution' of 1964 in which the army intervened to seize power, as it had done in 1889 and 1930. On each of those occasions the army returned power to the politicians and permitted the development of civilian politics. In 1964, however, the army did not stand aside but set out to construct a genuinely new state dominated by the military bureaucracy.

The First Republic, overthrown in the 'revolution' of 1930, was an oligarchy dominated by the coffee planters of São Paulo and Minas Gerais. These two states took turns in providing a President, but the regime was extremely decentralized. Different states kept their own armed forces and were empowered to raise foreign loans. The key problem of Brazil's international economic relations, the fluctuation of the price of coffee on the world market, was dealt with in a manner highly favourable to the coffee planters. From 1907 onwards the federal government carried out an effective price support policy, whereby losses resulting from the falling coffee price were 'socialized' by repeated devaluation.

The first challenge to the oligarchic republic of the coffee planters were the *tenente* (lieutenant) rebellions of the 1920s. The junior officers who gave their name to these armed insurrections did not represent an ascending industrial bourgeoisie. There are no signs that the bourgeoisie, at that time still predominantly commercial, was conscious of any substantial contradiction between its interests and those of the coffee planters. Moreover the social origins of the *tenentes* were almost exclusively in the traditional oligarchy. The *tenentes* were united by the generation gap which forced on them a consciousness of Brazil's backwardness which their parents could still ignore. The *tenentes* unfurled the banner of liberal democracy in its most abstract (and thus itself anachronistic) form, initially seeing this as the fundamental condition of Brazil's modernization. While their Garibaldian exploits in the 1920s, particularly those of the Prestes column, whose leader Luís Carlos Prestes later became the leader of the Communist Party, may have stirred the hearts of the São Paulo middle classes, their liberal democratic ideas, borrowed from the nineteenth-century European capitalism, had extremely weak social roots.

The occasion for the overthrow of the First Republic was a crisis of presidential succession. Washington Luiz's attempt to keep the presidency in the hands of São Paulo was no new phenomenon in Brazil. The military had previously had to intervene politically to hold the ring between the rival oligarchic groups. However, this time the disaffection of the São Paulo middle classes, the realization on the part of a growing section of the higher military of the need for reforms, and the revolutionary aspirations of the *tenentes*, were able to coalesce with the old oligarchic rivalries to produce a definite transformation of the Brazilian political structure. The final blow to the First Republic was provided by the 1929 Wall Street Crash, which produced a divorce between the political interests of the coffee planters and their immediate economic interests, expressed in Washington Luiz's refusal to devalue the cruzeiro any further. By October, 1930 the coffee planters were also ready to seek a new political solution. The presidential election held in May 1930 gave a narrow majority to Julio Prestes, the government candidate, against Getúlio Vargas, the candidate of the opposition *Aliança Liberal* bloc. Vargas immediately accused the government of electoral fraud – an allegation invariably made by defeated candidates under the First Republic, and just as invariably true. This time however, the losers were to act on their words. In September Vargas mobilized a rebel army in Rio Grande do Sul, where he was governor, to march on the capital (then Rio de Janeiro). Coordinated forces also marched on Rio from Paraíba and Minas Gerais. By 24 October the revolt had reached such proportions that the dissident wing of the higher military were able to seize power and transfer it to Vargas ten days later, when he entered the capital. The threat of civil war proved sufficient to neutralize the defenders of the Old Republic.

The very scenario of the 'October revolution' reveals its weaknesses. The two forces whose aims were avowedly revolutionary, the *tenentes* and the São Paulo middle class, had chosen to make a deal with the dissident political and military groups of the Old Republic rather than mobilize the popular masses against the old regime. This choice reflects the limitations of their revolution: the bourgeoisie was not revolutionary, the peasantry was still dormant after the last of the great *jacqueries* (the *Contestado*[1] of 1912–16), and the working class was still only a marginal presence. Getúlio Vargas himself was a big cattle rancher from the Southern State of Rio Grande do Sul, and a politician of the First Republic who had held both ministerial office in the twenties and the governorship of his home State.

The political compromise Vargas created which outlasted both the *Estado Nôvo* and his own death in 1954, was one in which the rural oligarchy continued to hold political office, yet conducted a policy of modernization and industrial development. 'Getulism', as his system was known, was a specifically Brazilian form of populism, appealing to the expanding working class in the towns from a base among the rural latifundists. What both classes had in common and what

---

[1] A peasant uprising in the Southern States of Parana and Santa Catarina. See below p. 135.

distinguished them from the strongest section of the bourgeoisie, was that their interests were not tied to foreign capital. Once Vargas had understood the positive role the state could play in promoting industrialization, he was able both to play the card of nationalism and appear to the working class as their direct benefactor by providing increased industrial employment and genuine improvements in working conditions. The loyalty Vargas built up served to deflect the working class from posing a revolutionary challenge to the rural oligarchy, while his latifundist support enabled him to ride roughshod, when necessary, over the short-term interests of the employers. All trade unions, moreover, were subordinated to the state, so that in return for decreed wage increases, capitalists both national and foreign received protection from the threat of a genuinely autonomous working-class movement.

Vargas did not construct his system from a ready-made plan, but approached it by trial and error, motivated throughout by the drive to maintain and consolidate his own power. The first steps in this direction were visible soon after the 1930 revolution, when Vargas gave signs that the programme of the *Aliança Liberal* would not be honoured. The victory of the October revolution had placed enormous powers in the hands of the provisional government, and Vargas was immediately able to manoeuvre between the genuine liberal constitutionalists, whose most vociferous section was the São Paulo middle class, and the *tenentes*, whose liberal rhetoric had been a useful weapon against the old regime, but which had vanished as soon as they found themselves in power. Vargas's desire to retain his full provisional powers coincided at this point with the *tenentes*' fears that elections would see the return of the traditional elite. To prevent this the São Paulo Democratic Party created a front of virtually all political organizations in that State, united on the question of States' rights and constitutional government. July 1932 saw the outbreak of the Constitutionalist Rebellion, but this was confined to São Paulo and easily defeated. Vargas's handling of these *Paulistas* was characteristic of his skilful opportunism. By announcing elections at once to a constituent assembly he presented himself as the true constitutionalist and the *Paulistas* as mere separatists.

At the Congressional elections in May 1933 Vargas's followers gained a majority but they still represented only a motley collection of local oligarchic groupings. Voting was still restricted to literates (the illiteracy rate was well above 50%) and only 3·5% of the Brazilian population were registered as electors. However, the combined effects of the 1930 revolution, the world trade depression, and the events in Europe, soon called to life new political forces. The fascist *Integralistas* were Brazil's first mass political organization, followed by the *Aliança Nacional Libertadora* (ANL), a front organization of the Brazilian Communist Party (PCB). The ANL broke historic ground, mobilizing mass support for an anti-imperialist and anti-oligarchic programme. It called for the liquidation of the latifundia, the cancellation of foreign debts and the nationalization of foreign-owned firms. By May 1935, 1,600 local branches of the ANL had been formed among the working class and the truly national sections of the middle class and bourgeoisie. But the PCB leadership, under the ex-*tenente* Luís Carlos Prestes, demonstrated in this period an adventurism quite blind to the realities of the situation. In July 1935 Prestes called for 'all power to the ANL' and Vargas used this as an excuse for its suppression. In late November, PCB militants in the North-East attempted a putsch based on the garrisons of Natal and Recife. This was easily suppressed, and the left was outlawed and ruthlessly persecuted. After the abortive Communist putsch,

Congress granted Vargas emergency powers to deal with subversion, and he exploited this position to the full in his bid for absolute power.

Vargas's economic and social policy paralleled his military policy. Following the 1930 revolution he announced that the 'labour question' would no longer be treated merely as a problem for the police, and until 1935 permitted limited trade-union activity. His economic policies, however, never threatened the interests of the possessing classes. His Minister of Agriculture, Oswaldo Aranha, designed the successful programme for the federal purchase and burning of coffee surpluses financed by currency issue, which unintentionally diverted investment capital into industrial growth. The Southern ranchers, and even the North-Eastern sugar planters who had opposed the 1930 revolution, were aided by federal measures. The policies that emerged from the 1930 revolution were not originally designed to further industrial growth at the expense of the latifundists. Rather the rapid industrialization which Brazil experienced from 1930 onwards was encouraged indirectly by government policies designed to support the latifundia.

Vargas's 'continuist' tendencies became clear in the course of 1937, when he refrained from endorsing José Americo, generally regarded as the government's presidential candidate. The two main candidates, Américo and Armando de Salles Oliveira, represented the two major tendencies that had crystallized within the Brazilian ruling class bloc after the 1930 revolution; the urban bourgeoisie and the rural latifundists. Salles Oliveira, the governor of São Paulo, was a free-market liberal and constitutionalist. Américo, a former *tenente* and radical nationalist, attempted to mobilize the working-class vote. Vargas however preempted the electorate's choice. On 1 October, the crude forgery of the 'Cohen plan'[2] was used to stampede Congress into approving the suspension of constitutional guarantees and, after preparing the ground with careful military and political manoeuvres, Vargas sent troops to close Congress. In a radio broadcast on the day of the coup, Vargas announced the abolition of all political parties and of the Congress. The constitution that soon followed established the *Estado Nôvo*, a 'new state', modelled on Italian and Portuguese fascism, giving Vargas himself decree powers for six years, when a new president was to be chosen by plebiscite.

Vargas had been able to suppress the popular forces by terror with the full support of the propertied classes but he could not rely automatically on the support of the army in dealing with his opponents among the ruling class itself. An influential section of the higher military, including Gomes, Vargas's own appointment to the War Ministry, opposed his plans for a coup. Faced nevertheless with an imagined threat from the left (they remembered 1935) and the potential threat from the *Integralistas*, they were prepared to let Vargas override the 1934 constitution in the general interests of the ruling class as a whole. Nevertheless a dictatorship set up by grace of the military could be overthrown by the military and they were to exercise what they considered their traditional prerogative as final arbiter in 1945, when they overthrew Vargas and again in 1964, when they overthrew Goulart.

At least until 1943 the *Estado Nôvo* represented the interests of the ruling class as a whole. It encountered remarkably little opposition from any section of the propertied classes, and any sign of resistance from the popular masses was suppressed by police terrorism. Vargas made no attempt to

---

[2] The 'Cohen Plan' was a document, almost certainly forged, allegedly proving that the PCB were planning a military take-over.

set up a political party, distrusting as he did political parties in any form. His power was built rather on the skilful manipulation of the different ruling-class groups, and on populist demagogy. This very lack of structured political mediation made possible the direct appeals to the working class which Vargas was to begin making in 1943. The *Estado Nôvo* strengthened the secret police and established a propaganda agency to reinforce Vargas's achievements in the minds of the people. Federal dominance over the States was ensured by replacing the elected governors with a new cadre of provincial bosses, called 'Interventors', who owed their careers to Vargas's patronage, and whose job was to carry out federal orders without threatening the economic power of the local oligarchy.

In the boom conditions of the Second World War, the *Estado Nôvo* enjoyed a period of rapid urban and industrial growth which was further encouraged by Vargas's expansionist economic policies. The federal government took over economic powers previously wielded by the States, and set up government-sponsored cartels in pinewood, tea and salt. Vargas nationalized some railway and shipping companies, and set up several mixed corporations in basic industries. Taxes on inter-state commerce were abolished in 1937, and low-interest loans, public works projects, and differential exchange rates were used to encourage the development of favoured industries. The eight-year dictatorship thus created not only a centralized state, but also a unified national economy, centred on the industrial triangle formed by São Paulo, Rio and Belo Horizonte. In 1941 Vargas openly committed himself to build Brazil into an industrial nation, and the National Steel Company was formed that year to operate the large Volta Redonda steel plant. The programme relied on loans provided by the United States in return for Brazil's contribution to the war effort.

The Labour Ministry, which was to become an essential pivot of Vargas's system, was founded immediately after the 1930 revolution. From 1937, and especially after 1941, the Labour Ministry encouraged recruitment into the government-sponsored unions, and placed government agents (*pelegos*)[3] in positions of responsibility. The official trade unions, the only legal ones, were organized by category of worker, and were controlled by the Ministry of Labour through the National Confederation of Industrial Workers (CNTI). In return for containing industrial unrest, the government provided a minimum wage, the eight-hour day, paid holidays and certain welfare benefits, codified in 1941 into the 'Consolidated Labour Laws'.

The analysis of Vargas's labour policies has tended to overemphasize the political role of the Ministry of Labour in the period before 1943. Until that time Vargas had not really needed to reckon with the working class. The rationale for the Ministry of Labour's operations had less to do with the borrowed fragments of corporativist theory than with a need to prevent the left from organizing the working class itself. Once the unity of the possessing classes began to break down, however, the state labour apparatus built up during the *Estado Nôvo* period provided Vargas with a much needed alternative base.

The *Estado Nôvo* was undermined more than anything else by the Axis defeat in the Second World War.[4] After the Italian defeat the Brazilian liberal bourgeoisie grew increasingly restive. In October 1943 a group of intellectuals and

---

[3] *Pelego* is the Portuguese for the piece of leather between the stirrup and the flank of the horse.
[4] Despite the *Estado Nôvo*'s fascist pedigree, Brazil was the only Latin American country to send troops to fight on the Allied side. Its expeditionary force fought in the Italian campaign.

politicians from Minas Gerais issued a statement calling for the restoration of democracy, the first open opposition since Vargas's 1937 coup. In response, Vargas promised political rights after the war. During 1944 the liberal opposition remained mainly covert, but early in 1945 it developed into an open torrent of protest. In February a call was made for elections in which Vargas could not be a candidate. In March the first student demonstration took place, and Vargas began to give ground, relaxing the censorship and announcing that elections would soon be held in which he would not stand. In April a political amnesty was declared and in May all political parties were legalized.

Since 1943 Vargas had begun to use the Labour Ministry to mobilize the working class as a new political base. Realizing that the *Estado Nôvo* was doomed, he had hoped to retain power within the framework of bourgeois democracy. The emphasis of Vargas's policies shifted accordingly. Social welfare legislation was extended, and the doctrine of *trabalhismo*[5] propagated by the regime's agencies. The working class was promised a prominent place among the 'new groups full of energy and enthusiasm that are capable of faith and of carrying out the tasks of our development.'

As 1945 progressed a showdown between Vargas and the liberal bourgeoisie became unavoidable. On 1 May Vargas formally endorsed the candidacy of his War Minister, the colourless General Dutra, and on 28 May he announced the presidential election for December. From this point on Vargas turned unambiguously to the left. In June his 'decree 7666' set up a commission empowered to expropriate enterprises whose operations ran counter to the national interest.

---

[5] *Trabalhismo* means literally 'labourism'. It was a vague doctrine intended to encourage working class political activity on the principles of economic nationalism and welfare.

In August the Ministry of Labour's *pelegos* launched a campaign to postpone the presidential election until a Constitutional Assembly could be held, thus allowing Vargas time for 'continuist' manoeuvres. The PCB, only recently legalized, began organizing the massive *queremista*[6] demonstrations on 3 October. Vargas himself addressed the largest of these, announcing that although he would not stand for re-election, he supported the demand for a Constituent Assembly.

Vargas's populist course, his continuist manoeuvrings and the unprecedented working-class mass mobilizations, gave the propertied classes reason enough to feel threatened. The successful re-election of Perón in Argentina served only to reinforce their fears. General Góes Monteiro, the architect of Vargas's 1937 coup, now arranged his deposition. The prompting of the US ambassador was scarcely necessary, and Vargas was overthrown by the generals on 29 October in a matter of hours. Eleven days after Vargas's fall decree 7666 was abrogated.

The three parties that were to dominate Brazilian politics for the next two decades were formed in 1945, as the *Estado Nôvo* crumbled: UDN, PSD and PTB.[7] None of these parties represented a straightforward class position; the relationship of each to its social base was complicated by regional disparities, and particularly by its relationship to Getulism.

The UDN was tied most closely to the urban middle class and developed directly out of the liberal opposition of 1943. Formed to promote liberal constitutionalism it rested on the twin principles of *laissez-faire* and pro-Americanism. The

---

[6] *Queremista* was a coinage from the slogan '*Queremos Vargas*': 'We want Vargas.'

[7] *União Democratico Nacional* (National Democratic Union), *Partido Social-Democratico* (Social-Democratic Party), *Partido Trabalhista Brasileiro* (Brazilian Labour Party).

UDN platform in the 1945 elections called for the collaboration of foreign capital in Brazil's industrialization, and rejected protective tariffs and government subsidy to 'unviable' new industries. Yet the legacy of the Vargas era and the lack of an integrated national class structure burdened the UDN with various secondary determinations. Formed as a broad alliance to combat the dictatorship, it inevitably became a rallying point for all politicians and officers whose careers had been checked at some point by Vargas. This network of ties extended the UDN's base to some dissident latifundist and merchant groups. The UDN also contained for some years a 'democratic left' based chiefly on European anti-fascist liberal reformism, which later split off to form the marginal Brazilian Socialist Party. Significantly, the UDN did not call for the abolition of the labour and welfare legislation of the *Estado Nôvo*, nor of the officially controlled trade unions.

If the UDN was the party of the united anti-Vargas opposition, the PSD and PTB represented the twin pillars of Getulism. Vargas himself, with unrivalled panache, managed to serve simultaneously as honorary president of both parties.

The PSD was the party of Vargas's provincial bosses, rallying the greater part of the rural oligarchy. It stood for the continuation of Vargas's strategy: maintenance of the *status quo* in the countryside, government control of the working class through state-sponsored economic development and the official trade unions.

The PTB was founded by Ministry of Labour officials at the time of the *queremista* demonstrations. Its social base was unambiguously working class, and its strength lay chiefly in the industrial metropoles of São Paulo and Rio. However, it never achieved an autonomous working-class politics, and remained the organized expression of Vargas's populism within the working class. Its growth into a national party, with Vargas's spectacular electoral victory of 1950, was achieved only at the expense of weakening its class character.

The strength of the newly legalized PCB was above all in São Paulo city, where it won an absolute majority of the voters in 1946. The PCB however, succumbed to a combination of repression (it was outlawed again in 1947) and populism, and was only to emerge as a major factor in 1963.

On 2 December 1945 General Enrico Gaspar Dutra, the joint PSD–PTB candidate, was elected with an absolute majority. His government attempted little except to hold the ring for five years and prevent the left from developing into a political force capable of challenging for power. In September 1946 a new constitution was adopted. Like that of 1934 it restricted the suffrage to literates. In the Congressional elections, constituencies were demarcated on the basis of total population, not size of electorate, thus giving the latifundist bosses an even greater political weight. The constitution preserved the 'consolidated labour laws' and the Dutra government attempted to uphold their most reactionary aspects (lack of freedom to organize outside the official union apparatus, very severe restrictions on the right to strike, compulsory arbitration in all conflicts between workers and employers, etc.). Both major parties agreed on the necessity of smashing the PCB, which after a promising electoral performance in 1945, was now consolidating its position among the working class. In 1946 the PCB formed the Brazilian Workers' Confederation (CTB), as an independent trade-union general staff, and won significant positions in several unions. When the PCB and the CTB were suppressed in 1947, the federal government had to 'intervene' in 143 out of the 944 trade unions to purge communist supporters.

Dutra's relaxation of economic controls soon led to an

acute balance of payments crisis. In 1947 the reimposition of exchange controls, combined with maintenance of an overvalued cruzeiro, although designed in the first instance to remedy the balance of payments deficit, had also, like the coffee policy of the thirties, the further consequence of encouraging industrial investment. With the rise in commodity prices and the world trade boom which came with rearmament and the Korean war, Brazil experienced an average growth rate of six per cent per annum from 1946 to 1951.

In his years out of office, Vargas made careful preparations for the presidential elections of 1950. The basis for his comeback was a bloc between the PTB, a section of the PSD, and the São Paulo PSP (Social Progressive Party) of Adhemar de Barros. The possibility of this combination attests to the continued strength of Brazilian populism, despite the rapid economic development in the São Paulo and Rio region. (In the decade 1940–50 alone, the population of São Paulo had almost quadrupled, from 587,000 to 2,228,000, while in the same period the industrial proletariat, the vast majority of which was concentrated in the São Paulo–Rio–Belo Horizonte triangle, had grown from 781,000 to 1,257,000.) Helped considerably by Dutra's suppression of the PCB in 1947, Vargas and his followers had been able to strengthen the PTB with an egalitarian and even anti-capitalist rhetoric, while keeping their real purpose evident enough to the propertied classes for Vargas to retain the allegiance of the majority of the PSD latifundists. (Vargas himself, in keeping with his social position, held his Senate seat as a PSD representative.) The economic nationalism which had become the core of Vargas's political programme undermined the UDN's hold over the urban petty bourgeoisie, and won Vargas a base of support in the army. Vargas ascertained that the generals would not oppose his taking office if elected, so long as he respected the 1946 constitution and the 'inalienable rights' of the military. In the presidential election in October Vargas won a strong plurality on the PTB-PSD ticket.

Vargas's nationalism in his second 'democratic' phase exhibited the same ambiguities as it had done during the period of the *Estado Nôvo*. But the question of economic development now exposed a contradiction within the ruling bloc which could no longer be surmounted by mere rhetoric. During the world depression and the Second World War Brazilian capitalism had taken full advantage of the resources released from coffee and of the cutting of normal trade channels. The process of import substitution continued to provide Brazil with rapid economic development until the mid 1950s. Towards the end of the decade, however, the growing penetration of imperialist capital posed the question of ownership for the ruling class in an acute form. The power of the 'associated bourgeoisie' – the sector connected with the foreign corporations – grew constantly at the expense of the national bourgeoisie.

Vargas's campaign oratory had stressed industrial development under Brazilian capital, public and private. Once in office, however, Vargas's cabinet was recruited almost solely from the PSD. The PTB, the only possible source of pressure for a nationalist policy, was given the portfolio of Labour. In December 1950 the Joint Brazil–US Economic Development Commission was established and this led in 1952 to the creation of a National Bank for Economic Development. The Bank's task was to encourage Brazilian investment in infrastructural projects, particularly power and transport, so as to render Brazil more attractive to foreign investors. Vargas's financial policy in the hands of Minister Horácio Lafer was 'orthodox' and 'responsible'. In 1953 import controls and a currency devaluation were abandoned and a multiple exchange-rate system was introduced which preserved some discrimination in favour of machine imports within the basic context of free trade. The one significant material expression of Vargas's nationalism at this time was the creation of the predominantly state-owned Petrobrás oil corporation which was given a monopoly on oil drilling and the operation of new refineries, although distribution and existing refineries were left in private hands. The Petrobrás project led to fierce debate over details, but some form of oil nationalization was supported by almost every section of the properties classes themselves, and even by the UDN.[8] In January 1952 Vargas imposed a temporary ten per cent limit on profit remittances, which had risen to 137 million dollars in 1951, but application of this limit was authorized only when there was undue pressure on the balance of payments.

Vargas's foreign policy led occasionally to token measures against imperialism, and only very rarely to measures of real significance. The development of the Cold War, in Brazil as elsewhere, drove the middle classes, and especially the military, into the imperialist camp. The Brazilian military has never displayed a high degree of ideological or political unity. Although it stands today for the most vicious reaction, it is significant that right up to the 1964 coup the Brazilian Left neglected preacutions against the forces of right because of its confidence in the democratic and progressive forces within the army, which were thought to preclude a right-wing coup.

The relatively open recruitment of the Brazilian officer corps has meant that the political tendencies represented within the officer corps have generally coincided with the

---

[8] The proposal was set before Congress in 1951 but only ratified in October 1953.

options open to the middle class as a whole, which range from complete integration with imperialism to a radical petty-bourgeois nationalism. The Military Club in Rio, an influential political discussion centre for officers, was dominated between 1944 and 1952 by a small but active nationalist caucus. Within the nationalist group there was a significant radical left, which in 1947 called for the abolition of the latifundia and criticized the US proposal for a continental military organization. In July 1950 the editor of the club's journal, *Revista*, provoked a crisis by denouncing the invasion of Korea, and warning against possible US attempts to involve Brazilian troops in the 'UN' operation. In the ensuing controversy, the journal was suspended and in March 1952 Estillac Leal, the nationalist general whom Vargas had appointed as War Minister, was forced to resign. Two months later new elections for the Directorate of the Military Club were held, in which the right wing, led by the so-called *Cruzada Democratica* group, defeated the nationalists by a two to one majority. The *Cruzada Democratica* group were to be prominent in the 1964 coup, and several of their number have since held ministerial office.

Vargas's response to the split in the officer corps in 1950–1952 illustrates the ambiguities of the class alliance he represented. He withstood US pressure to send troops to Korea, which had little support in Brazil outside the officer corps, but ratified the US-Brazilian military accords, which opened wide the Brazilian army to US political penetration. He also authorized the arrest and imprisonment of officers suspected of Communist sympathy.

In 1953 Vargas began once again to shift to the left. Inflation had grown substantially in 1951 and 1952. The PTB labour leaders who had returned with Vargas had won substantial wage increases, and middle class groups, particularly the government bureaucracy, felt threatened by their failure to gain equivalent benefits. In 1952 the balance of payments position became acute once more, and capitalist orthodoxy demanded deflation. But Vargas was concerned above all with the presidential election of 1955. Under the constitution he would himself be ineligible to stand, and in his bargain with the PSP he agreed to support Adhemar de Barros's candidacy, a pledge he did not intend to honour. Playing for a 'continuist' solution, Vargas now staked his future on promoting *trabalhismo* and attempting to undermine Barros's hold over the São Paulo working class.

In June 1953 Vargas reshuffled his cabinet, strengthening his personal following by bringing in José Américo as Minister of Transport and Oswaldo Aranha as Finance Minister, both old colleagues of his from the thirties. Most significantly, he appointed Joâo Goulart Minister of Labour. Goulart was a populist, a neighbouring rancher of Vargas from Rio Grande do Sul, and his demagogic use of the Labour Ministry was immediately suspect to the propertied classes. The *trabalhista* demand for an increase in real wages could only have been reconciled with anti-inflationary measures to solve the balance of payments crisis, with the support of foreign loans, but the Eisenhower administration instead cut back on its commitments to Brazilian public investment and wound up the Joint US–Brazil Economic Commission.

Vargas's position now became increasingly difficult. The rate of inflation had reached twenty-seven per cent, and 1957 saw a wave of strikes, beginning with one of engineers, glass-workers and typographers in São Paulo, who no longer heeded the restrictions of the labour laws. In Rio Grande do Sul strikes led to violent confrontations with the police, and there were even cases where the police refused to repress striking workers. The extent of middle-class discontent had been made apparent by Janio Quadros's election as mayor of São Paulo city in March 1953. Quadros represented a new form of populism which attacked government corruption (particularly blatant under Barros's governorship) and called for an 'honest' administration. The UDN, now led by the right-wing journalist Carlos Lacerda and actively supported by the anti-nationalist officers who had formed the *Cruzada Democratica*, mounted a carefully orchestrated campaign against the Vargas regime, concentrating in particular on the figure of Goulart.

On 8 February 1954 eighty-one colonels and lieutenant-colonels submitted an unprecedented memorandum to the War Minister which cited the 'danger of communist subversion' as a reason for raising officers' salaries. In the following two weeks the press campaign for Goulart's dismissal grew daily more intense. Senior officers finally warned of their 'inability to maintain army discipline' and Vargas realized at last that he would have to sacrifice Goulart. Goulart was replaced by an unimportant functionary, and Cardozo, the Minister of War was replaced by General Zenóbio da Costa, a dedicated anti-communist. But it was now too late for these concessions to the military to be effective. Moreover, by deciding to sacrifice Goulart, Vargas had opted against a radical mobilization of the working class. On 4 April his former Foreign Minister, Neves da Fontoura, claimed that Vargas and Goulart had secretly negotiated a pact with Perón between the 'ABC powers' (Argentina, Brazil and Chile) directed against the US. The UDN attempted a congressional impeachment.

On 1 May Vargas tried to win back some of the support he had lost from the working class by accepting the hundred per cent wage increase and by praising Goulart as an 'indefatigable friend of the workers'. But Vargas's bold words to his working class audiences – 'tomorrow you will be the governors' – were not backed up by any serious attempts at political mobilization. Aged seventy-two, Vargas was all too evidently tired, and had lost much of his old political skill. During the summer, the New York coffee dealers boycotted Brazilian coffee to protest against the high minimum price which the Brazilian Coffee Institute had set. On 5 August an Air Force major was killed in an attempt to assassinate Lacerda. Vargas was not directly implicated, but the event added impetus to the movement for his dismissal. By 23 August a consensus in the high command had been won and a 'Manifesto to the Nation' was issued calling for Vargas to resign.

The coup of August 1954 was a dress rehearsal for that of March 1964. Vargas's heroism alone stopped the proimperialist wing of the military from winning power for another decade. Confronted by the generals' ultimatum, Vargas committed suicide, leaving behind him his most uncompromising political statement. It denounced the imperialists and reactionaries who had together overthrown his government. The news of Vargas's death provoked an unprecedented response from the masses. They attacked American diplomatic buildings and anti-Getulist newspapers like *O Globo*. The sudden upsurge of the mass movement blocked any attempt to overthrow the constitution.

Vargas's political strategy had only been viable as long as he was able to implement his programme of state-sponsored industrialization. While this was compatible with Brazil's position in the international capitalist economy, Vargas could fend off the hostility of the bourgeoisie by using the trade union apparatus to control the working class, since industrial expansion provided enough benefits to contain industrial unrest. When, however, the allied victory in the Second World War and, eight years later, an uncontrolled inflation, made his regime intolerable for the bourgeoisie, the latifundists had no compelling reason to intervene in

Vargas's favour. The government-organized working class was a tempting weapon for him to use in pursuit of his own personal ambition against the propertied classes he represented. However, Vargas's mobilization of the popular forces was inevitably restrained by the fear that, once unleashed, they might escape his control. In both the crisis of 1945 and that of 1954, Vargas played for time until it was too late.

The weakness of Vargas when challenged by the propertied classes contrasts significantly with Perón, to whom he is often compared. In 1943 Argentina was already a developed country, with a sixty-two per cent urban population and a large working class. Perón's policy in the Ministry of Labour was to stoke up and unleash the trade union's energies against the employers, thus achieving an immediate and substantial increase in real wages at the expense of all other social groups. Perón had no base in the traditional ruling class or in the army. His power was based solely on his proletarian following. The gains the working class obtained from Vargas's regime, on the other hand, derived entirely from his successful development policies. Brazil's industrial development provided significant gains for the urban masses, but these were not wrested from capital in class struggle. Despite Vargas's *trabalhista* rhetoric, the only role which his system allowed the working class as an active political force was of intervening during crises to prevent a pro-imperialist intervention.

In 1945 Vargas appealed to the working class when the *Estado Nôvo* had outlived its original purpose of protecting the united front of property from the masses. Again in 1953, faced with the bourgeoisie's attacks on inflation and government corruption, Vargas turned to the left and obtained a year's grace before he was finally ousted. While Perón's regime was anathema to the Argentinian bourgeoisie and to US imperialism, Vargas never made a sustained attack

## The Legacy of Vargas 41

against imperialist exploitation, let alone against the Brazilian oligarchy. Yet by the heroism of his suicide, he reinforced his own myth, and gave not only liberty but also the populist tradition he had founded a further decade of life.

After Vargas's death Vice-President Café Filho, a conservative leader of Barros's PSP, was sworn in as president. Congressional elections had been held as planned in October 1954, and a year later a new president was elected. In the presidential election, the PSD and PTB nominated Juscelino Kubitschek for President, and Goulart for Vice-President. Kubitschek won the 1955 election on a narrow plurality, while Goulart won half a million votes more than Kubitschek on the vice-presidential ballot. Many UDN leaders had called for the postponment of the election, and Lacerda and the officers in the *Cruzada Democratica* now attempted to provoke a new putsch. Events were complicated when Café Filho suffered a heart attack two months before the inauguration, but General Lott, as War Minister, used his own *dispositivo militar*[9] to ensure the inauguration of Kubitschek and Goulart on 31 January 1956. The main body of the ruling classes and the officer caste were prepared to accept Kubitschek, since, although a politician of the Vargas regime and thus detested by the UDN in party terms, he was evidently reliable as a representative of his class, untainted by Getulist demagogy. Moreover, the events of 1955 had shown that if Goulart inherited the presidency and compromised the interests of capital and landed property he would be far more difficult to get rid of than Vargas. Goulart played his part by publicly denouncing Communism, and Kubitschek stood solidly by his vice-president. The choice offered in the election of 1955 had represented the economic options facing

---

[9] In Brazilian politics a *dispositivo militar* is a group of officers openly associated with a political group.

the Brazilian bourgeoisie: *entrega* or austerity. The continuation of development required the massive influx of foreign capital or radical social reform (an option which the fate of Vargas had already proved impossible). In choosing Kubitschek the electorate chose a regime of economic euphoria and imperialist take-over.

Kubitschek left his mark on the country as no leader except Vargas had since 1930. The late fifties saw an acceleration of Brazil's already rapid industrialization, with industrial output rising by eighty per cent between 1955 and 1961. Brazil's overall growth rate in the 1950s was three times that of the rest of Latin America. Kubitschek's economic strategy, unlike Vargas's, was explicitly based on encouraging massive foreign investment by creating an appropriate economic and political climate. Foreign firms investing in Brazil were even freed from controls over import of machinery to which Brazilian firms were subject. They received easy credit and guaranteed protection from foreign imports. The massive returns on investment made by such companies as Ford Motors of Brazil or Brascan led the Wall Street Journal to ask: 'Is there any other place in the world where such profits can be obtained?'.

Kubitschek's government put into action many of the infrastructural projects inherited from the defunct joint US–Brazil Economic Commission of 1951–53, and was able to take advantage of the greater availability of funds from US and IMF agencies and build up a gigantic foreign debt, repayments on which were to contribute to the crisis of 1963. Kubitschek's flair for improvisation and political gesture was epitomized by the Brasilia project. His economic successes, whatever their long-term cost, dampened temporarily the domestic class struggle which had developed in 1954. In addition, Kubitschek was quick to crack down on Communist influence in the trade unions. Goulart, operating through the Ministry of Labour and the PTB, had the task of reconciling his president's acceptance of imperialist penetration with the nationalist aspirations of the working class. Internationally, Kubitschek took care to follow closely the lead of the US, sometimes even keeping well ahead of their strategic thinking. In 1958 he proposed an 'Operation Pan-America' but was rebuffed by the Eisenhower administration. It was this plan which was later taken up by Kennedy as the 'Alliance for Progress'.

In the last years of Kubitschek's presidency, inflation again reached an intolerable level and provided at long last the occasion for an opposition victory in the presidential campaign of 1960. Kubitschek's attempts after October 1958 to carry out a disinflationary policy at the expense of the working class brought increased agitation for wage increases, while the privileges given foreign firms in an effort to maintain the high level of foreign investment brought him the opposition of São Paulo interests, understandably hostile to protectionism in reverse. In June 1959 Kubitschek sacrificed the control of inflation to the attainment of existing growth targets. He broke off negotiations with the IMF in Washington over a three hundred million dollar loan which was conditional on the imposition of severe inflationary measures. In August he reshuffled his cabinet, placing Pais de Almeida, a nationalist, in charge of economic policy.

Kubitschek left the problems raised by inflation to his successor, Jânio Quadros, a schoolmaster turned demagogue who had become governor of São Paulo. He won the presidential election in October 1960 as an independent with the backing of the UDN. His success was no doubt due in part to his independence and to the uninspired choice of General Lott by the PSD and PTB. The electoral weakness of the UDN and its reliance on Quadros's personal talents was shown by the result of the vice-presidential ballot in which

Goulart was once again elected on the PSD-PTB ticket.

Quadros's government was to last scarcely six months. His slogans of 'morality' and 'honest government' proved little help in initiating any definite reforms. His most decisive measures were to modify exchange regulations so as to effect a one hundred per cent devaluation and drastically to reduce government subsidies on wheat and oil imports. The Kennedy administration was impressed with Quadros and was prepared to invest several hundred million dollars in shoring up Brazil from any threat from the left.

By June 1961 Quadros had already succeeded in refinancing the foreign debt incurred under Kubitschek but the very success of this operation tempted him to shift his economic policy from retrenchment back to development. Moreover, Quadros's complete lack of any loyal organization, and his political ineptness, led him to cast around for idiosyncratic policies without calculating their political effects. Despite his dependence on the generosity of the Kennedy administration, Quadros refused to follow the US ban on all dealings with Cuba, and voted at the UN in favour of a debate on the seating of People's China. Though these token actions in no sense reflected a left-wing or even consistently nationalist course, they were enough to provoke the right. Lacerda and the UDN began the same tactics against their former protégé as they had earlier used against Vargas and Kubitschek. Quadros, in whom the bourgeoisie understandably had no confidence at all, was quick to capitulate. On 25 August he suddenly resigned the Presidency, leaving Goulart as his constitutional successor.

The struggle which Goulart fought to take office reveal the forces which were to overthrow him in the 1964 coup. Goulart was abroad at the time of Quadros's resignation, leading an economic delegation to China. The three military ministers were in effective control of the government and on 28 August they informed Congress that Goulart would not be allowed to return to Brazil. They claimed that he would transform the armed forces into 'Communist militias' and had already granted key trade union positions to 'agents of international Communism'. However, the very suddenness of Quadros's resignation had made it impossible for the military right to neutralize all the forces within the army hostile to a military intervention into constitutional affairs.

General Lopes, commander of the third army in Rio Grande do Sul, and Leonel Brizola, governor of the State and Goulart's brother-in-law, announced that they would support Goulart even at the risk of civil war, and mobilized all available forces to resist a possible invasion. In these circumstances, the ultras had to back down. A section of the middle classes rallied behind the legalist stand made in the South, and the Army decided to accept the compromise put forward by Congress to change the constitution in favour of a parliamentary system in which a Prime Minister at the head of a cabinet was intended to modify the previously absolute power of the President. Only after these precautions was Goulart allowed to take office.

Under his leadership the bureaucratic PTB had been riddled as always with corruption. In different circumstances Goulart might have had no hesitation in keeping a political course well within the limits set by imperialism and the Brazilian oligarchy. However, by the time Goulart took office, the economic basis of Vargas's system had been decisively changed. The unprecedented influx of foreign capital during the five years of Kubitschek's presidency drastically strengthened the imperialist hold over the Brazilian economy, transforming a whole section of national capitalists into associates of the international monopoly corporations. By 1961 foreign enterprises accounted for 33 per cent of the total capital of the sixty-six largest business groups, state enterprises 38 per cent, and private enterprises only 11 per cent (mixed companies accounted for 18 per cent). The Brazilian government owed more on loan capital from abroad than the 743 million dollars of direct foreign investment. Quadros's refunding of the short-term debt, though successful, only gave two or three years grace before an even more serious payments crisis, and in 1961 the rate of inflation reached 37 per cent per annum.

Under these conditions a continuation of Vargas's or even Kubitschek's development policies was impossible. The only alternatives to the drastic retrenchment and austerity demanded by the pro-imperialist UDN were either a development financed by an ever-growing inflation or the basic anti-imperialist and anti-latifundist reforms demanded by the PCB. Goulart shied away from the latter alternative until the last possible moment. As inflation mounted he had to concede ever higher wage increases to the working class to maintain his populist following, each time intensifying the hostility not just of the bourgeoisie but also of the professional middle class, increasingly unable to maintain its relatively privileged position.

Moreover the political conditions which had made Getulism possible were no longer present. The popular forces had begun to escape the control of the populist politicians. In the late fifties the forty-year quiescence of the peasantry was ended by the Peasant Leagues founded by Francisco Julião, which were particularly strong in Pernambuco and the North East generally. The last year of Kubitschek's presidency also saw a break-through towards a real autonomy for the working-class movement. The consolidated labour laws still precluded national trade union federations, but even so several unions did establish 'joint action pacts' which by-

## The Legacy of Vargas 47

passed this restriction by committing them to a common programme of struggle. The 'parity' strike of dockers and seamen in Rio de Janeiro at the end of 1960, escaped efforts to contain it made by the Ministry of Labour's *pelegos*.

By the time Goulart took office in 1961 the Cuban revolution had already renewed the strength of popular forces all over Latin America. In Brazil the impact of Cuba drew the embryonic Peasant Leagues into an unprecedented mass movement for agrarian reform, strengthened the radical forces within the working class, and inspired a new wave of nationalism among the intelligentsia and in sections of the army – junior officers, NCOs and lower ranks.

The PSD-PTB bloc, which united elements of the rural oligarchy and the working-class, could not survive in the face of the movement for agrarian reform or increasing union militancy. It began to break up, leaving Goulart poised between the pro-imperialist right and the popular forces. Goulart's only chance of political survival was to move increasingly to the left, provoking finally the military-oligarchic coup.

During the first fourteen months of his presidency, Goulart's powers were limited by the new form of parliamentary cabinet. At first he went out of his way to placate the right, but he was soon forced to change direction by the growing strength of the popular movement. In April 1962 he visited the US, and publicly stressed his opposition to 'Castroite totalitarianism'. Kennedy and Goulart issued a joint communique in support of the proposed Latin American Free Trade Area, which also payed tribute to the political co-operation of the Western hemisphere. Goulart did initiate certain nationalization measures but these were designed to have neither an anti-imperialist nor an anti-capitalist character. When Leonel Brizola expropriated a subsidiary of International Telephone and Telegraph in Rio Grande do

Sul early in 1962, Goulart's response was to discuss with President Kennedy, during his visit to Washington in April, a proposal for the Brazilian government to purchase US-owned public utilities at mutually agreed prices, with the funds realized being reinvested in less 'politically sensitive' industrial sectors. A year later the particularly generous agreement reached with the American and Foreign Power Corporation, the largest of the foreign utility companies, led to bitter attacks on Goulart from the left.

On 1 May 1962, however, when Goulart addressed the traditional working-class rally, he took up the cause of agrarian reform which had in the previous year become a focal demand of the popular movement, and called for a constitutional amendment to enable compulsory purchase of land without prior payment in cash. This immediately alienated the PSD latifundists, and when Tancredo Neves, Goulart's first Prime Minister (a post created by the constitutional amendment of September 1961), resigned in June 1962, Goulart had difficulty in finding a replacement acceptable to Congress. In this crisis the official trade union leadership in the CNTI, called an unprecedented general strike in favour of Goulart's PTB nominee for Prime Minister, San Tiago Dantas, whom Congress had rejected. This manifestation of the new strength of the organized working class led Goulart to seek the left's support for his own plans. In 1962 he allowed the formation of the CGT (General Workers' Executive), an independent political leadership uniting all trade unions and workers' organization, and thus illegal according to strict interpretation of the labour laws. The CGT for the first time bypassed the whole system of compartmentalized trade unions subordinated to the Ministry of Labour through the CNTI, and from then on the unions were politically led by an executive controlled jointly by the PTB and the PCB (which had been in practice legalized). Meanwhile Goulart had been manoeuvring for a return to a presidential cabinet, and in September 1962 introduced a bill to hold a plebiscite on the issue in December. He backed up this move by reshuffling his supporters in the Army into key positions, and emphasized that Brizola and the Third Army in Rio Grande do Sul threatened to revolt if Congress did not pass the bill. The plebiscite was finally held on 6 January 1963, and the presidential system restored by a 5 to 1 majority.

In the early sixties the popular forces developed in strength and confidence, though not at the level of organizational and tactical unity. Julião's Peasant Leagues spread extensively, demanding agrarian reform 'by law or by force', and spontaneous peasant occupations of latifundist lands began to increase. The student movement's efforts were largely directed into the campaign against illiteracy. A *Movimento de Educação de Base* (Movement for Basic Education) was sponsored by the Ministry of Education and had a very definite political dimension, officially intended to build a broad political base for Goulart among those sections of the masses newly awakening to political life, but also providing the UNE (National Union of Students) and the radical student groups with the opportunity for their own propaganda.

The new CGT acted as a powerful pressure group on Goulart, and was to organize the mass working-class rallies that marked the final phase of his regime. The left's strongest national figure however was the left PTB leader, Leonel Brizola, who after his term as governor of Rio Grande do Sul, was elected to Congress from Guanabara in 1962, with a record vote. Brizola's political style was firmly in the populist tradition set by Vargas, but the content of his politics represented a genuine break with his own class background. Under the impact of the Cuban revolution, Brizola – a nationalist first and a social revolutionary second

– embodied a Jacobinism shared by a large section of the intelligentsia, students and lower military whose aim was a national and popular revolution which would place a radical dictatorship in power on an uncompromising anti-imperialist and anti-oligarchic programme. The figure of Brizola was increasingly attractive to working-class militants of the PTB and PCB, impatient with Goulart's vacillations and Prestes's cautious advocacy of a popular front.

From the January 1963 constitutional plebiscite until June, Goulart kept his distance from the radical left and attempted a programme of 'positive' reforms which would disturb neither the balance of class forces within Brazil nor that between Brazil and imperialism. The Triennial Development Plan worked out by Celso Furtado, the Minister in charge of economic planning, aimed to combat inflation (which had reached fifty-two per cent per annum in 1962) while maintaining a high level of economic growth, by means of increased taxation on the propertied classes to provide funds for public investment. The Plan's success depended on a further refinancing of Brazil's short-term debts, repayment on which was now costing forty-five per cent of the total value of Brazilian exports, as well as on a stringent incomes' policy. However, the US government made any further loans conditional on a deflationary policy, while civil servants and army officers pressed vigorously for a seventy per cent salary increase.

In June Goulart had to admit his failure to check inflation and the proposed Plan was abandoned. He reshuffled his cabinet, though not as was expected by bringing in the PTB left. The PSD-PTB majority in Congress was now split wide open by the growth of the peasant movement, Goulart's plans for agrarian reform and Brizola's ascendancy within the PTB. During the summer Goulart played for time, while a wave of strikes in support of wage demands swept the country and provoked counter-agitation from the right. In September 1963 a group of sergeants under Brizola's influence revolted in Brazilia, protesting against their lack of political rights. This sign of subversion within the army itself was to set the professedly constitutionalist majority of the higher military, under Chief of Staff Castelo Branco, on the path of intervention.

In October 1963 Goulart attempted a second way out of the crisis, without mobilizing the left. He asked Congress to declare a state of siege, claiming that he needed special powers to deal with the growing wave of political violence. This was generally received both by the right and the left as a move towards 'continuism', particularly as Goulart had made no attempt to endorse a presidential candidate for the elections due in 1965. Faced with scepticism from all sides, Goulart withdrew his request.

The only course now open to Goulart was reliance on the left. At first this shift was merely a tactical response to objective conditions, but it finally led to a strategic alliance, and it was at this stage that the counter-revolution broke out. In November 1963 at a meeting of the Inter-American Economic and Social Council, Goulart made a rousing call for a united Latin American trade policy towards the developed countries. In his New Year's Day message for 1964 he promised agrarian reform and measures against foreign capital, and later that month promulgated a decree setting a strict ceiling on profit remittances, counting reinvested profits as national capital. In February 1964, he issued a series of decrees controlling prices of basic consumer goods. These measures themselves were radical enough to unite the bourgeoisie and the higher military behind a conspiracy to overthrow Goulart, yet at this stage Goulart showed his political weakness, postponing the crucial choice between the ruling class and the popular forces until it was too late.

San Tiago Dantas (the Minister of Finance whom Goulart had dismissed the previous June) made desperate attempts to rally the left and restore Goulart's Congressional majority by a negotiated popular front. The PCB alone favoured the project which Brizola and the rest of the 'Jacobin' left dismissed as the politics of opportunism and conciliation.

In December 1963, after encouraging the belief that he was about to appoint Brizola as Finance Minister, Goulart had lacked the resolve to make this move, and as late as February 1964 was conniving with the Fourth Army and the Pernambuco oligarchy in their manoeuvres against Miguel Arraes, the leftist governor who had shown his willingness to cooperate with the organizers of the Peasant Leagues. By March, however, Goulart was ready to move. With the Brizolists and the CGT he decided on a programme of structural reforms, to be announced at mass rallies. Congress would be bypassed if necessary with a plebiscite. On 13 March the first of these rallies was held in Rio de Janeiro. 150,000 workers attended with banners demanding agrarian reform and the legalization of the PCB. Brizola spoke first, calling for a constituent assembly. Goulart then signed two decrees before this huge crowd, one nationalizing those oil refineries still in private hands, the other authorizing the expropriation of certain categories of under-utilized latifundist land. He also announced plans for rent control, tax reform, and the extension of the suffrage to illiterates and soldiers, which were presented to Congress in the president's annual message two days later.

The 13 March rally lost Goulart what little support he still had left among the middle classes. In São Paulo on 19 March a hastily organized rally, the 'March of the Family with God for Liberty', called in the name of a Catholic women's organization, attracted a quarter of a million people. With the help of politicians of the right, the military conspirators had at last found their mass base.

The question of power was posed on 26 March, when the arrest of a Rio sailor active in organizing a Sailors' Association provoked a revolt of a thousand sailors and marines. In September 1963 Goulart had suppressed the Brasilia Sergeants' Revolt. This time his response was to dismiss Admiral Mota, the naval minister, to consult the CGT on his replacement, and to declare an amnesty for the sailors involved. This was the signal for a spontaneous revolt among the higher officers.

On 30 March 1964, while Goulart was addressing a televised meeting of army sergeants, General Filho in Minas Gerais mobilized his forces to march on Rio. Goulart sent the First Army to contain the attack, but it joined forces with the rebels on the roads into the city. The CGT called a general strike, but its key militants had already been arrested by the Guanabara political police, under the orders of Governor Lacerda. In the countryside the latifundists, organized in the Brazilian Rural Society, which had functioned as a second headquarters for the conspiracy, with its own militia, unleased white terror against peasant militants, thousands of whom were assassinated in the first days of April. In Rio Grande do Sul Brizola attempted to mobilize loyal sections of the Third Army but on 1 April Goulart ordered him to cease resistance. Goulart fled to Rio Grande do Sul and from there to Uruguay. Brizola followed him a few days later.

Power was now in the hands of the conspirators but the conspirators themselves were deeply divided. The civilian politicians expected the restoration of order and a return to constitutional government but the hard-liners within the military high command – a majority among the conspirators

– had no intention of following their predecessors' example in handing back power at once to the civilians. On 2 April General Costa e Silva appointed himself Minister of War and on 9 April, together with the three service ministers, formed the Supreme Revolutionary Council. Bypassing both the acting President, Mazilli, and the UDN and PSD leaders in Congress, they issued an Institutional Act – the first of many – which while appearing to uphold the 1946 Constitution in fact gave the executive near decree powers and enabled it to suspend the political rights of undesirables for up to ten years. It also made provisions for the election of a President by Congress on 11 April. For the first time officers would be eligible as candidates. One of the leading conspirators, Chief of Staff General Castelo Branco, was elected by a cowed and broken Congress by 361 votes to 2.

The success of the military coup had been assured by an alliance of the military command with politicians of the right and centre who used large sections of the urban middle classes and the petty bourgeoisie as their striking force. Once Goulart had decided to bypass Congress and appeal for power to the people themselves the right was forced to rally its own supporters. Adhemar de Barros and Carlos Lacerda orchestrated the hysterical campaign against Goulart which was mounted late in March, and the governors of two other states, Margalhães Pinto (Minas Gerais) and Ildo Meneghetti (Rio Grande do Sul) contributed their own political forces. Centre politicians in the PSD were able to rally public employees and professionals against administrative corruption and the threat to 'democratic' government which Goulart allegedly represented. The rural petty bourgeoisie were persuaded that his land reforms threatened not only the latifundists' huge properties but their own small holdings as well, and the small capitalist entrepreneurs were blinded by the campaign against Communism.

The military conspirators had completed their plans for the coup soon after Goulart's decisive speech on 13 March, but at this stage by no means all the members of the higher military supported Costa e Silva and Castelo Branco's plans for Goulart's overthrow. The influential General Kruel waited until the last possible opportunity before siding with the conspirators. Only when Goulart had refused for the last time to renounce the CGT did he move his tanks on Rio. Once the military command was united, Goulart and his handful of left-wing officers were effectively defeated. Goulart had mobilized the left too late and was now isolated.

The very speed of Goulart's fall and its alleged 'bloodlessness' deceived the civilian politicians who, like Adauto Cardoso, had been active participants in the plot. Many believed that the coup was merely another 1954 or 1961, a military intervention to restore 'democracy' and to protect the constitution. Those, however, who understood the true significance of the 'March revolution' fully realized that the military were unlikely to entrust power once again to the civilians. In the context of imperialism the Goulart years were not just another temporary failure but a complete refutation of the populist experiment. The ruling classes had tolerated political improvisation for too long. The traditional means for successful involvement of the masses, inherited from Vargas, were by now exhausted. The military announced its task as the 'restoration of order', but in the political vacuum of 1964 this required not a return to democracy but the creation of an entirely new state.

# Chapter 1

# The Ruling Class and its Transformations

## 1. TOWARDS 'GUIDED DEMOCRACY'

The Castelo Branco dictatorship went through two distinct phases. The first ran until 27 October 1965, when the Second Institutional Act was promulgated. The second, from then to 15 March 1967, ended with Branco abandoning power to his successor, Marshal Costa e Silva. In its first phase the regime still presented itself as the defender of the 1946 Constitution against the enemies of democracy: Goulart and the Communists. The 1964 coup was given legal reality by the First Institutional Act of 9 April 1964, which maintained the Constitution while suspending for six months those very constitutional guarantees that would have prevented the purging of Congress, the armed forces, the administration, etc.; the regime wished to be thought of as transitory. It is even possible that some of the putschists really believed in a rapid 'normalization' or 'redemocratization' of the country. They were soon to change their minds. The more the internal logic of the new regime became clear, the more its social base contracted. This process was not automatic. The heterogenous social forces that took part in the overthrow of Goulart had first of all to decide who was to play the hegemonic role in the 'March revolution'. It is customary to describe this dispute as a struggle between 'moderates' (supporters of a rapid 'redemocratization' and of a return to the 1946 institutions) and 'hards' (supporters of a new type of state altogether). The real course of the struggle for hegemony was much more complex, if only because a large section of the putschist soldiers had no other ideology than blind anticommunism, overlaid with the hypocritical moralism typical of the bourgeois official. The 'hards' won out decisively, and the purge within the ruling classes continued until it reached the real 'moderates' themselves, striking at the former Presidents Janio Quadros and Kubitschek, and the governor of Goiás state, Mauro Borges. In political terms this meant that the attack was widening to include leaders not only of the middle classes (Quadros) but leaders of the republican bourgeoisie (Kubitschek) and representatives of bourgeois nationalism, initially spared thanks to their prudent neutrality during the coup.

Insofar as it was only individuals who were affected it was possible however for the new regime to speak without blushing overmuch of the 're-establishment of democratic normality', and this is why the question of elections provided a decisive test. It was this that would decide in practice whether the regime was really heading towards the reestablishment of democratic liberties, as Brazil had known them between 1946 and 1964 (limited though these were in comparison to a fully achieved bourgeois democracy), or whether it was in fact heading towards the establishment of a military and oligarchic autocracy. Fearing this test, the dictatorship tried at first to gain time. The presidential election was due in October 1965, but Castelo Branco, who in April 1964 had committed himself to hand back presidential power to his constitutionally elected successor, obtained from Congress the extension of his mandate until March 1967. In October 1965 only the gubernatorial elections were held and the presidential election was postponed for a year.

In reality it was postponed for ever. The President of the 'Republic' was henceforth to be chosen by the military high command, while the role of Congress was reduced to 'ratifying' the generals' choice. The regime's euphemism for this was 'indirect election'.

If it was a comparatively easy task to bring to heel a Congress from which forty-two members had been expelled, it was more difficult to secure victory in a direct election where, despite police and military harassment and almost complete government control of the mass media, the consciousness of urban workers would still be an important factor and could give victory to the bourgeois-republican and populist opposition. Further repression was thus necessary. On 9 July 1965, the lower house approved an election reform bill declaring numerous individuals connected with the Goulart regime ineligible, and dissolved the smaller parties. Those that did not contain at least five federal deputies and had not obtained five per cent of the vote at the elections were automatically dissolved. Ten small parties disappeared in this way, leaving only the PSD, the PTB, the UDN, the PSP (Social Progressive Party) and the PDC (Christian Democrats). A 'revolutionary Parliamentary bloc' uniting the reactionary forces around the UDN, the pro-American party of economic 'austerity', guaranteed the dictatorship its Congressional majority. These were the conditions in which the electoral test of 3 October 1965 took place.

The opposition's victory was stunning. It won five States out of eleven, including the two most important: Guanabara and Minas Gerais (in twelve other States the gubernatorial elections were not due until later). In Guanabara the opposition candidate (supported by Kubitschek and Goulart) comfortably defeated the regime's candidate, Carlos Lacerda, who was himself to join the opposition some time later. The government's victories were predominantly in the poor and backward agrarian states (e.g. Goiás, Maranhão), of little political importance, where the majority of the peasantry do not vote, and where those that do are anyway under the influence of the local *coronel*.[1]

The victory of the bourgeois-republican opposition (which included more or less all the protagonists of industrial development), confronted the dictatorship with the need for a show of strength. The 'hards' exerted strong pressure on the government, going so far as to insist on military intervention in the states where the opposition had triumphed. They won the first round on 7 October. Castelo Branco announced the preparation of legislative measures designed to extend the power of federal intervention into States' affairs, and to limit still further the rights of the opposition, while declaring that 'the country must respect democratically the verdict of the ballot box'. This combination of anti-democratic measures in practice and protestations of democracy in the abstract did not succeed in placating the 'hards'. On 15 October, the 'captains' proclamation' was issued, calling on the colonels in direct command of units to overthrow Castelo Branco. These ultras were arrested, but their wishes were heeded. On 20 October the President of the Supreme Court, Ribeiro da Costa, published an article urging the officers to 'leave politics alone and return to their barracks'. The Minister of War, Costa e Silva, replied that 'the Brazilian army... left its barracks... to answer the call of the people. There will be no respite until the house has been put in order', adding that Ribeiro da Costa was 'an irresponsible minister'. This split within the ruling bloc was to be repeated three years later, in a quite different political conjuncture, and with Congress, rather than the Supreme Court, at the

---

[1] A *coronel* (meaning literally a colonel) is the name for the local landowner who exercises political control over those peasants in his area who can vote.

mercy of the executive. Each time the legislative or judicial organs acted as if they were a source of real power outside the executive and the army high command, a new coup reminded them precisely who was in power in Brazil.

In October 1965, negotiations between the Minister of Justice and Congressional leaders broke down over the approval of the constitutional amendments submitted by Castelo Branco. The attitude of the Supreme Court, which unanimously approved on 25 October the re-election of its acting president, Ribeiro da Costa, was pretext enough for yet another military intervention. The army had at any price to prevent the opposition's electoral victory from becoming a rallying-point. It manoeuvred rapidly and on 27 October engineered the passage of the Second Institutional Act.

Its most important provisions were that the President of the Republic was to be elected by Congress, thus abolishing universal suffrage; that although Congress was not dissolved, the President was empowered to annul the mandates of federal or state deputies without their being replaced by their substitutes; that the remaining political parties were dissolved, and the President was given power to intervene by decree into States' affairs, 'to ensure the execution of federal law and to prevent or suppress subversion'; finally, the abolition of the special status of ex-presidents was abolished. (The last measure was directed especially against Kubitschek, who had returned to the country after the opposition's electoral victory.)

Far from preparing 'the re-establishment of democracy', the regime of April 1964 had confessed its inability to survive without periodically destroying the 'legality' that it had itself claimed to defend. Because of this, the period from April 1964 to October 1965, was decisive for the republican bourgeoisie, that is for that fraction of the bourgeoisie which, while having opposed Goulart's 'popular front' and participated either actively or tacitly in the 1964 counter-revolution, did not want a militarization of the regime. It must be stressed that Castelo Branco himself was very conscious of the usefulness of a 'legal façade', and took pains to present himself as a mediator between the 'hards' and the 'moderates'. To this end he attempted to pursue the simple enough tactic of expelling the traditional leaders of the big bourgeoisie (such as Kubitschek) and the middle class (such as Quadros) from political life, so as to maintain the social base of the *coup d'etat* (latifundists, big bourgeoisie) within the institutional framework of a 'guided democracy'. The opposition's victory put an end to the usefulness of this tactic. With the Second Institutional Act the regime clearly and unmistakably set under way the construction a military-oligarchic state, a state of a new type which despite superficial similarities cannot be equated with previous fascist or colonial models.

If the political measures of the Castelo Branco dictatorship in its first period (April 1964 to October 1965) expressed a struggle between the militarist and 'democratic' tendencies with the regime, the same cannot be said of the economic measures adopted during this period. Reaction invariably sees the reduction of real wages as the simplest cure for inflation, and one of Castelo Branco's first decrees abolished the mobile wage scale which had compensated for the constant and sharp rise in the cost of living. But small and medium-sized Brazilian firms also earned the attention of Minister Roberto Campos (known in Brazil as Bob Fields for his sincere attachment to the great North American monopolies). Campos put into practice a method known as 'positive insolvency', which consisted of abruptly cutting off government credits to Brazilian firms which failed to show an adequate level of productivity. The method of 'positive insolvency' was a heavy blow to many Brazilian businesses, already affected by an economic stagnation which was to worsen with the effects of wage restriction. In São Paulo alone, the number of bankruptcies grew steadily from 838 in 1963 to 3,689 in 1967. According to Campos, this murderous therapy was the only means of substituting 'non-inflationary for inflationary forms of investment'. The fact that this 'substitution' also implied a substitution of the investor's nationality in no way disturbed him. The important thing was to achieve the 'financial health' of the firms concerned by means of a 'monetary correction of fixed assets and floating capital'. For those who, like Campos, view Brazilian society from the same reassuring perspective as North American monopoly capitalism does, there is certainly no more suitable means to effect the 'rationalization' of the capital market, monetary circulation and the Brazilian economy in general, than to give free play to the principle of 'natural selection'. Small and medium-sized firms could be ruined without too much fear of economic stagnation, since the 'friends from the North' were on hand to undertake massive capital investment. Nor was Campos disturbed by the fact that this capital would occupy strategic sectors of the Brazilian economy, and would export to its country of origin profits incomparably higher than its original investments. What was important was 'rationalization' (i.e. monopolist concentration) of production. If this particularly benefited 'our friends from the North', this was due, explained Campos, to the 'obvious fact that the world is unequal'.[2]

The culmination of Campos's policy of handing over the Brazilian economy to imperialism was the investment guarantee agreement signed in February 1965 by the Brazilian

---

[2] Roberto Campos, 'O ataque dos primitivos', in *O Estado de São Paulo*, 21 January 1970.

ambassador in Washington and the administrator of USAID, an agreement that flagrantly violated the 1946 constitution (which the military claimed to be defending against 'Castro-communist subversion'). 'Under the terms of this agreement, a North American firm can solicit from the Brazilian government a guarantee against every kind of damage to which it might be subject: inflation, breach of contract, revolution, etc. This guarantee being granted, the Brazilian government government loses all right of assessment of the damage. If the firm claims its interests have been prejudiced, the affair is dealt with by officials of the competent department of the US government, which thereby becomes a creditor of the Brazilian government for the sum paid, and reserves the right to recover this from any credit held by the Brazilian government in US banks. The settlement is always to be made in dollars. In the case of one of the governments wishing to rescind the agreement, investors will have six more months to solicit the concession of guarantees and, these being granted, firms will be able to present claims for twenty years from the date of rescinding the agreement.'[3]

II. COSTA E SILVA: CASTELO BRANCO'S LEGACY AND PERMANENT COUP D'ETAT

The second period of the Castelo Branco government saw the further militarization of the regime and the final defeat of those political currents which had supported the overthrowing of Goulart but which now baulked at the destruction of the bourgeois republic itself. The victory of the opposition in the election of 1965 had proved that the 're-establishment of democracy' would entail almost automatically a return to the pre-1964 situation in which the national and the reactionary factions within the bourgeoisie were split. The military and the big bourgeoisie were no more prepared to tolerate this than was the revolutionary left. The only groups interested in such a utopia were the nationalist fraction of the bourgeoisie and the reformists within the working class.

Those among the bourgeoisie not prepared to accept the continued postponement of democracy were swept successively from the political stage. The liquidation of the traditional bourgeois parties and the suppression of universal suffrage reduced the power struggle between the different factions of the ruling class bloc to intrigue and manoeuvre between the various warlords. After October 1965 – the promulgation of the Second Institutional Act – the only politician to offer a focus for opposition to the dictatorship from within the ranks of bourgeois democracy was Carlos Lacerda. It was to be his defeat at the hands of Costa e Silva in 1967 which set the seal on the hegemony of the military.

Castelo Branco's government came to an end in a festival of 'civilianization'. Its final months saw three elections (two indirect, one direct), two legal texts (the new Constitution and the law on national security), a fourth Institutional Act and two new parties[4] to replace the old parties which were disbanded. Such was the political legacy which the next President, Costa e Silva, would inherit from the first government of the new regime.

In the elections Castelo Branco did not trust to chance. A third Institutional Act was promulgated, which stipulated that the twelve postponed gubernatorial elections now due would also be held by 'indirect suffrage', i.e. by vote of the State assemblies. This amounted to holding no elections

---

[3] Miguel Arraes, *Le Brésil, le peuple et le pouvoir* (Maspero, Paris, 1969), p. 212.
[4] ARENA and MDB (see Appendix).

at all, since the State assemblies were just as decimated and intimidated by the expulsions as the federal Congress had been and could do nothing but ratify the dictatorship's candidates. On 3 September 1966 the legislative assemblies of twelve States nominated their new governors. All were men devoted to the new regime and all owed their political careers exclusively to it. The net effect was that civilian leaders of the 1964 putsch disappeared almost totally from the political scene, and the army high command established itself as the sole seat of power. On 3 October 1966, the federal Congress elected Costa e Silva as President designate 336 out of the 473 deputies and senators were present. The single candidate received 295 votes and there were 41 abstentions. The former politicians of the big bourgeoisie were represented in the new government by the Vice-President, a former deputy of the pro-American right in the UDN. Finally the Congressional elections were held on 15 November 1966. The two parties set up by the regime contended for twenty-two million votes which were to determine the re-election of a third of the Senate and the whole of the lower house and the State legislatures. The government party, ARENA (National Alliance for Renovation), brought together the old right (fascists and UDN) and the operators of the PSD and PSP (the latter a mere clique of swindlers, still led by Adhemar de Barros). The 'opposition' party, the MDB (Brazilian Democratic Movement), composed primarily of those former PTB deputies who had escaped the successive purges, together with the remnants of the small centre parties. It existed only to serve as ARENA's *alter ego*.

The results of the elections assured the government an absolute majority in Congress. ARENA obtained 260 seats out of 402 in the chamber of deputies against 142 for the MDB. The mass of the people observed the instruction to abstain given by the left-wing groups. ARENA failed to obtain an absolute majority of the popular vote, if blank and spoiled ballots are taken into account, even though it naturally benefited from the *cabresto*[5] in the countryside, particularly since any hopes of independence here had been dashed by the brutal suppression of the peasant movement in 1964. Moreover, the populist tradition of Brazilian politics leads the Brazilian elector to vote for the individual candidate more than for the party. Those ARENA candidates who received the most substantial majorities were by no means unconditional stooges of the government: Milton Campos for example, in Minas Gerais, who had resigned as Minister of Justice in October 1965 and so made clear his commitment only to the first, 'legalist' phase of the Castelo Branco government.

The Fourth Institutional Act, dated 6 December 1966, convoked deputies for an extraordinary session of Congress at which a new constitutional text, hastily manufactured by the scribes of the military high-command, was to be adopted. The 1964 putsch, the professed aim of which was to defend the 1946 Constitution, was finally revealed for what it was: a putsch to set up a state 'of a new type' with a new constitution, designed to 'legalize' the autocratic and military regime. This Constitution of January 1967 legitimized certain major transformations which had already taken place in the Brazilian state: the suppression of civil and political liberties; the effective elimination of an already weakened Congress; the centralization of power and the introduction of a brand of economic and social reformism peculiar to the military oligarchy.

All the restrictions on political and civil liberty contained in the four Institutional Acts were written into the Constitu-

---

[5] Peasant vote controlled by the local *coronel*.

tion. The 1967 Constitution promised the re-establishment of direct suffrage for gubernatorial elections, although this was never put into effect.

The powers of Congress were severely reduced. The President of the Republic arrogated to himself the right to legislate by decree 'in case of emergency for the public interest'. He acquired the exclusive initiative as far as laws on financial matters or any measures involving an increase in budgetary expenditure were concerned. The law on national security widened the powers and jurisdiction of the military tribunals, and provided the framework for the execution of summary justice.

The 'horizontal' extension of the executive *vis-à-vis* the legislature and judiciary was reinforced by a 'vertical' extension at the expense of the States and communal authorities. The official name of the country was changed from 'Republic of the United States of Brazil' to the simple 'Republic of Brazil'. This titular change echoed the increased importance of the federal police organs and especially the secret service (whose central organ, the SNI – National Information Service – became a Brazilian Gestapo), and the multiplication of permissible cases of 'federal intervention' into the States.

The peculiarities of military-oligarchic reformism were revealed in the following measures: on the one hand, the prohibition of all strikes in the public services; on the other, provisos to facilitate agrarian reform and the institution of 'planned budgets'. While the first of these measures had an unambiguous class character, the other two exposed important contradictions within the ruling class itself.

The need for agrarian reform had long been recognized in principle, though the big bourgeoisie had never been politically strong enough to break the 'united front' of reaction and expropriate the latifundists. In view of the fact that one of the decisive arguments used by extreme reaction to prove that Goulart was a communist was precisely his bill authorizing expropriation of land without prior compensation in currency, the constitutional enshrinement of this very proviso in 1966 reveals the contradictions of the present regime. The SUPRA (Superintendency of Agrarian Reform), designed by Goulart's government to coordinate the preparatory work, had survived the furious violence against the peasant movement which followed the coup. A situation was thus created, ridiculous were it not tragic, in which the latifundists tolerated the preservation of the very body designed for their own abolition. On 15 July 1964, the Minister of Agriculture handed over the direction of SUPRA to the latifundist José Gomes da Silva, who was moved to declare, with a cynicism bordering on naiveté, that SUPRA 'would not again become an organ of agitation and disorder.... That is why the government has entrusted it to a landed proprietor'.[6]

The agrarian policy of the ruling bloc has three main objectives: the first two are the distribution of land to *colonos*[7] in specially chosen strategic areas (the colonization of the Amazon) and the removal of the landless peasants from the North-East to the latifundia of the centre where they would become agricultural wage earners. Obviously the successful widespread implementation of both plans would depend on the prior agreement of different interests within the ruling bloc, and on the weakness of peasant resistance and their inability to dictate the size of their new holdings or the conditions of work. A third objective is the progressive weakening of the traditional landowners by fiscal means

---

[6] *Correio da Manhã*, Rio de Janeiro, 16 July 1964.
[7] *Colonos*, as will be explained more fully in section 111 of the next chapter, are poor peasants tied to land paying rent.

in particular. The proposed switching of the landlord tax from the local to the federal sector would be a heavy blow for *coronelismo* since the interests of the country municipalities have been in practice indistinguishable from those of latifundists themselves, and so municipal taxes never needed to change hands. The government intended also to encourage fixed capital investment by means of fiscal and monetary incentives, with the strategic aim of gradually transforming the old latifundia into large scale capitalist enterprises.

These few observations are not meant as a full analysis of the present regime's agrarian strategy. The major question of the political and economic possibility of a wide-ranging land reform under the dictatorship will be dealt with in section iv of this chapter when questions of the nature of the present state and the balance of forces within the ruling class bloc will be dealt with in detail.

The introduction of 'programmatic budgets' revealed contradictions as well. In the capitalist metropoles, the economic importance of the state continues to increase, so that state monopoly capitalism forms a distinct stage of monopoly capitalism in general. In a dependent capitalist country such as Brazil, however, the situation is different, since the big monopoly corporations are based abroad and are not directly concerned with the affairs of the Brazilian state. Provided that they can remit to their respective metropoles a maximal profit they are indifferent to the nature of the regime, its contradictions and conflicts. (It is the metropolitan capitalist states that are concerned with political and military control of the dependent capitalist countries, as part of their global strategies). Capitalist 'planning' in Brazil thus has a particular content, very different from its equivalent in the capitalist metropoles. It is not conducted for the benefit of a national monopolist oligarchy, but under the constraints of foreign penetration of the key sectors of the national economy. In this respect it is more accurate to speak of an adaptation of Brazilian capitalism to the new characteristics of state monopoly and international monopoly capitalism, insofar as these are reflected within the Brazilian economy.

Forms of capitalist 'planning' were no novelty in Brazil, which had already experienced the *Plano de Metas*, Goulart's Triennial Plan (not put into effect) and lastly the PAEG (Plan of Government Economic Action) which finally cleared the ground for imperialist occupation. Nevertheless, in so far as it subordinates the national economy as a whole to a global strategy (even if the final aim of that strategy is the transformation of the Brazilian economy into a mere extension of the metropolitan capitalist economy), planning enables the systematic use of the state's budgetary and financial resources for investments, unprofitable in the short term (infrastructure, research, etc.), but which permit international monopoly capitalism and its local associates to realize great profits in the most important industrial sectors. Military-oligarchic 'planning' thus provides the regime with a basic instrument for its policy of austerity, itself dictated by US imperialism. Such a policy was all the more necessary insofar as the industrial advance of 1968–9, made possible by the acceleration of the 'transfer' of Brazilian fixed capital to imperialist ownership, increased the already immense number of unemployed (due to the very high organic composition of capital in the modern factories), and rendered the consequences of the rural exodus still more catastrophic. Chronic, structural unemployment, typical of an underdeveloped country, was reinforced by technological unemployment.

The law on national security came into force on 17 March 1967, two days after Costa e Silva assumed the Presidency. The Minister of Justice himself presented the law as a major weapon in a preventive counter-revolutionary war. If in contrast to the repressive laws of 1969 it may still seem rather 'liberal', it is undeniable that it constituted the legal instrument for a police state. Its 'concept' of 'psychological warfare' for example is enough to raise a smile from the least democratic jurist, as it is painfully obvious that this 'concept' was intended quite simply to legitimate a reign of cultural terror. As the Minister defined it: 'Hostile psychological warfare is the use of propaganda, counter-propaganda and actions in the political, economic, psycho-social or military field aiming to influence or provoke among foreign, enemy, neutral or friendly groups, opinions, sentiments, attitudes, or behaviour counter to the achievement of national objectives.'[8]

The law, which ran to fifty-eight articles, was couched in the same tone. It provided sentences of up to six years imprisonment for all who take part in strikes in the public services or in 'essential activities' (whose definition was left to the goodwill of the military tribunals). It also threatened journalists, who could be condemned to two years imprisonment for 'publishing or divulging any news or declaration' considered as a 'threat to national security'. All 'offences' provided for by this law were to be judged by military tribunals. There is no need to stress further the repressive nature of this 'legal' instrument: even the bourgeois press was forced to make its vain protests.

Such was the end product of two and a half years of the government's 'cleansing' operation. During this period Castelo Branco had transformed the weakened institutions of a

[8] Mario Pedrosa, 'Seguranca Nacional contra o Brasil', *Correio da Manhã*, 19 March 1967.

bourgeois democracy and laid the groundwork for the construction of a military dictatorship. His Minister of War, General Costa e Silva prepared to succeed him as President. Though not Castelo's first choice, he knew how to flatter the nationalist and democratic sectors of the bourgeoisie hit hardest by the 'encouraged transfer' policy of Roberto Campos. Costa e Silva was, needless to say, an ardent supporter of the 'revolution' of 1964 and fully intended to pursue its consequences. In a message to Congress in 1967 he voiced his lucubrations on the nature of the new order: 'The Brazilian revolution is incomprehensible to the impatient, because it is a movement of depth which has reached the country's moral foundations before touching its structures. It is no superficial revolution, but one of ideas, of methods, customs and moral norms.' It was due no doubt to his ability to disguise continued repression with the mask of 'democratization' that he had emerged in the first place from the obscurity of a mediocre career.

Armed with the institutions inherited from Castelo, assured of support from an abased Congress and benefiting from an economic recovery after the critical years of 1964–6, Costa seemed certain to preside over the regime's consolidation. Now that the repressive apparatus of the military and the police was securely established he was able to take advantage of a full year of comparative social peace (1967) to reduce the regime's almost universal unpopularity and attempt 'to normalize national political life' with a measure of 'redemocratization'. But this government euphemism described merely those few brief pauses in a reign of growing terror. The left at this stage was still not ready for a direct assault on the dictatorship, and in the absence of enemies from outside the ruling bloc Costa was able to strike the final blow against the remnants of an opposition within. The last effective challenge to the military oligarchy from inside the ranks of the bourgeoisie had come from the *Frente Ampla* (Enlarged Front) reinforced by the allegiance of Carlos Lacerda (an active participant in the 1964 coup) and by the ineffectual support of a discredited PCB. This confrontation was not a trial of strength between the 'revolutionaries of 1964' and the 'counter-revolutionaries' (supporters of the old 1946 republic) but between the partisans of military power and those of civilian power. The failure of this civilian challenge was a decisive turning point in the political history of the regime for it proved that the preservation of bourgeois structures was now inevitably linked with the continuance of a military hegemony. Henceforth political debate within the ruling class bloc would only take place through the mediation of the army, which had now added a monopoly in politics to its monopoly of violence.

This unequal trial of strength had been provoked by the government itself when, to weaken the opposition still further for the legislative elections of November 1966, it annulled the mandates of six federal deputies. Following the lead of Adaúto Cardoso, President of the Chamber of Deputies and representative of an important tendency within the government party (ARENA), the Chamber refused to confirm the new expulsions. Castelo Branco's response was both rapid and effective. Colonel Meira Matos (already distinguished for his command of the Brazilian troops which took part in the occupation of Santo Domingo after the US invasion) closed Congress at the head of a military detachment. This episode convinced men like Carlos Lacerda of the direction in which the regime was moving, and emphasized the need to act before the 'March revolution' devoured all its non-uniformed children. Lacerda had no difficulty in organizing the whole of the bourgeois opposition around the slogan 'the soldiers to the barracks', and the PCB closed the ranks on the left. But since the hypothesis of the spontaneous withering away of the generals had been disproved by the facts, it was necessary to win the support of a section of the army. Hence the two open letters 'to a friend in uniform' which Lacerda wrote, aimed at the young officers whose ideologue he had been for so long. In these letters Lacerda accused the government of 'aiding communism' with its own corruption. These two letters were followed by the Manifesto of the *Frente Ampla*, published on 28 October 1966. Since one of the basic premises of Lacerda's policy was the reconciliation of all anti-militarist currents within the bourgeoisie, the Manifesto proclaimed that it would neither apologize for nor criticize the past. In fact its whole programme, calling for the 'participation of the people in the decisions that forge its destiny', and appealing to 'workers', 'students', 'the middle classes', 'entrepreneurs', 'directors and managers' on the basis of their oppression by 'reaction', not to mention 'women whose religious sentiments have been exploited by those who now turn themselves against the church', and 'soldiers, whose democratic tradition does not permit them to support the usurpation of the people's rights', was borrowed from the very adversaries against whom Lacerda had always fought – Getulism, populism and nationalism.

Costa e Silva's policy towards the *Frente Ampla* was just as effective. He understood that violence would transform Lacerda into the martyr of the 'revolution', while severely compromising his own programme of 'redemocratization'. Besides, it was difficult to gauge what repercussion the slogans of the *Frente Ampla* would have among the young officers and bourgeois politicians linked with the regime. Costa e Silva therefore preferred to leave the reputation of hangman and grave-digger of democracy to Castelo Branco, keeping for himself the role of champion of constitutional 'normalization'. He therefore tolerated the *Frente Ampla* and preserved for some time the government's democratic façade by taking up the most popular aspects of the *Frente*'s policy. For the middle classes, a little democracy and a little nationalism, granted smoothly and from above by the military regime, was preferable to the prospect of rather more democracy and nationalism offered by a clique of discredited politicians without the weapons to defend the country against the 'menace' of the left. This tactical manoeuvre succeeded in neutralizing one section of the *Frente*'s sympathizers while isolating the more 'radical'. In addition, compared with the violence of Castelo Branco and the policies of Roberto Campos, the vaguely nationalist proposals of his Minister of Finance, Magalhães Pinto, appeared to be a real change in policy. The *Frente Ampla* lost its credibility and in the end came to be considered merely as a venture designed to obtain amnesty for a number of bourgeois politicians. Its banning, in December 1967, caused no trouble: it was the consequence not the cause of its defeat.

The defeat of the *Frente Ampla* signalled a radical change. For the first time in contemporary Brazilian history there was no consistent opposition to the regime apart from the revolutionary opposition. The struggle for power ceased to be principally a struggle over the division of power between the various sections of the ruling class bloc. The latter finally understood that to maintain their economic domination they had to resign themselves to losing their political domination to the army. There would henceforth be no other political movements among the possessing classes than the different tendencies represented by the various cliques of generals. The only 'activity' possible for civilian politicians from now on would be to tail behind one of these cliques.

The liquidation of the bourgeois opposition presented

both the advantage of political homogenization of the ruling class and the disadvantage of cutting those demagogic and populist ties which formerly linked bourgeois leaders and parties to sections of the popular masses. The questions to which this account gives rise can only be dealt with once the whole problem has been posed of the balance of forces within the ruling bloc and the nature of the present Brazilian state.

While the dictatorship was completing its 'cleansing' of official political life, the forces of revolution were silently ripening among the student movement, the workers' movement and the most politicized sections of the peasantry. From March 1968 on, these forces took a concrete and visible form. On the one hand the mass movement, first students, then workers; on the other hand the direct actions of the revolutionary left. The ruling classes were divided before the upsurge of the forces of revolution, but divided this time not so much by different political interests, as by the question of what tactic to employ against the popular masses and the fighting vanguard detachments. Costa e Silva, ever prudent, tried to reserve for himself the role of arbiter between the ultras who advocated ever more repression, and the 'doves' preoccupied with preserving the regime's legal and constitutional façade.

However, in the climate of growing violence the regime was led during 1968 to an impasse. Domestically, as well as internationally, the military could only justify its stranglehold on the state apparatus on the pretext of 'restoring order'. The dominant sections of the ruling bloc had been quick to jettison bourgeois democracy when only a military regime seemed capable of maintaining internal order. But when the military showed signs that it might be unable to fulfil this task, they began to regret having made it a present of the state apparatus. The democratic opposition moreover regained some of its courage, and denunciations of police harassment were heard in Congress. The regime responded by attempting to crush the students. After several months of waiting, the military police finally invaded the faculties. Students were led away like prisoners of war, and teachers and students' parents – including an ARENA deputy – were viciously maltreated. Each day the press published photos of the 'defenders of Christian civilization' striking women and adolescents. There were massive abstentions in the São Paulo municipal elections and over twenty per cent of ballot papers were spoiled, the electors writing in either 'UNE' – the banned student union – or 'Guevara'.

Threatened from right and left, Costa e Silva finished by tearing up the 1967 Constitution which in the minds of its authors was the culminating achievement of the new regime.

The crisis which led in December 1968 to the promulgation of the Fifth Institutional Act (the *diktat* of the coup within the coup) was formally similar to the regime's earlier crises, but the balance of forces between the various social classes was quite different. The conflict between executive and Congress, which necessarily involved the defection of a fraction of the government party itself, was provoked this time by the resurgence of the mass movement. But far from leading the mass movement, of which it was now quite incapable, the bourgeois opposition could only tail behind it. The time when the nationalist and democratic bourgeoisie had been able to mobilize the masses against the antinational and anti-popular oligarchy had long passed. Now it could only neutralize one section of the reactionary forces by showing that the military regime had deprived the country of all liberty without for all that being able to guarantee order.

The government finally understood that the farce of 'redemocratization' was not paying off. The hour of final victory for the ultras was approaching. The survival of the regime depended on two things: silencing the Congressional opposition and removing from politics its social base – the republican bourgeoisie, and crushing the resurgence of the Left. The first condition had to some extent been met, but now that even government allies in Congress began to hesitate in their support the need for further 'militarization' became obvious. Only when Congress itself was effectively crushed could the military concentrate all its energies in the promotion of a counter-revolutionary 'state of war'.

The pretext was provided by the speech of an MDB deputy, Marcio Moreira Alves, in which he dared to criticize the Army. A storm of indignation, orchestrated by the army secret service, exploded in every barracks in the country. The most insignificant lieutenant felt personally injured by this terrible offence. The Constitution laid down that proceedings against a deputy required the authorization of Congress and, despite the advice of the ultras, the government requested this authorization. Either because they underestimated the generals' anger, or because they had succeeded in regaining some dignity, the old bourgeois politicians voted the request down. A large number of the ARENA deputies made common cause with the MDB. Immediately afterwards Costa e Silva signed the Fifth Institutional Act.

III. FROM THE FIFTH INSTITUTIONAL ACT
TO THE GARRASTAZU DICTATORSHIP

The Fifth Act (13 December 1968) prorogued Congress and suspended basic legal guarantees (including *habeas corpus*). It was accompanied by a new wave of expulsions of deputies and suspensions of political rights, and it reorganized the ill-famed commissions of investigation, designed to spread terror within the university, and among intellectual and professional circles in general. Some days after the Fifth Act, the army invaded the São Paulo university residential complex. Hundreds of students were carted off by the army and thrown into prison. In their almost puerile anger against the students, whom the military blamed most of all for discrediting the army in the public eye, an exhibition was organized in São Paulo of subversive material which the army had so courageously uncovered in the university. All this amounted to was a few volumes of Marx and some contraceptive pills. Hundreds of political opponents were sent to the *Ilha Grande* in Guanabara bay, together with those whom the regime regarded, in the best fascist tradition, as degenerates: inoffensive hippies and *'tropicalista'* singers.

However, the basic aim of the Fifth Act was the suppression of those legal and constitutional obstacles which still impeded counter-revolutionary war. December 1968 saw the launching of a vast police and military operation across the whole national territory, aiming at the liquidation of the revolutionary organizations.[9] In December 1968 and January 1969 hundreds of prisons were improvised throughout Brazil. The political police, coordinated by the SNI and aided discreetly at a distance by the CIA, wreaked severe damage on the urban guerrilla networks which the armed organizations had set up during the previous year. Torture became a weapon used sytematically by the regime, to which every prisoner suspected even vaguely of liason with the clandestine organizations was subjected. The first armed networks were discovered at the end of January 1969. In São Paulo and Minas the police and army began their

---

[9] In São Paulo this counter-guerrilla operation was given the name *Operaçao Bandeirantes* after the seventeenth century Paulista fortune hunters.

operation of 'encirclement and destruction': VPR (Revolutionary Popular Vanguard) and COLINA (National Liberation Commando) 'nests' were attacked with sub-machine-guns. They met with resistance; encircled, the revolutionary militants preferred death to capture, as they well knew what awaited them in prison. A few months later Lira Tavares, one of the military's theorists, explained in lucid fashion the regime's strategy in the conjuncture of 1968/69. It had been quite simply 'to crush subversion'.

Contrary to what the ultras, as well as certain ultra-leftists, would like to believe, the weakening of the mass movement was more the cause than the consequence of the Fifth Institutional Act, and of the white terror. In Autumn 1968 the student movement was already in retreat, and the arrest of eight hundred students at the UNE congress in October only accelerated a process recognised already by the students. The regime realized that it had to seize this opportunity to carry to a conclusion the annihilation of this advance detachment of the popular movement, whose dynamism had been one of the principal reasons for the scope and strength of the 1968 upsurge. For this reason the government supplemented the brutal repression of student activists by the military with a decree that punished any 'lapse of discipline' by a student with summary expulsion. The effect of this measure was far from negligible, and in 1969 'order reigned' in the student sector.

At the same time the unity of the armed forces had undergone a process of erosion. Costa e Silva's regime was notorious for its corruption, particularly among the most 'moralist' segment of the army, and his thrombosis in August 1969 served merely to reveal conflicts within the dictatorship which would anyway have not gone unconcealed for long. Earlier that year one of the leaders of the 'hard' pro-imperialist tendency within the high command, General

Moniz Aragão, had sent the Minister of War an open letter in which he denounced Costa e Silva's nepotism. He mentioned a number of cases of 'scandalous' corruption in the President's entourage, singling out the appointment of his relatives to sinecure positions and their use of these offices for private gain. He ended by calling for 'the re-establishment of the professional discipline and moral integrity of the military apparatus', warning, without perhaps the political strength to make good the threat, that there was 'still time to put things right' but that this would be 'very difficult next time'. Aragão was quickly relieved of his command.

The expected crisis was headed off by Costa e Silva's stroke. Struck dumb and half-paralysed towards the end of August he could obviously not continue in office. The constitutional provisions for such an emergency were perfectly clear: the Vice-President should take over the functions of the head of state. But the Vice-President was a cunning civilian politician, Pedro Aleixo, and no regime of generals could allow itself to be commanded by a civilian. The head of the President's household, the infamous General Portela, informed only the three military ministers of the President's condition: Rademaker (Navy) a known fascist: Lira Tavares (Army) and Souza Melo (Air), famous in Brazil as co-author of the plan to kidnap certain 'subversives' and drop them into the sea from military planes. After deliberation the four decided on the following way of ensuring the succession. Pedro Aleixo was placed under house arrest while Costa (muffled with a scarf to hide his swollen face) was removed from Brasilia and taken to Rio. Forming themselves into a junta with a Twelfth Institutional Act in order to side step the constitutional provision, they decided that only four star generals would be eligible for the succession. In this way the threat from the right-wing nationalists would be averted since their leader, General Albuquerque Lima, would be unable to stand. It was agreed without question that in this singular republic of soldiers only officers would be able to vote, but only after long and bitter argument was it decided to restrict the suffrage to generals alone. In the event a unique electoral college of 107 generals chose Garrastazu Medici, a personal friend of Costa e Silva and boss of the SNI. Congress, which had been dissolved now for almost a year, was convoked to 'ratify' the high command's candidate, and was more than ever ready to crawl before the military command, voted unanimously for Garrastazu. (The MDB's sixty-two deputies and five senators abstained.)

Garrastazu's 'election' was a victory for the inertia of the state apparatus over the various rival military cliques; he was considered a 'centrist', that is a compromise, but one between factions from which the nationalist option and the option of further democratization had already been excluded.

Garrastazu's 'election' marked the highpoint of the state's 'militarization'. At the height of the crisis, just after the publication of the Twelfth Institutional Act, the US ambassador Burke Elbrick was kidnapped by an ALN commando. To save this representative of monopoly capital the junta was forced to concede all the ALN's demands. Fifteen political prisoners were released and the ALN broadcast its manifesto over radio and television. The leadership crisis had weakened the dictatorship, and this further débâcle exposed them not only in the eyes of the Brazilian people, but in the eyes of their imperialist backers. Their ability to 'maintain order' was seriously questioned. There could be no possibility of liberalization, and an intensification of repression was inevitable. Thousands were arrested in Rio and São Paulo and tortured as a matter of course to extract information. Prisoners could now be held legally (as if the distinction mattered anymore) for ten days incommunicado – time enough, as Paulo Schilling remarks, to make a dumb man speak. The new law punishing subversion with death threatened not only armed insurgents but also editors, publishers and distributors of anything the authorities considered 'hostile'. The military turned on their own as well and conducted a purge of the government party – ARENA – and the high command. Admiral Rademaker was made Vice-President (so that Garrastazu could have as many thromboses as he pleased without provoking another constitutional crisis), and a seventeenth Institutional Act was promulgated with the intention of crushing further opposition from Albuquerque Lima and his clique of young nationalist officers. It authorized the President to reduce to the reserves officers who 'prejudice the unity of the armed forces'.

History has already repeated itself in Brazil. Costa e Silva and Garrastazu are avatars of the same regime. Their coups stabilized and preserved a state which could and can only survive by means of permanent *coup d'etat*. Although these torturers have no sense of humour, there is something comic about pronouncements such as that which Garrastazu addressed to the nation in his first public speech as head of state: 'The Brazilian regime is not completely democratic,' but 'I nourish ... the hope ... of permanently re-establishing full democracy in Brazil before the end of my presidential term.' Five months later, on the sixth anniversay of the coup of 1 April 1964, he was forced to resort to the regime's true language: 'There will be repression, and it will be hard and implacable ... This government is much too strong to let itself be intimidated by terror.'

The military junta bequeathed to the Garrastazu government a 'constitutional amendment' published on 17 October 1969, which was in fact a new constitution in all but name. The republican vestiges were minimal. Judicial powers had already been ceded to the military tribunals, the last vestiges of legislative independence were erased, and near decree power vested in the President in keeping with the military principle of the unity of command. In January 1970 the Minister of Justice Alfredo Buzaid announced that there would be no constitutional changes for another four years, and later that year Garrastazu let it be known that the dictatorship was content with the powers that it had managed to acquire adding that there would be no question of repealing the Fifth Institutional Act. Such is the new type of state that the military dictatorship has constructed in the six years since the 'revolution' of 1964.

IV. THE BALANCE OF ECONOMIC POWER
WITHIN THE RULING CLASS AND THE NATURE
OF THE PRESENT REGIME

Throughout this brief account of the consolidation of the generals in power the question of the nature of the present regime has been left unanswered. Moreover, though we have mentioned the different forces within the ruling class, the details of economic power have been postponed until now. In Brazil dependent capitalism has given rise to a society in which political struggle shows a remarkable autonomy in relation to the fundamental class structure, and in which the real interests of the ruling class need not reveal themselves obviously or straightforwardly at the political level.

Indeed the most striking feature of Brazilian society since the 1964 coup is its dual character: economic power is held by the dominant sectors of the ruling class while political power is exercised by a militarized bureaucracy. The exploiting class comprises five main sectors, each corresponding to a different stage of capitalist development in Brazil and each with its own specific interests which may or may not coincide with the interests of the class as a whole: the industrial bourgeoisie, the big coffee bourgeoisie, the latifundist oligarchy, the managers of Brazilian state capital, and finally international monopoly capital together with its domestic associates. Hegemony within this class belongs to the international corporations, their Brazilian associates and state capital. By means of a 'pact of dependence' made possible by the 1964 coup, this dominant bloc has established a division according to which heavy industry and consumer durables remain in the hands of imperialism, light industry in the hands of its domestic associates, while the state sector concerns itself with infrastructural investment and utilities.

The industrial bourgeoisie centred in São Paulo was never dominant and has been further weakened, as this section will show, by the regime's cessionist policies. The São Paulo coffee bourgeoisie is now a receding force as its share of the national product continues to fall. The latifundist oligarchy is the most backward sector of all and, politically powerful out of proportion to its economic weight, it presents the greatest barrier to the regime's plans of 'rationalizing' Brazil's declining agriculture.

Political hegemony on the other hand is exercised by a bureaucracy of officers and technocrats who, while placing the state at the service of this economically dominant bloc, are not the exclusive representatives of any one sector within it and who therefore enjoy a certain independence in their choice of political strategies.

The aim of this section will be to examine in turn the present role of each of these economic sectors and the consequences for each of the 'pact of dependence', and then to pose the question of the nature of the present regime. An understanding of these two things is of course essential for the correct estimation of armed struggle in Brazil and can be the only basis for a correct revolutionary strategy. For only when the displacement of forces within the ruling bloc are fully understood can the enemy's weaknesses be exploited.

*The position of agriculture and the economic relationship between agriculture and industry*

The decline in the relative importance of agriculture in Brazilian economic life has in no way been a uniform and linear process. The share of agriculture in the gross national product, which fell from 31·3% in 1950 to 28·3% in 1960, actually rose again to 31·0% in 1965. According to FAO statistics, Brazilian agricultural production increased by an average of 4·6% per annum between 1958 and 1964.

Although the share of agriculture in the gross national product has remained constant, the composition of agricultural production must be taken into account, in particular the balance between production for the home market and for export, and the division of home market production between traditional Brazilian crops and import substitutes (particularly wheat). It is common knowledge that for a whole century Brazil's role in the international division of labour was restricted almost exclusively to the production of coffee. The most important changes in the role of the coffee sector must now be analysed in more detail in order to define more accurately the position of the export-agricultural bourgeoisie within the ruling class bloc. Two variables – the share of coffee in Brazilian exports, and the share of Brazilian coffee in world coffee imports, illustrate the decline in the importance of agriculture for the Brazilian economy as a whole:[10]

---

[10] See John Brooks, 'The role of coffee in the Brazilian Economy', in Claudio Veliz's *Latin America and the Caribbean* (Anthony Blond, 1968), p. 634. The figures cited are from Edmar Lisboa Bacha, 'A politica cafeeira do Brasil, 1952–1967', in *Dados*, no. 5, 1968, p. 146.

|      | Coffee exports as % of total | Brazilian coffee as % of world coffee imports |
|------|------------------------------|-----------------------------------------------|
| 1952 | 74%                          | 49%                                           |
| 1960 | 56%                          | 39%                                           |
| 1966 | 44%                          | 34%                                           |

Coffee, which in 1952 made up almost three-quarters of Brazilian exports, today represents less than half. That is why, despite the 1964 coup, the 'coffee bourgeoisie' had to accept the so-called 'eradication policy' which reduced the number of Brazilian coffee bushes from 4·4 thousand million in 1962 to 2·6 thousand million in 1967. While still remaining the chief Brazilian export, coffee lost its position as the overwhelmingly dominant source of foreign currency. The relative decline of coffee exports brought in its train that of the export-agricultural sector as a whole. Although no single product has taken the place of coffee in the Brazilian export economy, it is iron ore and general manufactures, rather than any agricultural product, which have experienced the strongest export development in the past few years.

This expansion is connected to the growth of trade between Brazil and her partners in the Latin American Free Trade Association, which has particularly encouraged the production of capital goods. This change in the composition of Brazilian exports is very significant. The 'dynamism' of iron ore sales (not to speak of the pillage of atomic ores by US interests) is in fact a symptom of the intensification of cessionism after the 1964 coup, from which Hanna Mining and the Bethlehem Steel Corporation have particularly profited.

The position of manufacturing exports is quite different. Just like the loans granted the Brazilian government by the imperialist metropoles and international banks, this is one of the fruits of the 'pact of dependence'. Unable to promote the even development of its social productive forces, the Brazilian bourgeoisie could not find within its national frontiers a large enough market for the products of large-scale monopolist industry. It took on the role of a sub-imperialist bourgeoisie, with the still more underdeveloped bourgeoisies of the rest of Latin America as the clients of 'Brazilian' modern industry. The search for profits in the specific conditions of dependent capitalism in Brazil explains the monstrous fact that instead of concentrating on the production of tractors, in order to help rescue tens of millions of Brazilian poor peasants and unemployed from misery, Volkswagen of Brazil produces thousands of cars for the big and middle bourgeoisie of the rest of Latin America. While production of cars increased from 256,000 in 1968 to 326,000 in 1969, production of tractors has fallen from 12,000 units in 1961 to 8,500 in 1967. Brazil, with 8·5 million square kilometres and over 90 million people only possessed 140,000 tractors in 1969, while the German Federal Republic, with 250,000 square kilometres and 58 million inhabitants, possessed 1·3 million.

Agricultural production for the home market is the sector in which the regime's economic policy has shown least consistency. The reasons for this lie in the very nature of the ruling class bloc, more precisely in the political impossibility of breaking the unity of the ruling classes by a bourgeois-democratic type of agrarian reform, for the military-oligarchic regime does not feel strong enough to unburden itself of the latifundist oligarchy or even of its most backward and uneconomic sectors.

The regime's problem was what agricultural policy it could pursue in the context of a dependent capitalism which had been unable to industrialize the countryside. The general line of its tactic has been analysed by Celso Furtado, who defines it as the search for social stability through 'pastorization'.

The Brazilian version of pastorization presents the following features: (1) the under-employed population in the urban zones, and the surplus population in general, are encouraged to migrate to still unoccupied land, particularly in central Brazil. The agricultural production of this new land has to be absorbed by the towns ... The latifundia nearest the centres of consumption, and equipped with a certain infrastructure, are encouraged to modify the composition of their output. Arable crops are cut back and restricted to the best quality land, so that they can compete in the cities with the product of the newly cultivated regions of the interior. Land previously sown is turned over to livestock. The total value of latifundist production may fall, but not necessarily its profitability.... Urban investment is reduced particularly in the industrial sector, so as to put a brake on the movement of population to the towns. The expansion of the urban market for agricultural products will therefore tend to slow down. The latifundia will be able to adapt in the manner described. The new agricultural zones, faced with the slower growth of urban demand, will tend to fall back to subsistence production.... Once the attraction at present exercised by the cities is eliminated, by reducing public and private investment in the urban regions, migration to the great expanses of the interior will tend to extend the economy horizontally and reduce structural modifications to a minimum. The success of this pastorization plan would substantially reduce social tensions.[11]

Although the present development of class struggle in Brazil makes the success of this plan much less probable, analysis of the agrarian policy of the Costa e Silva and Garrastazu governments clearly shows that the aims pursued are very well summed up as the search for 'social stability through pastorization'. This policy, already outlined on various occasions by the different planning ministers since 1964, has been defined more precisely by the present government, which has begun to put into practice what it calls the

---

[11] Celso Furtado, 'Brésil: de la république oligarchique à l'état militaire', in *Les Temps Modernes*, October 1967.

'colonization plan'. This provides for the migration of 1·8 million people, 45% of the region's labour force, from the overpopulated North East to central Brazil.

These attempts at 'pastorization' are a dismal caricature of the agrarian reform which the regime will not carry out. The ruling classes only want to gain time, and they rely for this on the vast and almost empty expanses of central Brazil and Amazonas. By flooding these regions with poor peasants, 'voluntarily' uprooted from the North East, the ruling classes are trying to dilute the class contradictions in the countryside spatially, while in fact they are putting Brazilian society into a state of quasi-hibernation. Far from conflicting with the supposed 'dynamic' function of the 'growth' industries set up in Brazil by the international monopoly corporations, the policy of pastorization in fact complements this, since the 'dynamic' industries are just as unable to absorb peasant labour as they are incapable of raising the standard of living of the great mass of the population. The 'westward march' is intended to perform this function in two ways. On the one hand it is meant to take the edge off the class contradictions in the great North-Eastern peasant concentrations, especially as the 'volunteers' sent to central Brazil are chosen from 'strategic' areas. On the other hand it is meant to diminish the influx of hungry peasants to the *Favelas* of the urban centres.

The 'colonization plan' might also bring the ruling classes other advantages. It is common knowledge that land in Amazonas and central Brazil is being bought up on a large scale by Brazilian and foreign (especially US) latifundists, who know better than anyone that there is no other place in the world where land is as cheap. All that is missing is labour. The 'colonization plan' is there to provide this, at a price as attractive as that of the land. In the absence of wage labour the 'pioneer' latifundists will continue to buy slaves.

The evidence of slave trading between the North East and central Brazil is irrefutable, and is corroborated by the regime itself.[12]

What are the chances of success of this 'colonization plan?' We shall see in the final chapter that at the same time as the beginnings of rural organization by the left, there was a resurgence of the spontaneous peasant movement, especially in the North East, where the drought of 1969–70 was particularly severe. Will the poor and hungry peasants be strong enough to show in practice that the only social class in too great supply in the North East is the latifundist oligarchy? In strict economic terms, the colonization plan is just as realizable as the development of large-scale industry in conditions of dependent capitalism, but the last word will always depend on the progress of the class struggle.

The regime's attitude towards other branches of agriculture and other social strata in the countryside has been more hesitant. Wholesale prices in agriculture have fallen very significantly behind industrial prices in the last few years. The government has tried to attenuate the effects of this by such measures as reducing the interest rate on its loans to small and middle-sized farmers. The most remarkable result of these concessions was a great advance in wheat production in southern Brazil. In the late 1950s US aid had driven the smaller Brazilian wheat growers out of business, forcing Brazil to spend 820 million dollars on the import of wheat between 1961 and 1965, of which the US received 56%. The US thus not only managed to dispose of its

---

[12] According to *O Globo* children are sold for eighty new cruzeiros per head in the interior of Paraiba state in the North East. An article for 13 December 1969 reported the discovery of forty children bought in this way working on a rice plantation in Mato Grosso. This is not the place to discuss the genocide of the Indians which accompanies the 'march west'. A source on this question is an article by Gregorio Selser in *Marcha*, 30 December 1969

surplus wheat, but also to pose as the benefactor of hungry Brazilians. With the government's recent encouragement to Brazilian wheat growers, production of wheat, which had fallen in the early sixties to around 200,000 tons, is now well above its former peak of 700,000 tons.

Despite these partial successes – which to a certain extent express the government's aim of encouraging the development of intermediate bourgeois strata in the countryside (although its main concern is to save foreign currency) – the situation of Brazilian agriculture as a whole is very bad. The abundance of land and of unskilled labour prevents this colossal economic wastage from resulting at once in an unprecented agrarian crisis. For the time being the 'only' results are peasant poverty and the under-consumption of the urban masses. Moreover, the low productivity of agricultural labour limits the impact of any partial successes that the regime may claim. For example the average production of rice in Brazil is only 1,380 kilos per hectare, compared with 2,980 kilos in Chile, 4,180 in Egypt, and 4,340 in Turkey. The same goes for wheat, which is why representatives of the associated bourgeoisie complained that the Bank of Brazil, which has a monopoly over the wheat trade, pays Brazilian farmers the equivalent of 123 dollars per ton of wheat, while imported wheat costs only 52 dollars.

It was said at the beginning of this section that the landowners were the most backward sector of the ruling bloc and it was suggested that what stood in the way of the regime's removing this brake on development by means of agrarian reform was the latifundists' *political* strength. It is true that under Castelo Branco the landowning oligarchy had more than its share of political representation: it dominated Congress and secured a number of ministries. Since Castelo, however, the regime has been completely militarized and political power more and more centralized. Whatever influence the latifundists may have kept at the local and state level they are no longer able to exert any pressure at the centre. To the extent that they are politically dispensable, then, it is an oversimplification to say that agrarian reform is politically impossible.

What then stands in the way of a land reform programme for the present regime? Why cannot the regime expropriate the most backward and unproductive sectors of the latifundist oligarchy – the sugar producers of the North East? The answer is that they could do so but that they would not thereby lessen the contradictions in the countryside. For in the case of sugar production the only possible reform which would both lighten the misery of the peasants and yet keep the sugar industry productive would be to turn the agricultural-industrial sugar complexes into self-managed co-operatives. But of course only a radical democratization of the present regime could make this possible and even then it would still be improbable. In the absence of this unlikely change, the development of the social productive forces in the countryside would benefit only the grand bourgeoisie: a transition from traditional landlordism to large-scale agricultural capitalism.

Whether the likelihood of agrarian reform is a political or economic question is, one can now see, really a side issue. What matters is the content of the reform. Though the regime may have nothing to fear any longer from the latifundists themselves and though it may be fully prepared to dispossess them by slowly transforming the old latifundia into large scale capitalist enterprises, they still have everything to fear from an immiserated peasantry. Such a transformation of landless peasants into agricultural wage-earners could only make the situation in the countryside more explosive.

This analysis is borne out by the thread of rationality running beneath the hesitations and contradictions of the regime's agrarian policy. Under Castelo Branco even a land reform was made *legally* possible by the 'statute on land' passed in 1964. Without going into the details of this bill one can say that it was the legal instrument for a policy for liquidating the most backward of the latifundists to the benefit of capitalist entrepreneurs and large 'modern' tenant farmers. More recently the regime has provided finance for investment in agricultural plant and equipment (in the form of fiscal incentives to the more 'modern' landowners) and has centralized the collection of the latifundists taxes in order to ensure that they are indeed collected. (The latifundists had previously paid municipal and not federal taxes. These were levies only in name since the municipalities were in practice indistinguishable from the latifundists.) All this may go under the name of 'agrarian reform' but the fact remains that not an inch of land has been expropriated. If anything a land reform in reverse has been carried out. Peasants have been evicted from the land they occupied during the high tide of the peasant movement (1958–64) and to complete the irony the agency which supervised the evictions was the IBRA (Brazilian Institute for Agrarian Reform).

## The contradictions of dependent capitalism

A rigorous Marxist critique of the 'sociology of development' has still to be produced. The incompleteness and limitations of our analysis of Brazilian capitalism, of which we are only too conscious, are due to this absence.

Analysis of the contradictions of dependent capitalism must clarify a certain number of notions – empirical and ideological – which have been used to describe the historical development of capitalist relations of production in the era of imperialism and state monopoly capitalism. The most important of these are 'import substitution' and 'cessionism'. The relationship between 'import substitution' and 'cessionism' is extremely complex. In very general terms the significance of 'import substitution' can be said to have changed in Brazil from the moment that the great international monopoly corporations began systematically to install themselves. It ceased to be a function of the national development of capitalism and the loosening of the ties of dependence on the imperialist metropoles, and became just the opposite: the expression of anti-national capitalist development and the reinforcement of ties of dependence. In accepting the displacement of Brazilian industry by the imperialist corporations, the Brazilian industrial bourgeoisie renounced its pretensions of autonomy, and recognized *ipso facto* that it could not itself achieve the monopolist transformation of Brazilian capitalism, which in the era of the 'technological revolution' (or 'second industrial revolution') demands a technical base and capital accumulation which are only within the reach of the international monopoly corporations. However, those writers who reduce cessionism denationalization of industry alone, i.e. to the remittance abroad of an important part of the surplus-value produced by the Brazilian working class, inevitably underestimate the anti-capitalist content of the Brazilian revolution and remain within the ideological limits of petty-bourgeois nationalism.

Under the military-oligarchic regime, import substitution and cessionism have ceased to be alternative economic policies for the Brazilian bourgeoisie, and are now two interdependent aspects of the new 'pact of dependence'. It is important to realize the specific consequences of this interdependence for the historic development of Brazilian capitalism. Considered in relation to the dominant mode of social production, the particular characteristics of industrial development under the military-oligarchic regime derive above all from the very high organic composition of capital in the most important industrial sectors, which are generally those belonging to the international monopoly corporations. This has several consequences, particularly for the contradiction between labour and capital. The rate of demographic growth in Brazil is near or just above three per cent per year. The influx of poor peasants, without land or work, constantly increases the number of unemployed in every industrial city. The increase of unemployment and underemployment, not only in absolute numbers but also as a proportion of the population, is inevitable as the 'dynamic' industries require skilled labour which the rural immigrants cannot provide. Thus although there is no technological unemployment in Brazil, the proportion of the working class in the active population continues to decline. It is now 6·5% against 25% in Argentina. The table on page 88 shows in broad outlines the distribution of employment by sectors, as well as the relative productivity of labour in each sector (in relation to manufacturing industry) and the annual rate of growth of productivity.[13]

The proportion of industrial workers in the active population, which as this table shows fell from 9·8% to 9·1% between 1950 and 1960, fell again to 8·4% by 1964, and to 6·5% by 1968, while industrial productivity rose by an average of 6·8% per annum. These figures show to what extent the effects of capitalist uneven development are aggravated in conditions of dependence. The hegemony of the great international monopoly corporations over the

---

[13] 'A Industrialização brasileira: Diagnostico e Perspectivos', published by the Ministerio do Planejamento e Coordenação Geral, January 1969, pp. 119–121.

Brazilian economy thus demands a new type of population policy, able at any price to stem the rural exodus and the concentration of unemployed and underemployed in the urban zones.

|  | Relative productivity (Manufacturing Industry = 100) | | Annual growth rate of productivity (average 1950–60) % | Percentage of total employment | |
|---|---|---|---|---|---|
| Sector | 1950 | 1960 |  | 1950 | 1960 |
| Agriculture | 20·6 | 13·6 | 2·49 | 62·4 | 55·1 |
| Manufacturing industry | 100 | 100 | 6·83 | 9·8 | 9·1 |
| Mining | 24·8 | 33·5 | 10·05 | 0·7 | 0·5 |
| Construction | 19·0 | 13·8 | 3·48 | 3·6 | 3·6 |
| Electric power | 184·1 | 116·3 | 2·04 | 0·2 | 0·3 |
| Commerce | 123·2 | 75·6 | 1·74 | 5·8 | 6·9 |
| Transport | 96·2 | 64·7 | 2·69 | 4·2 | 4·9 |
| Services | 62·2 | 26·6 | −1·59 | 10·2 | 12·4 |
| Government | 113·3 | 24·1 | −8·50 | 3·1 | 7·2 |

But the effects of this hegemony, and the mode of development it implies, i.e. the increasing importance of the 'dynamic' industries, are not restricted to the relationship between labour and capital. As dependence under the military-oligarchic regime has changed the general direction of development of Brazilian capitalism, the search for profit can no longer be realized chiefly through import substitution. The exhaustion of the simple process of import substitution had long been inevitable, and it lost its 'dynamic role' as soon as the majority of goods previously imported from the imperialist metropoles came to be produced in

Brazil itself. The 'new course' of Brazilian capitalism, which we have already analysed in broad lines, dates from that moment.

The problem of the realization of surplus-value and the accumulation of capital could no longer be resolved in the old way. This problem was no longer one of the conquest of a pre-existing market by local industry. There certainly still remain imports to be substituted (petrol, wheat, certain types of machinery and modern raw materials), but the role of import substitution has become a completely secondary one, as far as economic growth is concerned. By associating itself with the international monopolies, Brazilian capitalism ceased to be chiefly a producer of consumer goods for the home market. The 'integration' of industry meant not only that heavy industry and the 'dynamic' industries as a whole acquired a preponderant role, but also that the home market (especially the market for the means of subsistence for the working class) was no longer able to guarantee the realization of surplus-value. The increasing unevenness of Brazilian capitalist development condemned the great mass of the population to under-consumption and under-employment, while bringing about an ever more acute danger of relative overproduction.

In the mind of the regime's technocrats, this immense human wastage (a striking example of the antagonism between the social character of production and the private character of appropriation) takes on the innocent form of a 'strategic choice' between different 'models of development'.

## The denationalization of industry[14]

The relative decline of Brazilian private capital in the face of imperialist encroachment does not necessarily imply the

[14] Contrary to its usual English meaning 'denationalization' here should be

weakening of Brazilian state capital. The relationship of the state sector to private capital on the one hand and to imperialism on the other is a complex one and there is no evidence that the state sector is being liquidated or abandoned. The difference between Kubitschek's cessionist policy and that of the present regime is not a quantitative one. Although Paulo Schilling speaks of the Castelo Branco government as aiming at 'total cession', at the elimination of all remaining obstacles in the way of total occupation of the Brazilian economy by the US monopolists,[15] this formula cannot pass as an adequate analysis of the military-oligarchic regime's economic policy, and it makes the role of the local ruling classes incomprehensible. It even hides the true nature of the problem, the actual content of the 'pact of dependence', and the division of functions – i.e. of the means of production – between the international monopoly corporations, their associated bourgeoisie and the state sector. Some whole industries, such as paper, textiles, wood and leather are still in the hands of Brazilian capital.

The new element introduced by the military-oligarchic dictatorship, in contrast to earlier cessionist policies, was not the simple acceleration of this process, nor simply the 'battle against inflation' (any government would be forced to tackle an inflation running at close on a hundred per cent per annum), but rather a coherent strategy of adaptation of Brazilian capitalism to the new conditions of the 'pact of dependence': integration and subordination of the national economy to the general requirements of state monopoly capitalism.

---

taken to mean a transfer of Brazilian capital to foreign ownership. 'Destatization' means the return of an industry from the state to the private sector.

[15] Paulo Schilling, 'Brésil: le cessionisme acceleré', *Tricontinental*, no. 2, 1969, p. 55.

The balance-sheet of denationalization is heavy. According to data worked out by a special commission of Congress in 1968, foreign capital controlled 40% of the Brazilian capital market, 62% of all foreign trade, 82% of maritime transport, 77% of international air lines, 100% of motor vehicle production, over 80% of the pharmaceutical industry, 39% of engineering production, 62% of vehicle component production, 48% of aluminium and 90% of cement. Half of all foreign capital came from the US, and then German, British, French and Swiss firms followed in order of importance.[16] The counterpart of denationalization was an influx of foreign investment. 'One hundred million dollars in new foreign investment was forecast for 1965, of which 74 million materialized. In 1967 actual foreign investment was 70 million dollars. In the same period foreign-owned firms remitted to their parent companies much higher sums in the form of profits and dividends: 102 million dollars in 1965, 127 million in 1966 and 130 million dollars in 1967, almost twice the amount of new foreign investment. To this total must be added the enormous sums paid out for management services, technical assistance, patent licenses, royalties and importers' commissions; in 1967, 170 million dollars was sent abroad under these headings. At the same time, the foreign debt reached four thousand million dollars, and in 1968 interest and amortization payments reached 500 million dollars.... In 1967 Brazil also paid 110 million dollars in freight and insurance charges, and besides all these payments, there is a clandestine export of capital to take into account. In its report for 1968, the central bank noted that 180 million dollars left Brazil illegally in 1966, and 120 million dollars in 1967.'[17]

[16] Eduardo Galeano, 'Denationalization and Brazilian Industry', *Monthly Review*, December 1969, p. 13.
[17] ibid., pp. 16–17.

Such is the price Brazilian capitalism has paid to raise its productive forces to a level compatible (in a relationship of integration and subordination) with those of metropolitan capitalism. Has this been good business? The practice of a social class can be judged either from its own particular interests or from those of the society as a whole. Campos's economic policy (and that of the military-oligarchic regime in general) has been one of shameful cessionism, but in no way one of suicide. It is wrong to conclude (as many Brazilian Marxists, both right and left-wing, have done) that Campos's policies have led the country to the verge of economic disaster, and that they have not even been in the general interests of the Brazilian bourgeoisie. It is understandable for the PCB theorists to make this mistake. Since their programmes have explained conclusively that the Brazilian revolution is anti-feudal and that its anti-imperialist content will be achieved within the limits of bourgeois nationalism, they are forced to show that Campos's policy does not correspond to the interests of the Brazilian bourgeoisie. But there are left-wing Marxists who make a parallel mistake, as for them every event must be interpreted to prove the imminent and final defeat of capitalism. In reality the Brazilian bourgeoisie's relationship of integration and subordination to international monopoly capitalism enables it to develop a viable and coherent economic strategy, although the price of this 'success' is a colossal waste of human resources, and despite the fact that the development of dependent capitalism adds to the general contradictions of the capitalist mode of production the specific ones of a relationship of dependence.

Nor should it be forgotten that the denationalization of industry is not a constant or absolute premiss of the 'pact of dependence'. One of the Castelo Branco government's most scandalous cessionist operations was the *purchase* (i.e.

nationalization) of the Brazilian branches of Bond and Share Inc. The dictatorship paid almost 400 million dollars for scrap metal. Bond and Share were able to use the assets realized by this sale for the purchase of Brazilian firms in profitable and expanding lines and, with the help of the customary methods of bribery, to buy these up at ridiculous prices. The sale of the Bank of Brazil's shares in the Companhia de Acos Especais (ACESITA) to Bond and Share for 18 million dollars was even denounced by the right-wing paper *Correio da Manhã*. Thanks to such anti-popular measures as the 'realistic tariffs' introduced for users of electric power, every capitalist sector – the international corporations, the Brazilian state sector and the associated bourgeoisie – had its cut at the expense of the Brazilian people.

The results of this policy of national humiliation were not at all bad from the bourgeoisie's viewpoint. In exchange for its accommodating policies, the Brazilian government received very substantial credits from the imperialist monopolies and their international organizations, in the most part for infrastructural development. In return for ceasing to encourage local capitalist development in large-scale industry, the Brazilian state acquired resources to use on infrastructural projects and for an 'industrialization programme' designed to attentuate the worst effects of uneven development within the country. It thus carried out its main task, that of ensuring the Brazilian ruling classes a new historical respite. We will now consider the significance of this respite and the contradictions to which it has given rise.

## The role of the state and the economic balance of forces between the imperialist metropoles, the state sector and the associated bourgeoisie

Eight out of Brazil's ten largest firms are state enterprises, one is foreign-owned and only one is a Brazilian private company. Significantly, the state enterprises show a substantially lower profit on their capital. In the rating of companies by their gross profits, foreign companies take four out of the top five places; no Brazilian private company appears in the first ten.

While in the capitalist metropoles the public sector is under the direct control of monopoly capital (hence the definition of the economic structure of these social formations as state monopoly capitalism), in the dependent capitalist countries the economic hegemony of *foreign* monopolies explains both the considerable, if relative, autonomy of the national state and the public sector of the economy in relation to national private capital, and the privileged relationship between the international monopolies and Brazilian state capital.

The dual question of 'statization' and denationalization is the pivot of the struggle for hegemony between the different factions of the ruling class. The outcome of this struggle will be decided by the balance of forces between the three main sectors of Brazilian capitalism. The 'associated bourgeoisie' willingly accepts denationalization, but is disturbed by 'statization'; its chief aim is the continued association of Brazilian private capital with international private monopoly capital. The newspaper *O Estado de São Paulo*, a mouthpiece of this sector, often insists on the need to 'finance development' not through government-to-government loans from the imperialist metropoles, but rather by the direct investments of the international monopoly corporations. The state sector, with its close links with military nationalism, is disturbed by denationalization but applauds 'statization'. This sector could be defined as a *new type of national bourgeoisie*, whose economic base is no longer national private capital and whose political strength derives not from the alliance between the bourgeoisie and the popular masses, but from military nationalism (backed up by the technocrats involved in the management of the public sector). The industrial and banking bourgeoisie wavers and will always waver between association with imperialism and this new type of nationalism, but in either case it will tail behind events. The third sector which, while not opposed to the denationalization of industry, favours the development of the public sector, is composed of a large section of the regime's technocrats who rely on the 'progressive' role of planning to carry through their anti-popular policies for adapting the Brazilian economy to the new conditions of dependence obtaining in the era of imperialist decline. The economic importance of the public sector can be seen from Costa e Silva's 'strategic programme' for the economy, which forecast for the period 1967–70 an overall investment of 32 thousand million new cruzeiros, of which 21·4 were to be provided by the public sector and only 10·5 by the private.

This section has so far analysed the Brazilian economy in order to discover which are the dominant and which are the recessive sectors. What political implications can be drawn from these findings? How in particular can they be used to answer the question of why an officer caste was able to *consolidate* itself in power? For what stands in need of urgent explanation is why the 1964 coup turned out not to be a mere 'accident' in the life of republican Brazil, and this in turn leads one to pose the question of the significance of the relative autonomy of the Brazilian state poised between a *local* ruling class whose instrument it is in theory, and international monopoly capital whose instrument it is currently in practice.

It is here particularly important to avoid all dogmatic simplifications. The military-oligarchic regime is not the only capitalist regime possible in Latin America. It is not the 'necessary' or 'fatal' culmination of an 'irreversible' process of 'militarization' of the Latin American continent. In other words it is not a world-historical phenomenon, but a specific historical one. In other Latin American countries the balance of forces between the different sectors of the ruling class, while not notably different from that in Brazil at the time of the 1964 coup, has produced bourgeois-nationalist regimes (Peru, Bolivia), and permitted the survival of bourgeois-republican regimes (Chile under Frei, Venezuela).

Among the main features of Brazilian society which have permitted the survival of a military oligarchy one may cite the following: firstly, because the hegemonic sector of the Brazilian economy (the international monopolist corporations) lives abroad and is only represented in Brazil by its local managers and straw bosses, the political dominance of the military is considerably strengthened. For it is one of the peculiarities of the Brazilian political system that power is increasingly concentrated in the hands of two categories of manager: the managers of international monopoly capitalism (the technocrats, of whom Roberto Campos is only the most complete example), and the managers of state capital and the Brazilian state sector in general. In contrast to these the Brazilian industrial bourgeoisie plays only an ancillary role. Secondly, though no parallel can be drawn mechanically between the economic role of state capital and the political role of the military, the interdependence of these two phenomena is undeniable. The need to 'rationalize' the

Brazilian economy implies the political need for increased centralization, and the army, both in its command structure and its neutrality between regions, fully satisfies this requirement. Finally one must cite the low level of institutionalization in Brazilian politics. The political history of Brazil repeatedly shows the weakness of the parties, the unions, and Congress. The struggle between the oppressed and the exploiters was not mediated through dependable and enduring institutions. We have already seen what this meant for the popular movement. For the bourgeoisie it has meant that the army has been able to marginalize it politically. In the absence of political institutions it has been possible for the intermediate sectors – neither exploiters as such nor exploited – to step in and occupy this political void. But this space could not be occupied by these sectors as such. What has happened rather is that an originally non-political institution – the army with its own very specific structure and its own social practice – has become political because it was the only institution on which the bourgeoisie could rely. It was in this way the military was able to become the arbiter of politics. Its specific weight in the exercise of power continues to increase. As long as it is the bourgeoisie that defines the legitimate use of violence, the armed forces are simply its armed wing. But as soon as the latter meet with the conditions in which they can define for themselves the role and limits of violence (when they become the sole source of their own social and political 'legitimacy'), then the bourgeoisie is confined to influencing the affairs of the bourgeois state only *indirectly*.

Having suggested answers to the question of how a military regime could have survived in 'republican' Brazil, we must now examine the precise nature of this military oligarchy. First of all one should not be misled by the slogans which heralded the 1964 coup, and which the dictatorship has continued to mouth ever since. The petty bourgeoisie rallied then to the defence of 'democracy' and 'honest administration' and the counter-revolutionaries were indeed only too pleased to make use of Adhemar de Barros's lumpen elements as a striking force in overthrowing Goulart. It would be grotesque however to conclude from the fact that the petty-bourgeoisie helped the army into power that the military oligarchy was a dictatorship of the petty-bourgeoisie or that it shared its ideology with the hysterical followers who made up the ranks of the 'March of the Family with God'. The hegemony of the military in Brazil is connected with the transformation of capitalism into state monopoly capitalism in conditions of dependence, and the regime's ideology is that of rationalizing technocrats, epitomized by the Minister of Finance, Delfim Neto and his 'intellectuals'. It would be impossible to mistake these planners or their military bosses for the hired crowd of 1964: 'that cortège of down and outs . . . that revenge from the provinces, small shopkeepers, fervent church-goers, prudes and lawyers'.[18] The regime has admittedly made concessions to these elements with the 'fight against pornography' and the rehabilitation of the old fascist Plinio Salgado. But this is all an irrelevance, it is only the pious homage of monopoly capital to the fetishes of its travelling companions.

An understanding of the present regime is no more advanced by calling it fascist than it is by calling it petty bourgeois, though its methods are as brutal as fascists' have ever been. Fascism, as a specific historical form of bourgeois society, has as its premiss both the defeat of the workers' movement, and the displacement of internal class struggle by means of an expansionist foreign policy, permitting the distraction of large sections of the population. In this respect

---

[18] See the article by Roberto Schwarz in *Les Temps Modernes*, July 1970.

fascism is a phenomenon typical of a precise phase of capitalist development: that in which monopolist concentration of production took place within the framework of the national state. In Latin America, however, even those political movements that were subjectively influenced by fascism, such as Peronism, ended up by conducting an anti-imperialist and anti-oligarchic struggle as soon as they attempted to realize a consistently nationalist programme. The anti-imperialist content of nationalism in the semi-colonial and dependent countries is still further reinforced in our present epoch, when the contradiction between capitalism and socialism is dominant on a world scale, and the contradictions between metropolitan capitalist *states* have lost their antagonistic character. Monopolist concentration of production does not cease, but takes place in the framework of a political integration of imperialism around its hegemonic centre, the USA. In this respect, even the nationalism of big capital has lost its completely reactionary character, at least where non-hegemonic capitalist metropoles are concerned (e.g. Gaullism). It is precisely the anti-national content of the Brazilian military dictatorship's policy that prevents it from becoming a fascist regime, for the economic and social base of the Brazilian military-oligarchic dictatorship is, as has been repeatedly stressed, the bloc formed by international monopoly capital, its domestic associates and the state sector. (Moreover it is a gross mistake to argue that a state is fascist merely because it is run by the army. Nazi Germany depended on the dominance of the party over the army, while in Brazil there are no parties which could dominate the army.)

Rather than follow these blind alleys in answering the question which we posed above we should examine first of all the nature of the military itself. One cannot interpret mechanically Lenin's dictum from *State and Revolution* that the armed forces are special detachments of armed men at the service of the ruling classes. In the barracks class contradictions become transposed: they determine the role of the army in the last instance but refracted through the functions and structure of the army. A general may represent the ruling classes but he remains a general.

In Brazil the military is by no means a homogeneous political force. Class struggle has penetrated the barracks: horizontally in the form of a struggle between pro-imperialist and nationalist officers. The former tend to be senior officers grouped around the Higher Military School (known as 'the Sorbonne'). They are divided on the question of tactics in confronting the urban guerrillas into 'hards' and 'moderates'. The latter group lead by General Albuquerque Lima, though temporarily defeated, still poses the question of the possibility of a military-nationalist transformation of Brazilian society. A third group should perhaps be included which comprises the young pro-imperialists who, in the tradition of generational struggle within the armed forces, oppose the government in the name of a social pseudo-moralism. They are partisans of ever greater institutionalized violence and they centre around the Officer Finishing School.[19]

Class contradictions within the army are expressed vertically in the conflicting interests of the officer class as a whole and those of the junior officers and the ranks (witness the Sergeants' Revolt of September 1963 and the Sailors' Associations formed at the same time). Despite these contradictions though, the authoritatian and pro-

---

[19] Miguel Arraes, op. cit., pp. 20–1. The Brazilian Army has about 200,000 men under arms, the Navy 43,000 and the Air Force 30,000. The close cooperation between the military and the police makes it difficult to estimate the precise size of the internal security forces (de Kadt, 'Brazil', in Veliz, op. cit., p. 55).

imperialist tendencies within the army are firmly in control. Besides it remains true that an army's function and its organization predisposes it towards *order*. Even supposing that the nationalist factions within the army were to recover from their defeat, this would not of course mean the transformation of a bourgeois army into a people's militia. Except in the conditions of a revolutionary civil war, except when the people themselves are in arms, the bourgeois army retains its identity as an institution. Considered purely as an institution it may swing either to the democratic or to the authoritatian sections of the bourgeoisie. But it will do this as a bourgeois army: with its organization, its discipline and its traditions: in short with its militarism. A bourgeois army may cut through the conflicts among different sectors of the ruling bloc in a historically progressive way but to the extent that it survives this process as a bourgeois army, it remains a decisive element in the maintenance of class society.

Despite the setback for the nationalists there are many opposition tendencies within the regime which still place their hopes in Albuquerque Lima, and in an eventual 'Peruvian-style' coup. What are the concrete pre-conditions for a nationalist-military take-over? We shall specify those which characterized the 'national revolutions' in Peru (in 1968) and Bolivia (in 1969):

(1) The prior liquidation of the revolutionary left (MIR and ELN in Peru, ELN in Bolivia).

(2) The exceptional weakness of the local ruling classes in countries where imperialist exploitation was mainly conducted through economic 'enclaves' (petrol, tin, etc.).

(3) The existence of a civilian government at the time of a nationalist coup.

This last condition is very important. The army officers' mode of social existence is that of a caste, which they are not anxious to destroy. This is why the different political tendencies within the army, though they invariably *intrigue* against one another, nevertheless abstain from *armed confrontation*. The struggle for mastery between these military groups is never a military struggle, even where, as in the South American countries, the military intrigue more than courtesans. The nationalist officers are soldiers first and nationalists second; they always respect the principle of the unity of command. It is only when they can count on the neutrality (if not the support) of the majority of their caste that they discount the risk of exposing themselves as 'divisionists'. In Bolivia, Ovando did not overthrow Barrientos, but the civilian government of Siles Salinas. Alvarado in Peru overthrew the reformist and cessionist Belaunde Terry.

This in no way means that military nationalism (the new form of bourgeois nationalism now current in Latin America) cannot be historically progressive. On this point 'left-wing' dogmatism is as blind as rightist opportunism. Understanding nothing of the balance of forces between the different social classes in Latin America, European 'left-wing' groups (and their kindred spirits in Latin America) persist in presenting Alvarado as a 'gorilla' pure and simple. If they were to read the Brazilian press, which daily insists that Alvarado is a dangerous totalitarian communist, they might perhaps understand who profits from their 'left-wing' chatter. It would be absurd to present Alvarado and Ovando as socialists, and absurd to claim that the class content of their policies is anything but bourgeois. But only those who learnt to repeat parrot-fashion Debray's thesis that any bourgeois-democratic transformation is out of the question in Latin America can 'explain' the nationalist policies of Alvarado and Ovando as an 'imperialist manoeuvre'.

In the light of these conditions, what are the chances of military nationalism in Brazil itself? Revolutionary warfare is in progress, capitalism is at present threatened neither with the exhaustion of its markets nor by economic stagnation, and the Brazilian oligarchy and military have kept up their alliance with US imperialism, despite growing political difficulties. It is this last factor that constitutes the regime's greatest weakness, and that might provide a basis for military nationalism. The succession crisis of September 1969 resulted nevertheless in a new compromise among the 'centrist' military tendencies, and the nationalists were yet again forced to wait.

Which faction will be the final beneficiary in the power struggle remains to be seen. The Garrastazu government has indeed adopted a nationalist stance, particularly in the sphere of foreign policy. It has extended Brazil's territorial waters and refused to sign the nuclear non-proliferation treaty. But these are no more than gestures. The real terrain over which the struggle for hegemony will be fought will be the future of the pact of dependence. The crucial question is whether Brazilian state capital will remain as a complement to foreign capital, providing only for infrastructural investment, or develop to replace foreign capital to the benefit of the Brazilian middle classes. It is against the background of these alternatives for the ruling bloc that the exploited classes must conduct the struggle for socialism against imperialism.

# Chapter 2

# The Exploited Classes under the Dictatorship

I. THE WORKING CLASS AND ITS ORGANIZATIONS

The development of the popular movement in Brazil is marked by the absence of strong and independent institutions able to articulate a truly working-class politics. Despite the massive influx to the towns and the very rapid industrialization of the post-war period, the Brazilian working class has failed to produce a party capable of a consistent class line and of organizing the class for struggle. In the crucial years of the Brazilian working class's political formation, the late forties, neither the PTB nor the PCB adopted such a role. The PTB was founded of course, not on Marxism, but on Vargas's nebulous doctrines of *trabalhismo*. Despite its mass support it remained Vargas's, then Goulart's, personal machine. It was the institutional expression of Getulist populism among the working class, and never generated its own cadre loyal to the working class alone. The PCB, during its brief period of legality – 1945–47 – rapidly developed its mass support. It was unique in Brazilian politics as the only popular force independent of ruling class hegemony, and its strength was further enhanced by the structural weakness of all rival parties. From the mid fifties onwards however, the PCB displayed an opportunism every bit as dangerous as its adventurism of the thirties. Correctly putting forward a minimum programme consisting of the liquidation of the financial and latifundist oligarchy, the expulsion of imperialism, the nationalization of key sectors of the economy, and universal suffrage, the PCB failed disastrously to understand that there was no national bourgeoisie in Brazil prepared to struggle consistently for these objectives, and that Goulart therefore could not be its representative. The PCB did not concentrate its efforts on building an independent workers' and peasants' alliance that would have been able to ally with a national bourgeoisie in a national-democratic revolution. If it had done so, it would have discovered that there was no genuine national bourgeoisie to ally with, and that the revolution could only be led by the bloc of workers and peasants. Instead it chose the 'short cut' of helping the 'national bourgeoisie' (i.e. Goulart) to take power, and then penetrating the state apparatus. The PCB saw its government-sponsored collaboration with the PTB in the CGT bureaucracy, and the increasing attention that Goulart paid to its advice, as the fulfilment of this alliance. But this disastrous miscalculation left it wholly unprepared for the events of 1964. Well after Brizola and the nationalists had realized the need for some organization against the threat from the right, the PCB continued on its suicidal course of pressuring Goulart from the left, in the utopian belief that he could lead a consistent struggle against reaction.

The only political current which seriously posed the question of revolutionary civil war was the 'Jacobin' left, and particularly Brizola and his followers. Through his network in the PTB and the army, and then late in 1963 with his newspaper *O Panfleto* and a radio station he had acquired, Brizola called for the formation of 'groups of eleven', as the nucleus of a new revolutionary organization prepared to defend the popular movement against a counter-revolutionary offensive. But there was not enough time for the nationalist left to remedy a fault of years.

Lacking not only a mass organization but also a clear and explicit revolutionary theory, the nationalists made a series of very serious mistakes. For too long they believed Goulart would respect the commitments he made to the people in August 1961. Taking an opportunist position, they overestimated the strength of the nationalist group within the armed forces. They underestimated the strength of the internal enemy – the latifundists, the big bourgeoisie and the reactionary officers, and they failed to realize that the Pentagon and the CIA were prepared to go to any lengths to liquidate what the Brazilian people had left in the way of self-determination.

After the 1964 coup the dictatorship proceeded to dismantle the reformist union structure controlled by the PTB and the PCB. The CGT was liquidated and the situation of the unions reverted to that of 1943. The most reactionary aspects of the Getulist 'consolidated labour laws' were reinforced while their progressive aspects were abandoned. The unions became one of the institutions with which the ruling class enslaves the workers' movement. Their 'militarization' was carried out partly by the appointment of soldiers as 'mediators' for the recalcitrant branches and partly by the development of a strain of lumpen-unionists whose task was to act as informers and terrorists.

The main aim of the dictatorship's economic policy was to contain inflation as quickly as possible, through the brutal reduction of real wages. Obviously constant and open violence was needed to 'convince' the workers to bear the cost of the 'deflation' which had been prescribed by the International Monetary Fund. As long as a new vanguard failed to arise from the ranks of the working class, the labouring masses could not fight back against this double exploitation. The extent to which their living fell and the weakness of their reaction can be gauged by the following figures. Between 1964 and 1966 the cost of living more than doubled while real wages fell by slightly more than thirty per cent. At the same time in the heavily industrialized São Paulo region stoppages due to strikes fell in 1965-6 from 1·6 million to 340,000 man hours. (See footnote p. 112.)

This deflationary policy, founded on the defiance, pure and simple, of the workers' most basic interests, could only have succeeded in the absence of institutions controlled by the workers themselves. A policy like this would have been unthinkable in Argentina or Uruguay where the regimes of Onganía and Pacecho, reactionary though they may have been, had at least to take account of the proletariat as an organized political force. In Argentina the working class were able to retain the benefits of Peronism even after Peron's fall because they exercised a large measure of control over their own institutions. In Brazil the workers lost even those moderate gains they had secured under Goulart precisely because they lacked any independence at all.

But though in the short term the working class was isolated and disarmed, this very isolation in the longer term helped create the conditions for a genuinely independent working-class politics. The logic of military repression stamped out reformism. In its place the embryo of a workers' movement free from all bourgeois influence could form.

## II. WORKERS' STRUGGLES IN 1968

By 1967 the opposition within the trade union had begun to emerge from silence. A movement known as the *contra o arrôcho* ('against the freeze') was organized in a number of places in working-class circles. The first wildcat strike took place at the beginning of April in the engineering industry in Belo Horizonte. It was provoked by a derisory wage increase which had anyway been postponed from the previous October. The strikers ignored the advice of the president of the Minas engineering unions (a government stooge), and established factory committees independent of the union apparatus with which to organize the strike. By the end of April nineteen factories were paralysed and 17,000 workers were on strike. The Minister of Labour rejected their claim for a sixty per cent rise (to make up the fall in the real wage since 1964) and threatened military intervention if the strike went on. Without the organization for a rapid generalization of the strike, the Minas engineers were forced to retreat.

The strike nevertheless was the first real protest against the regime. Others followed. It had been decided that the State governor of São Paulo would attend the annual May Day rally in order to demonstrate the regime's support for the union bureaucracy. The vanguard in the unions and the revolutionary left organizations decided however to organize a counter-demonstration within the demonstration. The plan was to storm the platform from where the governor and his 'unionists' were to speak, drive them out and then hand the meeting over to revolutionary workers. Whatever the outcome, it would be clear that the mass of the workers were at last demanding a firmer stand after four years of relative silence. Steps had been taken to protect the demonstrators against the police. At each corner of the square where the meeting was to take place groups were stationed, armed only with sticks and Molotov cocktails, but that was thought enough to delay the police attack while the masses withdrew from the square. A police or army charge against the whole demonstration was not thought likely.

The counter-demonstration was organized in the most democratic manner possible. In the factories and workers' districts small groups met to decide on specific details and to coordinate the counter-demonstration as a whole. Everything went according to plan. At the very moment the governor began trying to explain the unexplainable (i.e. that the reduction of real wages was for the workers' benefit), hundreds of workers and students advanced towards the official platform. A shower of eggs, placards and even stones, thrown from all sides, covered their advance. The platform was guarded only by a few dozen plain-clothes men. (The absence of obvious police measures was intended to prove that the lumpen-unionists were genuine workers' leaders.) The governor and his 'unionist' escort were forced unceremoniously to take refuge in São Paulo cathedral. It was then the new workers' leaders' turn to speak. Despite their political immaturity and even their 'ultra-leftism', they proved themselves as the embyro of a new revolutionary leadership of the workers' movement.

Two months later in July 1968 the São Paulo engineering workers took up the struggle from their Minas comrades. The strike took place in Osasco, an industrial suburb of São Paulo, and was spearheaded from the Cobrasma plant where the formation of illegal factory committees was already far advanced. The strike spread quickly to other plants in Osasco itself but though the organizers hoped it would engulf all of São Paulo's 215,000 engineering workers, it in fact never went further than the suburb. The government was given time to act. Two battalions were dispatched to Osasco, hundreds of workers arrested, union offices occupied and martial law threatened. The workers and their families showed exemplary courage. They refused to leave the factories which they had occupied and argued vainly with the invading troops: 'Soldiers, our hunger is your hunger'.

The Osasco strike revealed both the working class's spirit of revolt and the immaturity of its leadership. In a self-criticism made some months after the strike, two of its leaders admitted that they had launched the slogan of factory occupation prematurely and so had ended up tailing behind the mass of workers. The workers followed the most radical slogans (occupation, resistance to the troops) but were easily routed when the dictatorship responded with the full weight of its repressive apparatus. In Minas as well as São Paulo a rapid extension of the strike was the only way to compensate for the working class's low level of organization but this was made impossible by the intervention, as swift as it was brutal, of the police and army. The masses were easily mobilized but as easily demobilized.

The lesson to be drawn from the workers' struggles of April–July 1968 is the need for the complex revolutionary work of organization at various levels. There is first of all the need for legal work in the unions themselves. Despite the fact that Brazil's recent history has shown repeatedly the futility of union struggle, the unions cannot for this reason be ignored. The idea of abandoning them to the police and a handful of reformists is simply absurd. 'To refuse to work in the reactionary trade unions means leaving the insufficiently developed or backward masses of workers under the influence of the reactionary leaders, the agents of the bourgeoisie, the labour aristocrats, or workers who have become completely bourgeois' (Lenin). The persistent work of organizing must be carried out in those institutions in which the proletarian masses are to be found, and foremost among these institutions are the unions. Despite the 'militarization' of the unions under the dictatorship, the 1968 strikes offer concrete evidence of what can be done. During the Osasco strike the unions were made into centres of political agitation and propaganda. In stormy meetings of the engineers not only was the preparation of the strike discussed but also Guevara, Vietnam and the need for armed struggle.

Secondly, there is the need for illegal work in the mass

organizations. The confusion of the left about this issue centres on the role of the factory committee. (These of course are strictly illegal but should not on this count be confused with factory cells which are always clandestine.) Employers have been known (at the Lonaflex plant in Osasco for example) to negotiate wages directly with these committees. After realizing the weakness of union struggle by itself it is easy to fall into the error of treating factory committees as alternative rather than parallel organizations. The fact is that these committees are still a long way from winning over the great mass of workers, having so far succeeded only in implanting themselves among the most advanced sectors of the working class. This is why they should not be confused with soviets or even with the Spanish *comisiones obreras*, which represent a higher degree of working-class organization and revolutionary experience. In Brazil at the present time the factory committees are only one of the instruments for a new working-class politics. Only the future development of revolutionary struggle will give the true measure of their historic importance. Under present conditions, the vanguard's political work should be a combination of legal work in the unions (organizing the workers in the workplace and trying to develop a consistent trade union opposition) and illegal work in the factory committees.

Thirdly, there is the need for clandestine work. The role of the revolutionary vanguard and the transition to armed struggle will be discussed in the next chapter. Here it is enough to observe that while the most important question is to decide on the specific forms of *combination* of the *permanent objectives* of a Marxist-Leninist vanguard (education of the working class through a political Marxist-Leninist practice, propaganda for socialism, formulation of strategy and tactics *from the standpoint of the working class* and its historic tasks, etc.), with the immediate tasks of the struggle against the dictatorship and against imperialism (minimum democratic and anti-imperialist programme, protracted war against the oligarchy and imperialism), one should not uphold a *unilateral* conception of the tasks of the vanguard in asserting an abstract and therefore anti-dialectical opposition between 'classic' political struggle and the military struggle. It is quite wrong to suppose that *because* the traditional organizations have forgotten armed struggle, the armed organizations must therefore forget the struggle for immediate demands. One often hears it argued that the military dictatorship does not permit struggle for immediate demands. Did it not permit the 1968 strikes? (That it should *repress* them is to be expected.) Does Franco permit the *comisiones obreras*? Did Czar Nicholas II permit struggle for immediate demands? What is forgotten is concrete analysis of the concrete situation. More precisely, from the unexceptionable premiss that the Brazilian working class is not organized enough as a class for the proper conduct of economic struggle in the conditions imposed by the dictatorship, it is mistakenly concluded that economic struggle must be abandoned.

The comparative failure of the 1968 strikes and the success of the 1 May demonstration is cited in support of this thesis. But what is conveniently overlooked is that such success was only made possible by the patient work of organization around slogans of economic struggle like 'Strike against the *arrôcho*' and 'Wage increases now'. It is true that it was about this time that the most advanced and combative sections of the working class (as will be seen in the next chapter) were enthusiastically adopting the slogan of armed struggle and the principle of the strategic priority of guerrilla war. The problem however was to transform this enthusiasm into an immediate political practice instead of postponing its materialization to a future date (little matter as far as the masses' political consciousness is concerned, whether this future is near or distant), or until a vanguard detachment launched guerrilla warfare. Mass offensive actions like the 1 May 1968 in São Paulo play an important role. The working masses were tired of reformist politics and ready to follow a consistent revolutionary tactic. But – and this is one of the fundamental teachings of Leninism – revolutionary politics does not arise spontaneously from the masses, even if one 'stimulates' them from outside by sensational direct actions. Hence the necessity of a national organization able to develop continuous and coordinated political work and to direct the peoples' struggle as a whole. This conception inevitably contradicted the prejudices of the orthodox Debrayists and militarists, who saw in it survivals of the methods of the 'traditional left'. The Leninists replied that if the tradition in question is that of Lenin, there was nothing to be ashamed of in 'traditionalism'.

If the level of organization so far reached by the working class is assessed in order to evaluate its strength as a social force within the popular movement, it must be admitted that it is below that of the working classes of the neighbouring countries, particularly Uruguay, Argentina and Chile. In these three countries the working class *is already* the leading force of the popular movement, if only because it is already *organized as a class*. In Brazil however, there is no equivalent of the Argentinian CGT or the Uruguayan CNT. There is not even a definite tendency towards a unified national workers' leadership. What is more, the workers have not succeeded in regaining by their own efforts an equivalent to the trade union apparatus they received ready-made during the period of bourgeois nationalism.

In those countries where the working class constitutes an organized political force, the main tactical question is that of winning the struggles for power within the workers' movement (this is what is taking place in Argentina with the struggle between the collaborationist and the rebel CGTs, and in Uruguay with the struggle between bourgeois reformists and the CP on one side, and the 'Tendency', particularly the PS and the FAU, on the other ).

In Brazil the problem is to organize the working class in economic struggle and *at the same time* to lead it towards revolutionary positions. This work is more difficult in that it has to be carried out under conditions of illegality, or even clandestinity. The unions which already have a regular and organized opposition, such as the bank workers and the engineers, are still extremely few in number. But the strength of the workers' movement must also be assessed in the context of the present stage of Brazilian capitalism. The conclusions to be drawn about the economic crisis and its political consequences are far more complicated than those who indulge in predicting the final and speedy defeat of capitalism believe. In the context of the strategy of North American imperialism Brazil has come to play the role of a sub-empire and its industrial centres that of sub-metropoles. Brazil's resulting economic growth allows the ruling class a certain room for manoeuvre and for corruption of the 'labour aristocracy', which neighbours such as Uruguay do not enjoy. The policy of *arrôcho salarial* (wage freeze) is therefore not so much the result of the system's imagined stagnation but arises rather from tactical objectives of the ruling class such as the struggle against inflation and the acceleration of the process of accumulation in the framework of concentrated monopolist production.

The Brazilian working-class's role in the present stage of popular struggle against dictatorship and against imperialism is limited insofar as it has not even developed a *programme of struggle* against the regime. Its level of organization does not permit it to be *in the immediate future* the 'vanguard in the struggle against the dictatorship and against imperialism'. The conclusion to be drawn from this is of course not that one should turn one's back on the workers (a position supported, with more or less pronounced nuances, by the militarist current within the armed organizations). On the contrary, because the working class is in the long run the most decisive revolutionary class, it is necessary at this moment to make every possible effort to help it transcend as rapidly as possible its present limitations. But this must be done within the framework of a strategy which takes the struggle against the dictatorship and imperialism as its principal aim at the present stage of the revolutionary process. For how can we convince the workers that we want to build socialism, if we are not even able to mount an effective struggle against the dictatorship? If transitional slogans are forgotten, one is bound to fall into 'left' opportunism, which consists in sparing oneself in practice the politico-military tasks of armed struggle in the name of ideological proselytism and the 'build-up of strength' among the working class.

As against Argentina and Uruguay, where the working class has from the beginning taken the leading role in the popular movement, the Brazilian workers will only come to organize themselves as a class, and to take the leadership of all the exploited and oppressed, in the course of the struggle against the dictatorship and against imperialism itself. In the immediate future, revolutionary strategy cannot be based on the thesis of an imminent workers' insurrection. Revolutionaries therefore cannot save themselves an entire period of clandestine work in organization, agitation and propaganda.[1]

---

[1] 'Balanço Trabalhista-Sindical do ano de 1966' cited in *Revista Teoria e Pratica*, no. 3, p. 163. In Brazil statistics about the labour force are usually

### III. THE COUNTRYSIDE AND THE PEASANTRY

Half of the Brazilian people, in other words between forty-five and fifty million, live in the countryside. The most recent census, held in 1960, counted 15½ million persons active on the land, and 3·35 million rural holdings. The latifundia (holdings larger than 500 hectares) occupied 154 million hectares, that is 58% of the total agricultural area, though only 18·5% of cultivated soil. Besides this latifundist oligarchy, the census indicated the existence of 275,000 medium holdings (from 100 to 500 hectares), occupying a total of 57·8 million hectares (21·6% of the agricultural area), and including 23·4% of cultivated soil. Holdings of less than 100 hectares (which should not properly be grouped together, since this conceals the existence of two distinct social classes, the rural petty bourgeoisie and the poor peasantry) numbered about 3 million in 1960, or 90% of the total number of holdings. Although representing only 20% of the total agricultural area (i.e. 53·6 million hectares out of a total of 265·5 million), these smallholdings included 59% of the cultivated soil.

---

either unobtainable or unreliable. Bearing this in mind, a further indication of the fall in the standard of living for Brazilian workers can be given by these figures taken from the review *Veja* for May 1970. Figures show hours of work needed for purchase of one kilo of each of the following foodstuffs:

|  | 1965 | 1969 |
|---|---|---|
| Bread | 1 hr 18 m | 2 hr 27 m |
| Rice | 1 hr 15 m | 1 hr 47 m |
| Black Beans | 1 hr 35 m | 3 hr 19 m |
| Potatoes | 1 hr 16 m | 1 hr 34 m |
| Meat | 4 hr 24 m | 5 hr 54 m |
| Salt | 1 hr 14 m | 37 m |
| Sugar | 1 hr 16 m | 1 hr 02 m |
| Milk (1 litre) | 34 m | 46 m |

According to the same source, based on DIEESE statistics, the average salary (real terms) has fallen 35·5% since 1958.

The 1960 census operated with the categories 'farms' and 'active persons', although thousands of large and medium proprietors possess two or even several farms. Bearing this in mind, the ownership of farm lands is as follows: 0·4% of the active population own 47·3% of the land, 42·6% own 52% of the land, and 57% of the population active in the countryside own no part of the land on which they work.[2] In fact, if, from the 15½ million persons active in the countryside, the 3·3 million agricultural proprietors are subtracted, the figure of 12·2 million landless peasants is reached, still on the above mentioned assumptions.

What are the historical tendencies of the development of property relations in the countryside? The figures are clear. Consider the following statistics for the largest latifundia (1,000 hectares or more) for a sufficiently long period from 1920 to 1960:[3]

| Census | Farms larger than 1,000 hectares Number | % of all farms | Area occupied by these farms hectares | % of agric. area | Average size in hectares |
|---|---|---|---|---|---|
| 1920 | 26,315 | 4·0 | 110,980,624 | 63·4 | 4,217 |
| 1940 | 37,812 | 1·5 | 95,529,649 | 48·3 | 3,435 |
| 1950 | 32,628 | 1·6 | 118,102,270 | 50·9 | 3,620 |
| 1960 | 32,885 | 1·0 | 125,537,925 | 47·3 | 3,817 |

The area occupied by the latifundia increases in absolute terms and remains constant in relative terms (censuses of 1940 and 1960). The average size of the latifundium also increases. 1% of all rural proprietors – a sector that repre-

[2] *Panorama Economico Latinoamericano*, Vol. VI, Havana, 1967, p. 130.
[3] Paulo Schilling, *Brasil de los Latifundistas* (Editorial Dialogo, Montevideo), 1968, p. 57.

sents only 0·04% of the Brazilian population – possesses practically one half of all land so far brought within the property system. Moreover the average size of the super-latifundia (larger than 10,000 hectares) has tended to increase while that of the smallest units the minifundia has tended to decrease. Between 1950 and 1960 super-latifundia increased their average size by more than 10% while that of the minifundia decreased by about 7%. Although data on the average productivity of the 'minifundia' are lacking (and with reason), it is certain that with the exception of some specialized crops (for example market-gardening around the great urban centres), the immense majority of small-holders (who constitute the poor peasantry) are not even in a position to ensure the simple reproduction of the productive process. Hence a process of absolute pauperization takes place, which forces the peasants either to become agricultural labourers or to leave the land and swell the ranks of the unemployed, either crowded into the urban *favelas* (shanty-towns) – 'urbanization' is only exceptionally, as in the fifties, accompanied by 'industrialization' – or wandering in the countryside.

The following table shows the figures for small-holdings as a whole (i.e. those less than 100 hectares):[4]

| Census | Farms of less than 100 hectares Number | % of all farms | Area occupied by these farms hectares | % of agric. area | Average size in hectares |
|---|---|---|---|---|---|
| 1940 | 1,629,996 | 85·58% | 36,005,599 | 18·21% | 22·1 |
| 1950 | 1,763,491 | 85·41% | 38,588,119 | 16·61% | 21·8 |
| 1960 | 2,994,093 | 89·39% | 53,620,936 | 20·30% | 17·9 |

[4] ibid., p. 59.

The constant decrease of the agricultural area in the hands of the small peasantry, and especially of the poor peasantry, is one of the chief causes of the wretched conditions of life and work in the countryside. It explains the fact that the urban population grew by 54% between 1950 and 1960, whereas the rural population grew by only 16%, in a country where the productivity of agricultural labour remains stationary.

There is a reactionary argument, which, however absurd, is none the less frequently found. As Brazil is a country of continental dimensions (over 8,500,000 km$^2$ in area, i.e. 851,196,000 hectares), the land problem is said to be above all one of occupation and colonization of virgin land.

The fact that 61% of available land is unoccupied (the percentage has certainly decreased since the 1960 census, though it still remains very high), far from attenuating the class contradiction between the big landed proprietors and the poor peasantry, only means that the contradiction between latifundist oligarchy and peasant masses is reproduced on an even larger scale. In 1940 latifundia of 1,000 hectares and above occupied an area of 95·9 million hectares, or about 48% of that occupied by all rural holdings. In 1960 these 'super-latifundia' occupied 125·5 million hectares and about 47% of the total area of rural holdings. This indicates that the latifundium has maintained its relative position while the area occupied by all rural holdings has increased (and the excess of virgin land consequently declined). Thus it only reproduces its privileges on an enlarged scale. The occupation of virgin land (of which a good part is situated in tropical forest, especially in Amazonas) requires investments which are only at the disposal of an oligarchy. The forest must be cleared on a large scale and means of communication established with the urban centres, often with light aircraft. In Brazil there is virgin land only for those who already have plenty of land – or plenty of money. The genocide of entire Indian tribes, and the sale of large quantities of land to North Americans, shows who is cornering the 61% of 'free' land.

Class contradictions in the countryside become more acute the further that uneven development between different regions of the country is pressed. In this respect the North East, dominated by the latifundist class, is without doubt the 'weakest link' in the Brazilian agrarian structure. This does not mean that other regions of the country do not show signs of the violent contradiction between latifundists and poor peasantry. On the contrary, study of the figures for the division of land by geographical region by itself can give the false impression that the agrarian crisis is the same over the whole country, the only noticeable difference being that between the more densely populated regions (South, East, North East) and the sparsely populated regions (West Central and North). The figures on the next page refer to 1960.[5]

North-Eastern agriculture is nevertheless more backward than the rest of Brazil's. Despite the fact that 72% of the active population there work in the rural sector, this only provides 41% of the regional revenue. Thirty-six per cent of the population active in the rural sector live in the North East, yet although it includes almost 27% of the cultivable land, it produces only 19% of national agricultural revenue. The 1950 census showed that the soil actually cultivated did not exceed 5·4 million hectares. Productivity is very low. That of cotton is only 0·07 tons per hectare in the North East, whereas in São Paulo state it reaches 0·214 tons, and in the USA 0·304 tons per hectare. Cane sugar in the North East yields some 38 tons per hectare, compared with 47 tons in São Paulo and 69 tons in Puerto Rico.

[5] *Panorama Economico*, p. 134.

| Size of holding | South A | South B | East A | East B | North East A | North East B | West Central A | West Central B | North A | North B |
|---|---|---|---|---|---|---|---|---|---|---|
| Less than 10 hect. | 34·3 | 3·4 | 39·1 | 2·5 | 66·3 | 4·0 | 18·6 | 0·2 | 52·0 | 0·8 |
| 10 and less than 100 hect. | 58·0 | 31·6 | 48·5 | 24·4 | 25·5 | 17·7 | 46·8 | 4·8 | 40·8 | 4·9 |
| 100 and less than 1,000 hect. | 7·0 | 34·3 | 11·6 | 43·9 | 7·5 | 42·5 | 28·0 | 24·7 | 5·8 | 6·8 |
| 1,000 and less than 10,000 hect. | 0·6 | 25·0 | 0·7 | 22·5 | 0·6 | 27·0 | 6·1 | 42·3 | 1·1 | 14·1 |
| 10,000 hect. and above | 0·01 | 5·7 | 0·01 | 6·7 | 0·01 | 8·8 | 0·5 | 28·0 | 0·3 | 73·4 |

(The columns 'A' give the figure for each class of holding as a percentage of the total number, columns 'B' indicate the area occupied by each class as a percentage of the total area.)

Though the highest percentage of 'super-latifundia' (more than 10,000 hectares) are found in the West-Central regions (Matto Grosso, Goiás) and in the North (Amazonas), 0·5% of all holdings occupying 28% of the land in the West-Central region and 0·3% occupying 73·4% in the North, the density of population per square kilometre was only 0·8 in the North and 1·9 in the West-Central region, compared with 17·6 in the North East.[6] Great as the disparities are between the average sizes of latifundia and small-holdings the North and the West-Central regions remain a vast 'hot Siberia' in which only the geography and the density of forest cushion the shock between antagonistic classes. Ex-

[6] See the *Anuário Estatístico do Brasil*, 1969, p. 73.

ploitation is indeed fiercer there than in the North East. Apart from the genocide of the Indians, there are all the 'ill-disguised forms of slavery' especially in the Amazonas *seringais* (rubber plantations), known as 'cemeteries of the living', and in the West-Central latifundia, where the latifundists' private police prevent the escape of peasants enenslaved to the owners by their debts to the *barracão*.[7] But precisely because they form a 'hot Siberia', the Northern and West-Central regions do not exhibit that historical phenomenon which, for want of a better term, can be described as an 'Asiastic peasantry': great concentrations of poor peasants and especially of landless peasants who, although producing for the capitalist world market (cane sugar, cotton, cocoa, etc.), undergo an unbridled economic exploitation, combined with pre-capitalist forms of social and political oppression. The most widespread of these are:

(1) *Labour rent:* poor and landless peasants pay the rent for parcels of land belonging to a latifundium by working some days a week on the latifundist's land. This practice, in the North East called *'cambão'*, is even found in the most highly developed parts of the country (for example on coffee plantations in São Paulo state).

(2) *Product rent:* this takes the form of share-cropping. Rent for the land is payed in the form of goods produced by the peasant on the 'rented' land (in fact, a fixed proportion of the harvest). An investigation carried out by the National

---

[7] Schilling defines the *barracão* as follows: 'A variation of national economy insofar as it abolishes, in practice, the monetary system ... (the *barracão*) is an obligation imposed on the wage-labourers and sharecroppers to make their purchases in the rudimentary bazaar belonging to the latifundist, by means of tokens (*vales*). ... In the 'accounts' of the latifundist's store the worker is always a debtor. The latifundist, of course, controls the price of the goods which he sells 'on credit' to the workers' (Schilling, op. cit., pp. 63-4).

Committee for Agricultural Policy in 1952 indicated the main forms of share-cropping as follows:
 (a) the peasant gives the latifundist half of the harvest ('*meia*'): 87·11% of all cases.
 (b) the peasant gives him a third of the harvest ('*terça*'): 10·61% of all cases.
 (c) he gives him a quarter: 1·92%.
 (d) other forms: 0·36%.

As Paulo Schilling points out: 'It is not only the poor landless peasant ... who, reduced to famine, submits to such an absurd form of exploitation. Even certain capitalist entrepreneurs, for example the rice growers of Rio Grande do Sul ... undergo this type of exploitation: 74·9% of rice cultivation takes place on rented lands, of which 72·7% are under a share-cropping system, paying the rent with a part of the harvest. This rent, the latifundist's revenue, ... constitutes an average 31% of the harvest. Given the high level of productivity, up to five or six thousand kilos per hectare, share-cropping enables the proprietor to pocket in a year the equivalent of twice or even three times the selling price of the rented land ... Share-cropping thus gives rise to a further kind of exploitation, for the share-cropper is often forced ... to sell the latifundist his own share of the harvest at a price very much lower than that of the market.'[8]

(3) *Money rent:* Schilling characterizes this in the following terms: 'More widespread in the Southern states, it already represents an evolution in the direction of capitalist agriculture. It nevertheless constitutes a great obstacle to capitalist development, since the entrepreneur is forced to deduct from his capital the rent of the land, which decreases

---

[8] This and the following quotations are all taken from Schilling, op. cit., pp. 60–3.

his investment capacity and to that extent his possibilities of rationalizing production'.

Relations of production in Brazilian agriculture are changing however. Attempts to diversify agriculture by eradicating coffee plantations have led in many cases to landowners' turning over their land to pasture and to the eviction of peasants from the land. In the agriculturally most advanced parts of São Paulo and Paraná the traditional *colono* – a peasant tied to a particular farm and paying rent in one of the three forms mentioned above – is being transformed into an agricultural day labourer – a *volante*. The *volante* takes a wage for agricultural work but no longer lives on the farm. He lives in the city, or rather in the *favelas* (shanty towns) which ring the large cities. Each morning he is trucked to work by a contractor who owns the trucking company and who therefore more or less decides who works and who does not. Workers will pay as much as 30% of their daily wage of six cruzeiros ($1.30–40) just to be taken to work.

Some indication of how fast this form of exploitation is growing can be given by a comparison of figures from São Paulo state for 1964 and 1966. It was estimated in 1964 that there were 2 million agricultural workers of which 1·7 million was classified as 'residents' and 300,000 as *volantes*. By 1966, though the number of people in agricultural production had fallen by 100,000, the number of *volantes* had risen to 375,000. Making the conservative assumption of a ratio of workers to non-workers of about one in three in each family, the number of people dependent on the work of the *volantes* was then about 1·2 million.

In Paraná state *volantes* make up about 30% of the agricultural labour force. The eradication of coffee plantations was started there in 1964 and more than 500 million plants disappeared releasing about 150,000 workers. Few of them were absorbed in the transition and though a Rural Workers Statute was introduced in 1967 requiring *fazendeiros* to pay their workers a minimum wage, the majority of them responded to this reform by throwing the peasants off their land. This growing stratum of agricultural workers constitutes a definitely proletarian sector among the peasantry. While rendering peasant misery more terrible the *volante* system increases their proletarian characteristics. Instead of living in their places of work they are forced to live in the *favelas* where they are no longer able to cultivate their own small patches of land. As will be seen later this sector is of great political importance.

IV. PEASANT STRUGGLES

Brazil has a strong tradition of peasant struggles. For a long while, though, their content was quite particularist, taking sometimes the form of a religious sect with a charismatic leader (for instance, the Canudos war in which thousands of peasants led by Antonio Conselheiro fought a long war to the death with the federal power), and sometimes that of banditry (Lampião and his *cangaçeiros*).[9] Early in the century the southern states of Paraná and Santa Catarina saw a peasant revolt (*do Contestado*) led by José Maria, which started when the foreign owned Brazil Railway dispossessed the peasants on its land. At its height there were 20,000 peasants involved in the struggle living under a primitive communism and fighting a guerrilla war against the federal government. They survived five years from the beginning

---

[9] Virgulino Ferreira da Silva, or Lampião as he was known, led a band of outlaws in the backwoods during the twenties and thirties of this century. He was killed in 1938. Antonio Conselheiro's rebellion was celebrated in Euclydes da Cunha's epic novel, published originally in 1902, *Os Sertões* (*Rebellion in the Backlands*).

of 1912 to the end of 1916 and were finally crushed by a well-equipped army of 7,000 men.

Heroic though this action was, it was the last in a cycle of isolated peasant wars and not the beginning of a peasant movement. The peasantry did not return to the surface of Brazilian history until forty years later and then only as an organized part of the popular movement. The historic context in which these first struggles developed made the defeat of the peasantry almost inevitable. The conditions were lacking not only for the workers in the countryside to organize around their specific interests, but also for other social classes (the industrial bourgeoisie for example) to profit from the peasant revolt to further their own interests. When these conditions did obtain (first in 1930 with Vargas, then from the fifties and up to the 1964 coup with the alliance between bourgeois nationalism and the popular movement), the Brazilian bourgeoisie, which was unable at the international level to sever its links with imperialism, was no more able at the internal level to lead a consistent fight against the latifundist oligarchy. Neither Vargas (although he had the means, especially during the period 1930–45), nor the other reformist leaders of the industrial bourgeoisie, dared to lead the struggle against the masters of the land. Each time peasant mobilization placed the question of agrarian reform on the order of the day, fear of a popular revolution led the reformist sectors of the ruling classes to patch up their quarrels with the latifundists. The united front of property organized itself against the front of the exploited, and the 1964 *coup d'etat* was only the most recent example of this.

But the fifties brought a new element to the history of the class struggle of the poor peasants and agricultural proletarians. For the first time they began to be organized as a class, even if their fight involved only a minority of the immense

Brazilian peasant masses. The first attempt at organization was the work of the Communist Party. It set up the ULTAB (União dos Lavradores e Trabalhadores Agrícolas do Brasil), which however never succeeded in playing an important role in the peasantry's political struggle, although its contribution towards the formation of a first nucleus of revolutionary militants in the countryside was by no means negligible.

In 1955 a peasant, João Firmino, working in the Galiléia sugar mill, organized the first of the Peasant Leagues (*Ligas Camponêsas*). It was impossible at that time to imagine how large this movement was to become. (Its first aim was modest enough, and as Josué de Castro noted, concerned rather with death than life: the Galiléia peasants initially demanded only a few inches of land to bury their dead.) Nevertheless, the tactical elements of a new stage of peasant struggle were already present: agitational work, a rudimentary mass organization resulting from it, and direct mass action – occupation of land. It did not matter that the land occupied by the Galiléia peasants was for burial and not for planting crops. Wishing to die with dignity means wishing to live with dignity. Francisco Julião, a young lawyer, arrived in court to defend the Galiléia peasants guilty of occupying the land of their cemetery. He soon disengaged himself from the purely legal aspects of peasant defence to become the main organizer of the Leagues.

These rapidly acquired first a regional (in the North East) then a national dimension. Here and there throughout Brazil (in the North East, in Minas, in Espírito Santo, in the state of Rio de Janeiro and in Bahia) Peasant Leagues were formed. In 1960 Julião became known as a leader throughout the country, and the Leagues organized the most advanced sections of the peasant masses on a national scale. Agitation and propaganda around the slogan 'agrarian reform by law or by force' (*na lei ou na marra*) was combined with a movement for the occupation of land belonging to the largest latifundists. Cities in the rural zone served as meeting-points between the urban workers and those of the countryside. In 1961 a national congress of Peasant Leagues was held in Belo Horizonte, in the state of Minas Gerais, in which over a thousand peasant leaders took part. In the extreme South of the country it was the governor of the state of Rio Grande do Sul, Leonel Brizola, the most prominent leader of revolutionary nationalism, who undertook to mobilize the peasant masses. In 1962 Julião attempted to bring the leaders of the Leagues into a single political organization, the Tiradentes Radical Movement. The attempt failed and the movement split some months later. Other political organizations also participated in the peasant movement, without for all that managing to give it a political leadership capable of transforming agitation and organization among the peasant masses into a revolutionary workers' party of the countryside and the city. The attempts of Popular Action (AP), of the Trotskyists, or of the PC do B (Communist Party of Brazil, pro-Chinese), had still not born fruit when the reaction moved to the counter-offensive.

According to Paulo Schilling (himself a fighter for agrarian reform, who took part in the organization of MASERT – Movement of Landless Cultivators – in Rio Grande do Sul under Brizola's governorship), the defeat of the Peasant Leagues, which were completely crushed after the 1964 coup, was due to 'Julião's inability to form a political organization that could give material support to his revolutionary exhortation. The great success obtained by his agitational work was not translated ... into organizational terms. The structure necessary to capitalize on the immense revolutionary gain that the whole agitation represented was lacking.'[10]

[10] Paulo Schilling, op. cit., pp. 89–90.

The role of the peasantry in Brazil's revolutionary war will be discussed in the third and fourth chapters. It is enough here to summarize the findings of this section by saying that, though there is a vast revolutionary potential contained in the Brazilian peasantry, it is buried deep. Without a continuous tradition of struggle to help bring it to the surface it will only be directed into revolutionary action when the peasant masses have been mobilized as an organized force against their exploiters and against the dictatorship.

### V. STUDENTS: A LEADING ROLE IN THE NEW VANGUARD

The Brazilian student movement came to maturity as an organized political force within the popular movement towards the end of 1963 when it became obvious that the armed counter-revolution was preparing for civil war. As a member of the Popular Mobilization Front which grouped together the majority of political currents demanding a popular democratic transformation of Brazilian society it was, however, limited in two ways: its connection with the people was effected through the left wing of the national bourgeoisie and there was little participation from the student base groups. Two political organizations shared the hegemony of the movement at that time: Popular Action (AP) which marshalled the left-wing catholics and those susceptible to 'Christian democracy', and the PCB.

In the aftermath of the 1964 coup the students were spared at first the repression suffered by the rest of the popular forces. As the only organization on the left which emerged from the defeat of April in a position of comparative strength, it was to the student movement that fell the immediate task of fighting the new regime. The organization of 'groups of five' was proposed, modelled on the 'groups of eleven' which Brizola had tried to organize. This was the first attempt at clandestine organization among the student mass. The result was fairly limited, but the groups of five nonetheless provided the first experience of a generation of revolutionaries who were to be among the initiators of armed struggle.

The first congress of UNE (National Students Union) after the coup, in July 1965, was held quite legally, and so the political conditions for effective student mobilization through illegal struggle were lacking. It was only after the July 1965 Congress that the dictatorship moved to the offensive against the student movement, through the famous 'Suplicy law', named after the arch-reactionary Minister of National Education. But the 'militarization' of the student organizations proved much more difficult than that of the unions, if only because it was far more difficult for the big bourgeoisie to strike at intermediate strata of the population. The 'Suplicy law' banned the student organizations and in particular the UNE. It transformed the regional sections of UNE into so many apolitical 'directorates', subordinated to the control of the universities, which controlled their funds and sought to limit them to organizations simply concerned with the students' 'leisure and cultural activities'. At the national level the Suplicy law only allowed 'meetings' to be held during the vacations, when hypothetical 'seminars' could take place.

The struggle against the Suplicy law was a decisive moment in the political development of the student movement. The question was whether it should be boycotted at once, or accepted for the time being, to be sabotaged later. The Popular Action group which to begin with had supported the second alternative had by the time of the July 1965 Congress swung round to the first. The PCB on the other hand supported the boycott to begin with but ended up by defending 'participation'. At the Congress this position was defeated and the PCB badly discredited. Its role in the student movement was taken over by POLOP, which had been firmest in its support for the boycott and which together with AP (the majority) came to form a new national leadership. By 1967 indeed the Communist party had practically ceased to exist as a force within the student movement. In a country where the working class is a nationally organized political force this would have been of no great importance but in Brazil it placed the PCB at an even greater distance from the real struggle.

The decisive test for the Suplicy law took place in August 1965 when the elections for 'directorates' provided for in the new law were held. To intimidate the boycotters the government announced severe measures against students who did not vote. The student leadership therefore recommended students to cast blank votes. The boycott of the 'official' election was not complete, but it was nevertheless significant enough to prevent the directorates from enjoying any genuine representativeness. The experience of the following months was in this respect decisive. Only the illegal organizations had an effective existence, while the directorates became no more than a legal fiction.

This victory guaranteed the independence of the student movement, and was one of the preconditions for the upsurge of the popular movement in 1968. Only a year later, in September 1966, the political progress of the student mass was given striking expression in the streets of São Paulo. Some days before, the police had invaded the university in Rio de Janeiro after a peaceful demonstration there. Students who had occupied the medicine faculty were brutally evicted by police using the 'Polish corridor' method (a double line of policemen armed with truncheons through which the victim is forced under a shower of blows). The São Paulo students replied by a street demonstration, the first since the coup. Ten thousand demonstrators confronted the unsurpassed brutality of the government forces for several hours. From this demonstration the students obtained practical apprenticeship in clandestine organization. They assembled rapidly in places fixed five minutes earlier, then dispersed again to regroup later in another area. The entire town centre was paralysed. In the eyes of the population it was politics itself that had been reborn after two years of silence.

1967 was the year of the great ideological turning-point for the Brazilian left. All parties and political groups, including the 'left-wing' Marxists (the POLOP and the POR – Revolutionary Workers Party, affiliated to the Fourth International) suffered its consequences. From a so-to-speak morphological aspect this was the year of fragmentation, splits and opposition. The student movement by its objective social situation provides the laboratory conditions of ideological debate. The groupuscules, the tiny factions (there are those in Brazil which call themselves, seriously, *dissidencia da dissidencia* – opposition to the opposition) found in the student movement possibilities for survival (naturally a very artificial, almost imaginary survival )which they could not find in other strata of society. But when this 'overestimation of ideas' is backed up by an effective political practice and when therefore theories and sects have to show the worth of their political positions in action, the fragmentation of organizations takes on a positive aspect especially if it calls into question a party like the PCB and hastens the creation of organizations better suited to the immediate struggle.

The upsurge of the 1968 student struggles was sparked off by the death of Edson Luis, a student, at a Rio demonstration in March of that year. He was murdered in cold blood by a shock troop of the military police. During months of increasingly violent confrontations between students and the forces of repression, the students led the popular movement and succeeded in mobilizing hundreds of thousands of people all over Brazil around such slogans as 'Down with the dictatorship' and 'Drive out imperialism'. The movement acquired a special depth in the main urban centres of the South East: São Paulo, Rio, Belo Horizonte, and in Brasilia where the specific slogans of the student movement were added to those of the political struggle (against the dictatorship, against imperialism).

The first struggles were against the 'MEC-USAID project', which sought to transform the universities into foundations directly controlled by the Ministry of Education, by 'representatives of the productive classes' (a euphemism which the employers like to use) and by 'American aid', the nature of which was not too well known. In short, the universities were to be transformed into extensions of private industry. They would be devoted to the training of technical cadres as well as imparting a sub-imperialist, technocratic, elitist and viciously anti-communist ideology. The struggle against the 'MEC-USAID project' was thus from the beginning a struggle of important ideological character, with the aims of resisting the new attempt at 'militarization' of the university (not being able to liquidate the student movement's independent organizations, the dictatorship fell upon the university itself as an institution). It was a political critique, at the levels of organization, agitation and propaganda, of the present regime, and in general, helped to advance the struggle for socialism. Surprised by the size of the movement, the dictatorship hesitated at first. In São Paulo in particular, where the governor was playing at redemocratization, police and army repression only really began with the Osasco strikes in July 1968, and the student movement itself was not attacked openly until September. In Rio and Brasilia, on the other hand, the struggle was more violent from the beginning, and in Rio especially the urban masses – state workers, white-collar workers, petty bourgeoisie – came out from the start on the side of the students. In São Paulo – business centre, 'city of work and order' – the combined effects of petty bourgeois individualism and what empiricist sociologists call 'the aspiration of social ascent, and 'social mobility' conspired to give the mass movement a more restricted and plebeian character. The intermediate strata of the population were only represented by students and intellectuals, although organized sections of the working class also took part.

The students used every form of popular urban struggle: rapid assemblies, groups of agitators touring the popular quarters at busy periods, large street demonstrations, faculty occupations, confrontation with the police and military forces of repression, and so on. In the month of June 1968 the movement reached its maximum intensity, when the 'march of a hundred thousand' took place in Rio to protest against the police and military violence of the dictatorship. The importance of such a demonstration must be measured against the savagery of the Brazilian regime's repressive methods. When housewives decide to leave home at the risk of being hit by a police truncheon, then the government's unpopularity has reached a dangerous level. It was thus forced to remain on the defensive, and the demonstration was permitted.

In São Paulo, the last days of June 1968 saw the student movement's passage to revolutionary warfare. This formula may astonish the reader and make him believe that, like so many other partisans of armed struggle in Latin America, I am taking my desires for reality, but here is a description of a demonstration from the bourgeois paper *Folha de São Paulo* (25 June 1968):

'The president of UEE (State Students Union) announced the beginning of a march and shouted the slogan 'the organized people will overthrow the dictatorship'. The demonstrators changed it: 'Only the armed people will overthrow the distatorship'. Cars and buses stopped.... The people were asked to participate.... They headed towards the Education Secretariat. Stones began to break the plateglass windows. The glass door of the Education Secretariat was shattered. A Molotov cocktail was thrown.... Dense flames climbed up the wall.... Walls and monuments were covered with slogans. Thunderflashes exploded non-stop. ... The demonstration reached the City Bank. Students threw stones and ... charged with thunderflashes.... Six students hurled themselves at the main door, ramming it with wooden beams.... Further on the Army pharmacy was stoned'. For two months the Brazilian press described dozens of similar demonstrations which took place in the main Brazilian cities.

The occupation of the São Paulo Philosophy Faculty during the July vacation was no less a test of the student movement's strength. The government was reluctant to invade the faculty by military force. The student's own 'security apparatus' guarded it night and day, and it was ready to fight, if only to cover the occupants' retreat. Courses on political philosophy, in which all forbidden topics from *Capital* to Debray were discussed, brought together hundreds of students and a number of teachers. Young highschool students also took part, even in the 'military' tasks. No one could remain unmoved at the sight of these revolutionary adolescents keeping watch from the top floor of the Philosophy Faculty, or from the barricades surrounding it against the incursions of the fascist militia (the CCC, *Comando de Caça ao Comunista*, Communist Pursuit Commando).

The occupants' main demand was for parity control of the university. The university institutions at all levels were to be controlled by parity committees of teachers and students (with representation for administrative functionaries and of all campus workers). In some departments of the Philosophy Faculty parity was put into practice. Even in faculties as reactionary as the Law Faculty, there was a significant minority of teachers favourable to the measure, but it was apparent enough that the dictatorship would only wait for the ebb of the wave to move to the counter-offensive. The federal government must be credited with a certain intelligence in its fight against the university. It was certainly forced by the very scale of the movement against the dictatorship to have recourse to violent measures previously reserved for workers and peasants. These measures only increased its unpopularity (and the list of its victims – there were at least a dozen students killed or severely wounded between March and September 1968). But altogether, it knew how to retreat in the face of pressure from the student movement and wait for better days to try and destroy it. Those 'better days' were not long in arriving.

During the upsurge of the mass movement, fascist terror groups made up of officers from the armed forces, policemen, members of oligarchic families and declassed elements of every kind, revived. (They had previously been particularly active during the 1963-64 conjuncture.) These well-dressed bandits were organized under two titles, the CCC, mentioned above, and the MAC (Anti-Communist Movement). At first their violence was exercised against intellectuals and artists. In 1968 numerous invasions of theatres where plays critical of the regime were being performed took place. The fury of these 'defenders of Western culture' spared no one. Actors and actresses as well as the audience were brutally assaulted on several occasions. The fascist commandos stripped the actresses (a singular method of restoring morality, but fascism has its own logic).

In September 1968, after successive provocations and under the benevolent eye of the police, a CCC commando, armed with revolvers, a sub-machine gun and Molotov cocktails, destroyed the São Paulo Philosophy Faculty in a battle that lasted a whole afternoon. They did not hesitate to fire on the students. A seventeen-year-old high-school student was murdered in cold blood and many others were wounded. Thus the fascists settled their accounts with the Philosophy Faculty.

The dictatorship's next blow struck at UNE itself. Important decisions were expected from the UNE Annual Congress that autumn. Earlier congresses had been clandestine, UNE being an illegal organization, but clandestinity in the case of a mass organization is a rather ambiguous notion. The students actually met in 'neutral' territory, most often in monasteries, which the police did not then dare invade. The 1968 Congress was also to be clandestine. But the faculties were no longer occupied, and besides, conscious of their political strength, the student movement leaders wanted a congress that reflected the recent broad development of the popular struggle. As a consequence, more than a thousand delegates met at a farm outside a village in São Paulo state. It was impossible not to be discovered by the Army's secret service. But the UNE leadership seems precisely to have thought that the government would not dare to imprison a thousand delegates. (This is only a hypothesis, as the student leaders have never made this point clear.) The government did dare. The Congress had hardly begun when an Army detachment encircled the farm and led off to prison almost eight hundred students (some others managed to escape). The student movement leadership was for the time being decimated. The most prominent leaders are still in prison, except for those who were freed a year later in exchange for the American ambassador kidnapped by an ALN-MR8 commando (see pages 212–13).

The 'coup within the coup' of December 1968 was finally to make 'order reign' in the university for a whole period. The time of the catacombs returned, though for all that, the regime's threats to the independence of the student organizations were never successful. The military-oligarchic dream of forming 'democratic' student unions (generally financed by US aid and by the Ministry of Education) was not transformed into reality. Despite its retreat, the student movement remains, after December 1968, an independent political force and a fighter in the struggle against the dictatorship and against imperialism. It is the most militant sector within the popular movement and indeed a large majority of the militants in the armed organizations are drawn from its ranks. These organizations gradually discovered the need to find ways of supporting the student struggle, of developing it and deepening it politically. They discovered – or at least they tried to discover – the specific characteristics and role of the student movement as the most sensitive and organized sector of the popular movement, in the special conditions of present Brazilian society.

Students belong to what have been called the 'intermediate' strata of the population.[11] They are not members of the ruling bloc, neither are they workers or peasants. But what distinguishes students from other members of this hetero-

---

[11] As of 1968 there were about 278,000 students enrolled in colleges of higher education throughout the country. Broken down according to regions the figure is: São Paulo 82,000; Guanabara (this includes the city of Rio de Janeiro): 38,000; Minas Gerais: 32,000 and Rio Grande do Sul: 29,000. The remainder is made up from the smaller states. The federal district, Brasilia, where the movement became particularly important in 1968 has about 4,000 students.

geneous group? They are neither producers nor government workers and so cannot be said to belong either to the economic or political moment. Rather they are the productive consumers of the dominant culture. They are quite distinct from the mass of workers (including intellectual workers – a group to which they are doubly tied both as consumers and as pupils) since the student *qua* student is a non-worker. They are not for the most part future owners of property but rather future intellectuals and this means that they are not future members of the dominant class. Their relation however with the culture of that class is ambiguous, since in order to criticize it they must first consume it. As cultivated plebeians they are economically oppressed but culturally privileged. Their oppression explains why they are on the side of the people, while their privilege explains in part why they are capable of political intervention.

Correct though this analysis may be in outline, it is still too schematic. In particular it may lead one to confuse the question of students' potential for revolutionary struggle with the question of the specific role of the student movement in that struggle. It is easy to treat students merely as a source of revolutionary cadres – as some of the fighting organizations have done – while totally ignoring the role which students may play as an organized movement. But it is equally easy to make the opposite mistake – just as ultra-leftists like the POC (Communist Workers Party) have done – of over-emphasizing the specificity of student struggle, by stressing in particular students' cultural privilege. Because students are best placed to master and teach Marxist science and method, it is argued, their proper role in the revolutionary struggle is therefore ideological. This is not of course their theory as they themselves understand it but it does reflect the logic of their practice. While ignoring the nature and requirements of the revolutionary struggle in general they claim that they are vanguard parties. These they may be – but ones which exist only on the base of the student body itself. This said one must reject also the position to be found all too often among the armed organizations which treats the student struggle as no more than a training for clandestine warfare.

VI. THE MARGINAL SECTOR

Though the majority of Brazilians now live in the city, there is a vast mass of urban under-employed who remain for most of the year on the fringes of the money economy. These 'marginals' form a lumpenproletarian stratum within Brazilian society. They live in the slums of São Paulo or in the *favelas* which ring Rio and Brasilia. They are the product not of industrialization but of urbanization, a process which in Brazil means the flight to the cities from famine in the countryside.

The rural population of Brazil is growing at a rate of 1·6 per cent per annum while the urban population is increasing at the rate of five per cent. Part of this increase is of course an expansion of the existing urban population, but a growing proportion is the result of a 'rural exodus' of starving peasants. Some indication of how large a proportion this is can be given by the following figures[12] for the growth of the *favelas* around the new capital in Brasilia. The present population of Brasilia is about 510,000 and it is estimated that its *favelas* contain 80,000 people, or fifteen and a half per cent of the total. Brasilia has only been in existence for ten years. (There are more than a million *favelados* in Rio and the proportion is far higher in the cities of the North East.)

[12] *Veja*, 8 October 1969.

It must be borne in mind that the *favelados* and the marginals do not necessarily coincide as groups. Many industrial workers are forced by the appalling housing shortage to live in the *favelas* and so are many of the new stratum of semi-proletarian agricultural workers – the *volantes*. Neither of these should be thought of as marginal sectors. In São Paulo, on the other hand, there are few *favelas* and the marginals – as well as many others – live in slum tenements. (According to the Head of the Social Welfare department for the city of São Paulo, these slums house more than 60 per cent of the city's population.[13]) *Favelas, bidonvilles* and shanty towns are not peculiarly Brazilian. They exist on the outskirts of many Western European cities, but this is the consequence of economic growth not underdevelopment. It is a housing problem – the foreign workers who inhabit them at least have jobs. The marginals in Brazil are produced by uneven development which condemns a vast mass of its population to starvation in the countryside or unemployment in the towns. Peasants are either thrown off their land by landowners in the process of 'rationalizing' and diversifying production, or they leave quite simply to escape starvation. This need not, in the latter case, be an irreversible process. In the North East, in particular, peasants will flee to the towns during the long droughts to which the area is prone and then return to the land. Nevertheless for the vast majority that stay, there are no jobs – either in industry or in the service sector.

Official statistics disguise the existence of this stratum by listing a large proportion of marginals as employed in 'services'. According to the 1960 census there were about a quarter of a million people employed in the 'tertiary sector'. Assuming the same rate of growth between 1960 and 1970

[13] *O Estado de São Paulo*, 16 August 1970.

as there was between 1950 and 1960 one can calculate the present size of this sector as near one million. To this must be added the number of small family shops and businesses, which, using the same projection, amounts to another million persons employed in distribution and in services. According to the IBGE Statistical Yearbook for 1968, however, there were 2·3 million people employed in distribution (wholesale and retail) and 4·2 million people employed in services.

The sudden appearance of 4·5 million people listed as working in the services sector is an indication of the extent to which the nature of this marginal stratum is distorted. The marginals are not 'employed' but exist on the fringes of the economy selling oddments in the street, washing cars or shining shoes.

The purposes of this fiction are not hard to detect. The marginals play an important part in the ideological products of the bourgeoisie. As the above statistics show they figure in the ideology of development by serving to disguise as productive a sector which produces no surplus value.

They figure also in the myth of the reconciliation of classes, which is alleged to take place when the *escolas de samba* descend from the *favelas* into the streets of Rio to sing and dance with the bourgeoisie at Carnival time. (The same thing occurs in the football stadium. Garrastazu holds up the World Cup to the cheering crowds and is embraced by Pele. Everyone realizes that despite appearances they are all, underneath, 'true Brazilians'.)

There is a theory shared by Brazil's technocrats and certain tendencies on the left which asserts that the working class is no longer capable of playing a revolutionary role and that this task has fallen to the ever growing mass of 'marginals'. The theory rests on a mistaken interpretation of the present dynamics of Brazilian society. On this analysis rapid industrial development together with vastly increased productivity in agriculture will continue to neutralize the proletariat as a revolutionary force. At the same time however a growing number of the urban masses and poor peasants will become economically 'marginalized', and so replace the proletariat as the main revolutionary force.

It must be realized that the marginals have no privileged role to play in the fight against the dictatorship for socialism. They have no organizations with which to develop the struggle. They are proletarianized in the most negative sense of that term. They are separated from the means of production, as a result of the increasing organic composition of capital both in industry and agriculture, but they have not thereby become workers. They are not grouped in a factory. They do not even constitute an industrial reserve army.

One of the main conditions for a class to play a political role is that it displays a certain minimum 'collectivity'. The importance of its political role does not depend in the first instance on its role in the production of the material conditions of life. The political importance of such groups as the Army or the Church do not depend on this in any way. Nobody, on the other hand, would deny the economic importance of the peasantry at the time of Louis Bonapoarte, even though the social conditions of their existence – namely their dispersion – prevented them from playing anything but a marginal role politically.

The marginals are not a collection of equal particles scattered evenly through the country, but are gathered into cities. Within the cities they are still dispersed. In general the marginals have no internal unity whatsoever but are masses in the basic sense of that word. They have not even the minimal political strength to win for themselves the smallest of their demands. A strategy which bases itself, therefore, first and foremost on this stratum is fundamentally mistaken. It is a *reductio ad absurdum* of the vanguard role of the working class to the vanguard role of the oppressed and exploited.

# Chapter 3

# The Passage to Revolutionary War

## I. THE CRISIS OF THE LEFT AND REORGANIZATION FOR ARMED ACTION

The preliminary stage of this analysis is now complete. We have examined the strength and dispositions of the forces of the counter-revolution as well as those of the mass of the people, and now we must examine how the forces of the left in their struggle against the dictatorship made the transition from reformist politics to armed struggle.[1] This was of course no simple process; the revolutionary vanguard was not formed according to some pre-ordained plan, and where the slogan of armed struggle was applied mechanically it tended to lead to disaster. It would of course be a gross caricature of the situation in which the left found itself after the coup to suggest that they faced the dictatorship without a theory of how to conduct their struggle. They had the example of Cuba. They had Guevara's theory of guerrilla war and later Debray's theory of the *foco*. This was a rich strategic heritage and the revolutionary left did indeed follow in broad outline Debray's two cardinal principles that the old parties of the left must be abandoned and armed

---

[1] See the Appendix for a list of the names, and a brief account of the origins and actions of the organizations of the left in Brazil.

struggle begun without delay. But they were forced in the years immediately after the coup to pose and answer a whole series of questions which had not been successfully answered before, and for which they had to find their own answers. Where is it best to begin armed struggle? The country or the city? Can one set up a guerrilla *foco* without first making lengthy preparations in the city? Is armed struggle in the city limited to preparing for the rural *foco*? Does the poor record of guerrilla *foco* lead one to revise one's view of the city as a secondary zone? What organization does the revolution need? In abandoning the old parties of the left should one jettison their apparatus as well? How can the various local urban guerrilla groupings be coordinated on a national scale? Once most militants become engaged in armed struggle how is the traditional political work of mass mobilization to be carried out? Or are armed actions in the cities themselves enough to mobilize the people?

It was the different answers to these various questions which caused the many splits and alliances within the fighting organizations which militants from the old left were to form. Before these problems could be confronted, however, armed struggle had to be put on the agenda. However, the first attempts to do this were not the result of any theoretical debates within the traditional parties, but actual armed actions mounted by the 'Jacobin' left which grouped itself around the impressive figure of Brizola. The Revolutionary Nationalists had not been strong enough to answer the counter-revolution of 1964 with the threat of revolutionary civil war, and Brizola's rearguard action in Rio Grande do Sul was, as explained earlier, a failure.

The lesson drawn from this defeat was that what was needed was a revolutionary party which would organize the most combative sections of the popular movement in resistance to the dictatorship. But how, it was argued, could such a party be constructed except through armed struggle? Following the slogan 'Action builds organization' the militants decided that their primary task was preparation for the military aspect of the struggle, and in 1966 accordingly began setting up the minimum clandestine infrastructure needed to launch armed operations.

The inadequacies of their analysis were demonstrated only too well a year later when their *foco* in the Caparáo mountains[2] was surrounded by a battalion of the First Army and a whole guerrilla detachment captured. This single disaster was enough to wreck their entire project. The *foco*, it seems, was intended as part of a wider scheme planned on a national or even continental scale. (According to an editorial in the Uruguayan Review *America Latina*, the Caparáo *foco* and the Bolivian guerrilla struggle were together meant to mark the opening of armed struggle throughout the Côno Sur – the southern portion of Latin America.) In the event the whole project turned out tragically enough to be little more than a vast conspiracy. The moment armed actions began it had been intended to announce the birth of the Revolutionary Nationalist Movement (MNR) based on 'insurrectional *focos*' planned for other parts of Brazil and on the urban support networks. Needless to say such a movement failed to appear. In their belief that the possession of excellent military cadre and equipment absolved them from the task of *building* an organization, they succeeded only in isolating themselves entirely from the rest of the revolutionary left. The coherence of their plan was purely internal: a great apparatus assembled by the general staff of the MNR alone. It only needed the removal of one of its cogs – like Caparáo – for the whole thing to collapse. (It must be said that, despite the Caparáo disaster, the MNR was able to

[2] The Caparáo mountains are on the border between Minas Gerais and Espírito Santo.

retreat in good order and not waste human material that could be relied on. This is why 'MNR survivors' can be found among the organizations that led the transition to direct action in 1968.)

The lessons of Caparáo were not lost on the Brazilian left. As the partisans of armed struggle broke from the PCB or from POLOP, the other major party of the old left, the disaster of Caparáo, as well as those in Bolivia and Peru stood out as stark lessons: the transition to direct action might be immediate but henceforth the rural *foco* would require preparation in the city.

It was after the OLAS conference in Havana in August 1967 that the Brazilian left explicitly adopted the slogan of armed struggle. By this time partisans had won their independence from the traditional left, and even though the PCB had refused Havana's invitation to attend, it too had by then become a supporter 'in principle'.

With the exception of the breaking away of the Trotskyists, who never grew beyond a weak Marxist fraction, the PCB's political decomposition can be dated from the beginning of the 1960s. There had been a severe internal conflict at the time of the Soviet invasion of Hungary, but the militants who left the party at that time retreated into private life, for there was no possibility of their turning their differences into a political alternative. In 1961 the POLOP was founded, which took over (and with rather more success) the old Trotskyist ambition of regrouping revolutionary Marxists outside official communism. In 1962 the break-up of the PCB began, one group on the central committee founding the Communist Party of Brazil (PC do B) and drawing close to the so-called 'Chinese' position. The fragmentation of the left halted there until the 1964 *coup d'etat*. The sorry role of the PCB during the counter-revolution destroyed it completely as a revolutionary workers' organization. Only the apparatus continued to obey the central leadership. The base organizations effectively ceased to belong to the party and developed into separate dissident groups. But the divisions within the PCB were as much vertical as horizontal; in December 1966 Carlos Marighela, the future initiator of urban guerrilla warfare, resigned from the Executive Committee (equivalent to political bureau), explaining his reasons in a long letter in which he questioned the party's policy *in toto*. Other leaders of the PCB also prepared to carry the 'internal struggle' to its final consequences. Those whose differences were above all over the methods of work of the old leadership inclined towards constituting a new party, and when it proved impossible to overthrow the party apparatus they proposed the formation of the Brazilian Revolutionary Communist Party (PCBR). Marighela on the other hand was completely opposed to substituting a new party for the old. What he considered necessary was to begin armed struggle, and he therefore made no attempt to win control over the innumerable dissident communist groups which broke from the party like splinters of broken glass. The support he enjoyed from the São Paulo state federation of the PCB provided him with the minimal organizational apparatus needed for the transition to direct action. He relied on the polarizing effect of armed struggle to regroup revolutionary cadres of the PCB, and was unconcerned by the appearance of the PCBR.

The PCB meanwhile, after discussions with the Argentine and Uruguayan CPs, decided not to take part in the OLAS conference, scheduled for August 1967. This position was also taken by the Argentine CP, though not by the Uruguayan, whose general secretary, Rodney Arismendi, played an important role at the conference as the main representative of 'official' communism. Marighela accepted the invitation refused by the PCB leadership and went to Havana. A break with Marighela now became as indispensable for the PCB as a break with the PCB was for Marighela. The sixth PCB conference later in the year only confirmed a separation already accomplished in practice.

The process of fragmentation of the PCB during this period cannot be understood without avoiding the tendency of over-simplification. The party had been completely inoperative, a purposeless machine that tried to survive by mediocre manoeuvres, such as support for the *Frente Ampla* (see page 74 above). The question of immediate transition to armed struggle was not the only one responsible for the vast crisis that led in 1967 to the formation of the PCBR on one side and the Marighela grouping on the other. Not all 'left' criticisms of the PCB's policy implied the adoption of the slogan of transition to direct action. One of the best known leaders of the PCBR, J. Gorender, did not hesitate to criticize what he called the 'infantile disorder' of Marighelism. In fact, one section of the militants who left the PCB were concerned above all to criticize its programme (PCBR), while the other (Marighela's group) were concerned rather to change the method of struggle. One could say that the former preferred the weapon of criticism, the latter the criticism of weapons.

A similar process took place within POLOP. As long as armed struggle was not on the agenda it had no internal difficulties. Its origin and its predominant milieu (the student movement) predisposed it towards stagnating in ideological criticism of the PCB's reformism, which stressed the historic role of the working class and of the socialist character of the Brazilian revolution, without being able to develop a practice conforming to its theoretical positions. Its critique of reformism and revisionism was predominantly verbal. POLOP managed neither to fulfil the historic requirements of a revolutionary vanguard nor to become the

Marxist-Leninist alternative to the PCB. Partisans of armed struggle hoped to have a majority at its September 1967 Congress, but they were defeated by 16 votes to 14. The theses adopted reaffirmed that the principal task of the vanguard was to construct the 'proletarian party', and while not rejecting the principle of armed struggle the majority reduced it in fact to nothing more than a principle. They failed to pose the question of power and fiercely denounced what they termed the 'rightist' conceptions of the POLOP section from Minas Gerais, which linked the necessity of armed struggle with that of *national liberation*. This section, which left POLOP after the Congress (in Minas the great majority of the base followed the regional leadership), adopted the conceptions of Guevara and Debray while trying to give them a concrete interpretation developed from the specific situation of the Brazilian class struggle. The Minas Gerais group replied to the slogan of 'construction of the revolutionary party' launched by the POLOP majority and the PCBR with the thesis that the party would be formed during and through armed struggle.

The POLOP split also had important consequences in São Paulo, where the tendency standing for transition to direct action, though not in a majority as in Minas, counted on the support of the most combative militants. The São Paulo opposition, combining with the 'MNR survivors', was also the first Brazilian organization to cross the Rubicon of armed action.

Towards the end of 1967 the crisis of the Brazilian left had lead to the break up of the two organizations: the Communist Party and POLOP. The splits were both on questions of strategy and on geographical lines. Differences of strategy focused of course around the question of armed struggle, but almost everyone was a partisan of direct action 'in principle'. The real division was between those who placed organization first and those who considered this problem quite secondary to the task of beginning armed struggle. Within the old parties these divisions were expressed geographically. As the old parties broke up and as the base ceased to obey the leadership it was only natural that the regional groups should take their own independent line. Marighela, partisan of armed struggle, dominated the CP in São Paulo; the opposition within POLOP (again the partisans of armed struggle) was divided into the Minas Gerais and the São Paulo opposition.

## II. THE FIRST ARMED ACTIONS

The privilege of receiving the first bomb of the revolutionary war fell in March 1968 to the US Consulate in São Paulo. This assault was the work of the MNR network, then in the process of fusing with the São Paulo POLOP opposition. Sticks of dynamite were used, and like the greater part of the terrorist attacks that were to follow, it was notable for its technical perfection. The police and army realized immediately that this was not the work of amateurs.

The bank raids began soon after. This initiative was taken by the grouping of the São Paulo MNR and POLOP opposition. The MNR survivors centred on São Paulo had joined forces with the partisans of armed struggle within POLOP. After an initial miscarriage, it pulled off its first stroke in an action that has become a model of its kind. A group of five or six men occupies a bank. The employees are rapidly locked in the lavatory, except the manager, who is forced to open the safe. The action usually lasts no more than a few minutes, five on average. The group arrives in a large car, stolen the day before. During the action this car is parked in front of the bank, with the driver, also armed with a submachine gun, at the wheel. The raid accomplished, the group leaves in this car. Two other cars are parked a few hundred yards away, in a district chosen beforehand, which must be relatively empty. There the car used for the raid is abandoned and the group transfers to the 'relief' cars.

Actions of this type were to become more and more frequent in the course of 1968 and 1969. Their technical and military characteristics remained almost unchanged; commandos, armed with one or two sub-machine guns, acted rapidly and with precision. Following the POLOP opposition/MNR, the Marighela group also moved to the offensive. In 1967 Marighela had formed an organization called ALN (Action for National Liberation) grouping together the ex-communist São Paulo militants who favoured armed action. (In February 1968 the ALN produced the *Standpoint Manifesto* published as the political statement of the 'São Paulo Communist Grouping'.[3] This was the first attempt to theorize the specific requirements of the Brazilian struggle.) In August 1968 it effected the year's most spectacular expropriation, the hold-up of the *trem pagador* (the train which carried pay to the workers on the Santos-Jundia railway), Five men boarded the train at 6.50 a.m. At 6.59 the train stopped at a small suburban station, departing one minute later. At 7.01 three men, one with a sub-machine gun, entered the carriage where the money was kept; there were 108,000 new cruzeiros (somewhat less than 30,000 dollars). They seized the money, pulled the emergency stop and jumped off the train. It was 7.03 a.m. Two cars were waiting,

[3] ALN texts were all published originally in Portuguese. *Les Temps Modernes* published a number of documents in the November 1969 issue. Marighela's letter of resignation from the PCB together with a biography and the *Manual of Urban Guerrilla Warfare* were published by Tricontinental in July 1970 under the title *Marighella*. The *Manual* was also published in the French edition of *Tricontinental*, no. 16, as well as in *Pour la libération du Brésil* which appeared under a collective imprint in Paris in July 1970. This volume included other writings by Marighela, translated into French, among which were his 'Letter to Fidel Castro' and his 'Interview on Revolutionary War'.

parked beside a large palm tree which had been used as a landmark. Without hesitation, the police and army publicly attributed the raid to the 'communists', even though neither the POLOP opposition nor the Marighela group had claimed responsibility for the past month's wave of expropriations. (Their attitude was to change only around December 1968, when Marighela's manifesto spoke of 'armed actions of every kind, surprise attacks and ambushes'.) In fact they considered it advisable to use their tactical advantage of surprise (the famous 'surprise effect' often mentioned in Marighelist documents). This type of action was completely unprecedented in Brazil, and the police were still not entirely convinced of the political significance of the raids. This was only ascertained beyond doubt around the end of the year.

Restricted at first to São Paulo (which one might almost call the true guerrilla *foco* in 1968), the expropriations soon spread to the city and state of Rio and the state of Minas Gerais. The idea of a 'subversive plot', minutely planned in some 'communist country' and in which the bank raids were only the first move, began to haunt both the imagination of the bourgeois press and the sleep of the '*gorillas*' charged with national security. At first the armed organization's silence prevented the police from completely jettisoning the hypothesis of a 'crime syndicate'. But expropriations of money were not everything.

Towards the end of June 1968 a small group of revolutionaries surprised the guard at the São Paulo army hospital. For the first time the army itself was attacked. The action was a total success; revolutionary commandos of the POLOP opposition/MNR penetrated the barracks after overpowering the sentry on duty at the side entrance. It was almost 11 p.m. The commando of ten militants, two of whom carried submachine guns (the other were armed only with revolvers) divided into two groups, each with a car. The first group had the task of subduing the guard (ten soldiers) who slept in the main building at the barracks, the other had to overpower the sentry at the main entrance. As expected, the first group found the guard half asleep. They ordered them to surrender and seized their arms (ten of the latest FAL rifles, just acquired by the Brazilian army). The second group meanwhile left for the main entrance. (Both groups, in their respective cars, had entered by the side gate; the second group thus approached the main gate from within the barracks.) Three militants emerged from the car, one dressed as an army officer. The problem was to overpower the sentry without noise, and avoiding useless violence. A simple trick was used: 'Did you fire? I heard a shot. Let's see your gun,' said the 'officer' as the sentry saluted, and the well-disciplined soldier handed over his gun. Immediately after, the first group arrived at the main gateway. The action had lasted less than ten minutes, and there were neither dead nor wounded. But from that time on the *gorillas* knew that a clandestine organization was at work, affecting its 'primitive accumulation' of automatic weapons.

This action attained by chance a quite unexpected significance. Some days later the commander of the Second Army made known the theft of 'a few old rifles', in an interview broadcast on radio and television. He added, in the bragging style of Latin American '*gorillas*', that the 'arms robbers' were only able to attack such small detachments and that they would not have the courage to come 'to my quarters'. For there they would be received, 'not in the Russian style, nor in the Chinese, nor in the Cuban, but with *cabocla*' (i.e. with a peasant roughness). Late one of the following nights the general received a spectacular reply. A truck stuffed with dynamite was driven against the Second Army HQ in São Paulo. To cover the driver's escape (he had to jump out of the moving truck before it crashed into the HQ building) the POLOP opposition/MNR used the automatic weapons it had recently acquired. A section of the building was destroyed by the explosion, which unfortunately caused the death of a sentry who approached the truck a few seconds before the explosion.

This event had considerable repercussions, but aside from arousing the excitement of that part of the left which already supported armed struggle, and demoralizing the old *'gorilla'* with his *'cabocla'* method, the action served to show up the dangerous tactical oscillations of the POLOP opposition/ MNR. If the dictatorship had replied by imposing a state of siege (and this question did indeed arise in the National Security Council), such a measure, far from aiding the preparation of armed struggle in the countryside (the avowed objective at this stage), would only have made it more difficult. The first direct actions had been supposedly 'logistic' (a vogue expression among the clandestine left). For the POLOP opposition/MNR this was definitely a matter of principle. Money, arms, equipment, urban infrastructure, trained cadres, were all destined, directly or indirectly, for the rural guerrilla. In this sense the 'preparatory phase' was not an objective part of revolutionary struggle, but rather the 'subjective' preparation of the vanguard detachment that was going to set up the *foco*. That at least was the initial idea. But as direct action developed the revolutionary groups fell into a double paradox. In the cities, they encountered a growing and combative mass movement, sections of which were definitely favourable to armed struggle. In the countryside however, they faced unforeseen difficulties even in fixing the 'strategic area', i.e. the region in which to deploy the main guerrilla effort.

The bank raids themselves, initially not even presented as revolutionary actions, ended up acquiring an objective meaning way beyond their original financial aims. But this very success, both military and political, posed difficult problems for the armed organizations. Up to what point did the tactical detour that urban actions represented correspond to the objective requirements of the guerrilla war as a whole? Were bank raids not rather a pure and simple deviation from the principle, always recognized in theory, that only the rural guerrilla detachment can become the embryo of the peoples' army? The activists may have believed they were still striving for the strategic objectives initially posed (formation of a peoples' army in the countryside via the development of rural guerrilla), but they began *in fact* to follow *another path*. The struggle they began in practice was based on the idea that a small vanguard organization can provoke a crisis of the military-oligarchic state by means of efficiently mounted armed blows.

Thus the very dynamic of the urban actions threatened to lead the revolutionary organizations onto a strategy based on the city, even if in theory they upheld the thesis of the rural guerrilla as strategic detachment and embryo of the peoples' army. Departing from the *explicit* theory, practice came to be guided *implicitly* by a different theory.

### III. RURAL GUERRILLA WARFARE

In order to understand the problem posed at the end of the last section we must return to the strategic debates that followed the decision to go over to armed struggle in the first place. It was relatively easy for the left to adopt the slogan of armed struggle, but difficult to answer in practice the questions of what form it should take, what base it would require, or how it would coordinate with a mass struggle. The theses of Debray arrived in Brazil at the right time to give answers to all these problems. Together with the Cuban example, and the writings of Guevara, Debray's theories gave the slogan a semblance of concrete content. Armed struggle would take the form of the rural guerrilla *foco* and its social base would be those strata that could be mobilized round a 'minimum anti-imperialist programme'. The development of the struggle itself would ensure the growing participation of these groups in the revolutionary process.

To revolutionaries faced with the question 'what is to be done?' Debray's reply was simple: set up the military *foco* (since 'one goes from the military *foco* to the political movement'[4]). To the tactical question of how to set up the *foco* the reply was just as simple: obtain cadres with military training, money, material and kit, arrange depots in the zone of operation, explore and await the arrival of the enemy to engage him in a war of movement.

In reality things were not so clear and the inadequacies of applying these straightforward formulae without considering the particular situation to which they were applied soon became only too apparent. Major problems were left unanswered: how could militants break from the party without losing all ties with the working class? How was one to prevent the guerrilla column from becoming merely its own vanguard? On the crucial question of preparing for the *foco* Debray has very little to say. The success of this stage is simply taken for granted and relegated to a heroic prehistory whose paradigm is the fitting out of the 'Granma'.

Despite their imprecision and their omissions, Debray's theories won wide acceptance and when they were criticized this was often only after they had failed in practice. Perhaps the major reason for the impact of these theses on the left in Latin America was the sharp distinction, on which they all rest, between revolutionary and opportunist politics. In

---

[4] Régis Debray, *Revolution in the Revolution?* (Monthly Review Press, 1967), p. 119.

*Revolution in the Revolution?* this distinction comes to coincide with the distinction between the guerrilla *foco* and any politics centred on the city. It was no doubt the attraction of its polemic against 'parties', their endless round of congresses and meetings, their bureaucratic apparatuses, their publications and their mass fronts, that won the book its acceptance and disarmed immediate criticism of its positive theories. Once the political choice became 'guerrilla fighter or opportunist', old leaders accustomed to the undisturbed inertia of the peaceful road could no longer silence young militants with well-chosen quotations from Lenin.

However, the positive theories of *Revolution in the Revolution?* deserved closer critical scrutiny than they at first received. They were developed as strict corollaries of the basic distinction between reformist and revolutionary politics. Two principles inform the whole work: the primacy of the military over the political and the primacy of the countryside over the city as the fighting ground for guerrilla warfare. As the struggle developed it became necessary to question both of these principles, and to see how they applied in the concrete situation in which Brazilian revolutionaries found themselves at the start of their offensive against the dictatorship.

This is not the place to summarize the experience of ten years of rural guerrilla warfare in Latin America. The balance would not be positive. For three guerrilla movements solidly entrenched (Guatemala, Colombia, Venezuela) but unable to go beyond the stage of strategic defensive, numerous defeats must be listed: Paraguay, Argentina, Peru, Bolivia, not to mention Caparáo and others less well known. The causes of these defeats (and of the relative stagnation of the struggle in those countries where the guerrilla is solidly entrenched) are many and varied: basic errors have been committed. The fact that Guevara himself launched guerrilla struggle in Bolivia without respecting the 'indispensable' condition of the support of the peasant masses shows clearly the gap between theory and practice. The basic accent of the theory of the guerrilla has been displaced. Presented at first as the Latin American form of peoples' war, it has been progressively transformed into a sort of rural conspiratism in which the military elements gained the upper hand over the political. In 1967 Guevara did not put his own theory of the guerrilla into practice but that of Debray as expounded in *Revolution in the Revolution*?

'In underdeveloped America, the countryside is the basic area for armed struggle.'[5] According to Guevara, this is one of the three basic contributions of the Cuban revolution 'to the conduct of revolutionary movements in America'. He criticizes 'those who maintain dogmatically that the struggle of the masses is centred in city movements, entirely forgetting the immense participation of the country people in the life of all the underdeveloped parts of America'.[6] This contribution of the Cuban revolution to the Latin-American revolution is a 'fundamental of strategy', Guevara specifies. He intends by this formulation to criticize strategies centred on urban struggle. Now it is obvious enough that the requirment 'not to forget the peasantry' is not by itself enough to justify a strategy founded on rural struggle. What really is at issue is not so much the question of forgetting the peasantry and so mistaking the class content of the revolution but rather the manner of conducting the struggle: the question of tactics, of what to do and how.

The basis of Guevara's position is that the bourgeois state is weakest in the countryside and it is for this reason

---

[5] Che Guevara, *Guerrilla Warfare* (Monthly Review Press, 1961), p. 15.
[6] ibid., p. 16.

that the countryside is the fundamental terrain for armed struggle. He does not base his argument on the greater importance of the peasantry as a force in the revolution. But nor on the other hand does he reduce the primacy of the countryside to a purely military question. Guerrilla warfare for Guevara remains a war of the masses of which the guerrilla detachment is only the vanguard. The countryside has many military advantages over the towns but it is not only there that the weakness of the bourgeois state lies. The bourgeois state is weak also because the peasants can be mobilized for the struggle. The advantages of the countryside for Guevara are therefore both military and political and he does not reduce the one to the other. One must launch armed struggle in the countryside because only there is it possible both to fight the forces of the bourgeois state and to mobilize the masses. It is for Guevara in the very nature of guerrilla war for it to be both armed struggle and mass struggle.

Lucid though this thesis is, it is far from guaranteeing the unity of the political and the military. The first question that arises is the following: what is the specific relationship between the social role of the peasantry and the military role of the countryside in guerrilla warfare? In his writings Guevara put the accent above all on the conditions for political mobilization of the peasantry, while for Debray the decisive factor – in *Revolution in the Revolution?* at least – was the military survival of the guerrilla *foco*. It is useless in practice to say that the guerrilla must fulfil both conditions, since in practice the question is always that of knowing which of the two factors is determinant, and on the correct solution of this question success or failure depends. There is a Cuban outcome, but there is also a Bolivian one. The question then is whether the *principal* objective of rural struggle is the revolutionary mobilization of the peasantry or the military demoralization of the ruling classes. It goes without saying that the two goals are interdependent, that it is by struggling arms in hand against the exploiters that one will best succeed in mobilizing the peasantry. But this interdependence in no way means that there is a *coincidence* between the military actions of a guerrilla *foco* and the political movement of the peasant masses. There is no lack of examples to show this in practice. Revolutionary struggles led well militarily (for instance Bejar's ELN in Peru or the Bolivian ELN) did not succeed in mobilizing the peasantry. On the other hand, there are plenty of examples of struggles led well politically but unable to survive military repression, such as Hugo Blanco's peasant unions in Peru and the Peasant Leagues in Brazil.

The growing importance of purely military considerations and the corresponding underestimation of political tasks becomes all the more clear when one considers the characteristically Debrayist *foco* variant of rural guerrilla war. The experiences of the POLOP opposition/MNR, of a splinter of the PCB based in Rio state and Paraná which later came to be known as MR-8 (Revolutionary Movement of 8 October) and of MR-26 (or MAR – Revolutionary Action Movement) are particularly relevant here. At the start of the revolutionary war the decision was taken to start guerrilla war in the countryside and for this purpose special sections were set up entrusted with the task of '*foco* preparation'. Groups set out looking for the right strategic area in which to begin rural guerrilla. But it is difficult to find something when one is uncertain what one is looking for. In Brazil there is unfortunately no pre-established harmony between the regions where the peasantry had developed its political struggle and the regions where geographical conditions exist for the survival of the *foco* as described by Debray. The North East where the Peasant Leagues arose, possesses neither high mountains nor extensive forests, the agricultural proletariat being concentrated in the *Zona da Mata* near the sea and the urban centres.

It is true that between the almost absolute geo-military security of the world's greatest forest (Amazonas) and the political importance of one of the world's largest peasant concentrations (the North East) many intermediate situations are to be found on the Brazilian sub-continent. The vast expanses of Goiás and the Mato Grosso on the one hand, the peasant concentrations of the Centre and South of the country on the other, provide as many intermediate situations in which the factor of military security is combined in varying proportions with the factor of liason with the masses. But the problem is not to find *intermediate* strategic solutions, but to formulate the *determinant strategic principle* that governs the principle objective of revolutionary warfare in the countryside. Either this principle is one of *military* order (mountains, forests, vast semi-desert expanses, difficulties of encirclement, etc.) or of *political* order (nature of the class contradictions and degree of their development, level of consciousness).

The MR-8 had to face all these problems when it began its *foco* search. Its members travelled thousands of kilometres looking for the 'strategic' zone which should in principle have been located in the state of Paraná. Ground explorations multiplied and the group financed them with a raid at Niteroi in Rio state. They bought a jeep and a small farm – both necessary parts of the guerrilla infrastructure. Later another farm was bought. This was in October 1968. The growing need for arms and other equipment led to a second raid in January 1969 and third later in March. Finally in April two militants returning to the clandestine farm from duties in the 'plain' were involved in a car crash. The police were called to the scene and they discovered arms and ammunition. The militants were hideously tortured, confessions obtained, and arrests made in Paraná and in Rio. After rounding up the 'urban support' network the police raided the farms and the conspiracy was effectively smashed. The MR-8 survived this disaster. (They were signatories to the communiqué put out by the kidnappers of the American Ambassador in Rio later that year in September.) But their experience led them to abandon 'orthodox Debrayism' and to realize that by trying to start revolutionary war directly with the guerrilla *foco* one reduces its preparation to a conspiracy pure and simple which usually ends in discovery by the police, before the guerrilla has had time to organize its own defence.

A similar fate overtook the hastily prepared *foco* in the Angra dos Reis forests south of Rio de Janeiro. The *foco* was planned by militants from MR-26 (Revolutionary Movement of the 26th, named after the Cuban organization of the same name and known also as MAR – Revolutionary Action Movement). This organization was made up of survivors from the MNR network based in Rio, who were left without work (like their São Paulo comrades) after the Caparáo débâcle. They were mostly ex-NCOs and sailors expelled from the forces after the 1964 coup.

They began armed struggle in 1969 with one of the most spectacular urban operations mounted in Rio: the springing of six militants from the military prison of Lemos de Brito. Five of these were former leaders of the sailors' association while the sixth was ex-sergeant Antonio Prestes de Paula who had directed the Brasilia Sergeants' revolt in September 1963.

The escape took place in broad daylight. The fugitives were met at the prison entrance by an MAR commando unit, and though the prison guard was alerted the only casualties were on the enemy side. After liberating its leaders from prison the MAR carried out a series of bank raids to finance its projected *foco*. It was then mid-1969 and the battle between the urban fighting detachments and the police was at its peak. The MAR met opposition during their first raid. Many of their militants were arrested and the urban support network was penetrated. Those who had already reached the countryside seemed safe in the mountainous forests of Angra dos Reis. But when their presence became known a large military force encircled the area and there were a series of skirmishes. Most of the MAR cadres managed to break the encirclement but rather than continue the struggle in the countryside they returned to Rio where they were soon active again. (Because their urban support network had been crushed they formed an alliance with the PCBR which had by that time been won over to armed struggle despite its initial hesitations.)

Both organizations were fortunate enough to be able to draw the lessons of the dangers of a premature *foco*. The case of the POLOP opposition/MNR was different: whole areas of Brazil were scoured by their '*foco* preparation' cadre, farm houses bought and suitable strategic areas carefully mapped. In the end the ideal place was never discovered and the search was abandoned. They themselves were quick to refute their own bucholic romanticism.

On the question of *foco* preparation one should add that, even among the 'militarists' for whom only military factors are of any importance, there are still severe problems when choosing the strategic area. They may ignore the question of whether or not there are peasant masses nearby but they must still find a region which is both wild enough to protect them and yet important enough for the army of the ruling class to be drawn into a fight. One solution to this problem would have been to set up not one *foco* but many. (This would of course have contradicted the very notion of a *foco* as explained by Debray. For according to him one should never dissipate one's forces but concentrate (focus) them since in that way fire power would be all the greater and the unity of command easier to maintain.)

However, those who continued to insist on balancing the military with the political had come to realize that the whole problem of 'one or many *focos*' was a false one. A new formulation of the problems of revolutionary war in the countryside was reached. Instead of starting from an aprioristic definition of the specific forms by way of which peoples' war must develop (there will at first be one or several *focos*, the strategic zone – or area – will be in one sort of place and not another, the *focos* will be made up of 40 and not of 200 militants, the support network will be fixed or mobile, and so on), the vanguard takes on as its preliminary task the work of revolutionary organization among the peasantry.

The experiences of the POLOP opposition/MNR cadres assigned to the task of finding a *foco* site were on *this* score far from negative. They failed to find the ideal strategic zone but in the process they were forced to confront their own preconceptions about how the struggle was to be waged with the opinions and experiences of the small revolutionary groups scattered over the whole country. They discovered that the most advanced sectors of the poor peasantry, though convinced of the need for armed struggle, insisted on the need to adapt armed struggle to the specific characteristics of each region. In fact several of these regions already sported an irregular guerrilla movement (i.e. one conducted by armed groups of peasants on the spot), although they offered very little opportunity for a regular ('mobile' and 'strategic') guerrilla detachment, operating on a permanent basis. Obviously the military and political development of 'irregular' guerrillas depends on the coordination of this struggle at the national or at least regional scale. But in any case it was a gross mistake that these regions should be deprived of a revolutionary organization just because they could not support a permanent or regular *foco*.

The slogan 'Prepare the *foco*' came to be heard less and less and in its place came 'Adapt armed struggle to local conditions'. This 'political' success was reinforced by the practical successes obtained with mass work among the peasants and especially among agricultural wage-labourers. In the state of São Paulo, for example, the POLOP opposition/MNR was able to find a base in the new concentrations of *volantes* which, as was seen in the previous chapter, have grown up around the cities. Political work among them has shown how it is possible to mobilize agricultural workers in economic struggle without at the same time having wholly to neglect military tasks.

This is just one example of the way in which the one-sidedness of Debrayist conceptions can be overcome. For the real problem which must be solved is what form should the preparation of people's war in the countryside take, once one has abandoned the *foco* model? How can one provide a revolutionary – political *and* military – reply to the class contradictions in the countryside?

As Debray said in another context, one must go from the simplest to the more complex. One cannot launch a rural guerrilla action right away, but only after one has built up enough strength on the basis of revolutionary organizations among the peasants. The simplest thing in this case is organization by *peasant cells* responsible both for political and military work. Instead of maintaining teams of militants scouring the countryside in search of that Eldorado of armed struggle, the strategic zone, one should start rather with the construction of political-military cells in all regions where it is possible, entrusting them with all the tasks which have to be carried out in that region. Obviously this will not correct the lack of pre-established harmony between regions with the best military features (suitable terrain, low population density, etc.) and regions of highest political importance (proletarian and semi-proletarian peasant concentrations, traditions of struggle, etc.). But there can be no question of developing the struggle just as one pleases, but rather as one can. It is the *foco* that must correspond to reality and not reality that must correspond to the *foco*. This method of work eliminates subjective and aprioristic elements in the preparation of peoples' war in the countryside. It also provides a practical way of cutting short the interminable discussion on the tactics of rural guerrilla, on the need for one single or for several *focos*, etc. The central leadership would be in a position to take decisions based on a global view of the possibilities of struggle that each region provides. Further, the need to prepare one (or several) permanent ('strategic and mobile') guerrilla detachments would no longer contradict the need to prepare the peasantry as a class for armed struggle.

Neither would this method intensify 'security problems'. The clandestinity and security of the preparatory military work would be guaranteed by the fact that only the militants of each region would know the whereabouts of their 'apparatuses'. The VPR for instance lost an entire rural network because one militant, who knew all the contacts, was imprisoned when he took part in an 'action' in São Paulo city. A rigorous separation between political work and preliminary military work (exploration of the terrain, training, excavation of depots, etc.) is needed to assure the success of the military work during the preliminary period. This is all the more important because it is impossible to remain *socially* clandestine in the countryside (except in completely remote places, where constant and firm relations with the peasantry cannot be established, simply because there are no peasants).

Consequently the cadres entrusted with military preparation work must be protected by a support network which can only be organized by a political cell already entrenched in the region.

Everything that has been said so far about the nature of revolutionary war in the countryside has been to some extent abstract in that the question of winning power has not been posed, let alone answered. Guerrilla war is a struggle for power and its stages cannot be correctly determined unless this is kept constantly in mind. What is the effective relationship between guerrilla struggle and the struggle for power? Up to what point can it be said that the guerrilla movement *is in itself* (and not just by virtue of its future programme) a 'red power' co-existing antagonistically with the 'white power'? In military terms this question is the question whether guerrilla warfare is really a revolutionary civil war.

In a class society power is inseparably bound up with violence which is usually monopolized by the ruling class. From the moment that, thanks to a crisis, a social class antagonistically opposed to the ruling class succeeds in organizing its own military forces (its own 'special bodies of armed men') then there exists a situation which Lenin called 'dual power'. Non-pacific coexistence between two armies and two states within the 'same' state is an unstable situation, and is necessarily ended by the destruction of one of the two antagonistic powers. The specific forms that such dual power can assume are very varied, since they depend on the specific character and balance of forces within each particular society.

In Latin America dual power takes most often the form of a division of power between city and country (hence the overestimation of the revolutionary role of the countryside, seat of red power). Colombia, where the weakness of the central state enabled independent peasant republics to exist, provides the best example of this special form of dual power which we will call 'division of power'. The Bolivian revolution of 1952 on the other hand approximated to the classical model of dual power and urban insurrection (workers' militia, workers' radio, etc.).

What are the conditions for dual or divided power to exist in Brazil, and what forms can this take? We have already examined one term in the relation: the military oligarchy. The Brazilian state has become more and more centralized under the dictatorship, thus making it more and more difficult to find enclaves in which white power does not operate. The state moreover is a military state and the central power exercises complete control over a nationwide police and military apparatus. The smallest peasant uprising, the weakest guerrilla *foco*, can call down the full weight of the ruling class's repressive machine. The Brazilian state is to this extent modern, post-Cuban. Once the nature of the enemy is fully understood, it becomes clear that dual power in the weak form of a geographical division of power between the country – the red zone – and the city – the white zone – is completely inconceivable. What form it *can* take, and whether revolutionaries can rely on the extension of inter-imperialist contradictions within Brazil, are questions which we will deal with in the final chapter.

## IV. URBAN GUERRILLA WARFARE

Having examined the theory of the rural guerrilla we must return to the question which was posed at the end of the second section of this chapter: how is it that despite the fighting organizations' unanimous agreement in theory on the primary role of rural guerrilla, armed struggle is still in practice restricted to partisan warfare in the city, the limitations and dangers of which, as well as the successes, have been constantly stressed by the urban fighters themselves? The armed organizations have become centres for regrouping the most combative sections of the popular movement and they have evolved a political and military structure that has enabled them to hold fast for two years despite heavy losses. They have in other words become a real force in Brazilian society. But this partial success cannot be explained by the difficulties of launching revolutionary warfare in the countryside. Nor can the 'obstinacy' of the revolutionaries in staying in the city. *Militarily* the city can only be the guerrilla's secondary zone. On this no one disagrees. But why is the 'secondary' struggle carried on so persistently, while the 'principal' struggle it is supposed to support is not even begun? In other words, how has the ALN slogan 'action builds organization' been corroborated? And why has this 'action' had to be urban guerrilla?

The answer is simple. In 1968 and 1969 the political and social basis for armed struggle existed only in the city. This might seem a banal truism, yet it pins down the basic contradiction of armed struggle in Brazil: while it can only advance militarily in the countryside, its social base is in the city. In Brazil as almost everywhere else in Latin America this 'neglect of the peasantry', which Guevara himself complained of, reflects the inability of the revolutionary vanguard, whether revolutionary-nationalist or Marxist-Leninist, to connect peasant struggles and workers' struggles except in the realm of theory. Class contradictions in the countryside are undoubtedly explosive. But they will only be detonated if certain political conditions are met without which neither the initiative of rural *focos* nor the spontaneity of the peasant masses will have revolutionary consequences. The obstacles to the realization of these conditions are 'classic' and well known to all Marxists: the dispersion of the peasantry, the particular oppression that the agricultural proletariat is subject to, in short, the backwardness of the countryside in comparison with the city. Thus, even though the countryside is the principal area of revolutionary warfare, it is predominantly in the city that the revolution has up to now found not only its professional militants, but above all the minimal level of consciousness and mass organization without which any revolutionary project is doomed to failure.

It is for this reason that the most correct slogans in the mass struggles of 1968, which best expressed the aspirations of the urban masses, were those that called the people to struggle against the dictatorship – 'The organized people will overthrow the dictatorship.' These slogans were aimed neither specifically at the working class nor at the peasantry (although the role of the most advanced sections of the workers' movement was a particularly important one, especially in São Paulo and in Minas, as we saw in Chapter Two), but corresponded rather to the demands and aspirations of the popular masses as a whole, especially the urban masses.

It is quite true that the peasant movement was badly hit by the 1964 coup. The Peasant Leagues were almost entirely liquidated; police and army intervened in the rare peasant unions; peasant leaders were massacred, and land occupied by the poor peasants was returned to the latifundists. But it must not be forgotten that the poor peasantry and the agricultural proletariat have always been the most oppressed social strata of Brazilian society and that consequently the change of regime in 1964 affected them relatively less than it did the urban masses. Urban workers know precisely how their economic situation and their political rights have been badly damaged by the 1964 regime. This is less visible in the countryside, where misery has always reigned. This then is the secret of Brazilian revolutionaries' 'obstinacy' in remaining in the city. Perhaps, as Guevara claimed, struggle is indeed less difficult in the countryside. It is in the city nevertheless that the masses can be more easily mobilized.

There are objective limits to the development of revolutionary politics in the city. In the first place there are limits imposed by the manner in which the bourgeoisie exercises its class dictatorship. With the military-oligarchic transformation of the Brazilian state, and the suppression of all bourgeois-democratic gains that the Brazilian people had been able to extract from the ruling classes in the course of class struggle, the popular movement could not develop its political struggle within the bounds of 'legality'. (This thesis, which to us appears indisputable, must not be confused with 'refusal to participate in the system', the ultra-left slogan which is a modern version of anarchism.) Since all popular and workers' organizations are either banned, or controlled by the regime's repressive apparatus, the question of armed struggle is automatically *posed*. In Brazil we find, though obviously in different forms, the same degree of violence and oppression which the workers of certain capitalist metropoles experienced during the Nazi-Fascist period. For the opposition and especially for the revolutionary opposition, the practical consequence is clandestinity, and if possible armed resistance.

Secondly, urban armed struggle, as opposed to rural guerrilla warfare, cannot be simultaneously guerrilla action and mass struggle. The rural *guerrilleros* can enter into direct contact with the peasants, they can recruit them into their ranks, without difficulty, thus enabling them to participate in the principle form of struggle. The *guerrillero* detachment's transformation into a people' army is intended to be a *continuous process*, hence the expression 'insurrectional *foco*', which signifies both that this is a detachment of professional revolutionaries – *foco* – and that this detachment is supposed to transform itself into the people's army and so is insurrectional. It must not be forgotten, however, that to start with the *foco* is only potentially insurrectional. There is no advance guarantee that it will succeed in recruiting the great mass of the peasantry. More precisely, it will do so only in the course of a *protracted war*, in which it makes up for its strategic inferiority by its tactical superiority.

The *mobility* of the guerrilla *foco* is in this respect a decisive element. It provides the military *sine qua non* for the *foco*'s transformation of its strategic inferiority into a tactical superiority. An urban guerrilla group on the contrary is condemned to the most complete clandestinity. It does not enter into direct contact with the urban masses and cannot recruit them into its ranks. Besides it is not mobile in the same sense as the guerrilla *foco*. Guerrilla warfare in the city is actually impossible without a *fixed base*. The 'concrete forest' hides only those who have the key to an apartment or a house. Houses cannot be changed like shirts, and one cannot take up a position in an apartment as one does on the grass or under a tree. These considerations may seem insignificant to the reader ignorant of the specific conditions of urban guerrilla life, but they are decisive for those involved in it. The importance of these considerations cannot be stressed too much particularly when one considers the nature of the enemy against which the struggle is being fought, the strength and depth of his repressive apparatus. Let us consider first of all the anti-guerrilla troops.

The Brazilian regime's ordinary political and military apparatus would have attracted the Gestapo's envy. It would have been strong enough by itself to deal with the urban guerrillas if they had been only two or three groups of enthusiasts cut off from the masses. But as armed struggle threatened to take on national dimensions, and as the developing political crisis of the regime made it indispensable to its survival to 'wipe out subversion', repressive operations had to assume an *offensive* character, so as to seize the tactical initiative from the urban partisans. For this, shock troops had to be found, something like an urban equivalent of the Rangers.

However, partisan warfare in the cities is a war of its own, with neither a fighting front nor a rear (exccept the 'fixed bases'), and where 'offence' and 'defence' are difficult to distinguish. It is a *war of total interpenetration*, where the enemy is simultaneously in front, behind and beside the revolutionary fighter. It often happens that the revolutionary fighter must disguise himself as his enemy and the enemy as a revolutionary fighter; in a war of total interprenetration, infiltration and espionage play a fundamental role.

All other things being equal, these characteristics of urban partisan warfare would work in the revolutionaries' favour. The revolutionaries have neither positions to defend nor a state apparatus to administer. They can always choose the time, place, form and method of infiltration (or of attack, in the case of a commando unit). The dictatorship's problem was to find suitable forms of counter-offensive, to discover the armed organizations' weak points, and to recruit the new style of 'Rangers' able to exploit them. In a bourgeois republic such a question would not even arise. Where the ruling classes enjoy a strong social and political base, the ordinary measures of police and judicial repression are enough by themselves to put an end to 'subversion'. But Brazil is not a bourgeois republic – if the objective historical content of this concept is taken at all seriously. It is a country where violence assures the exploiting classes an historical respite. The means with which to deal with the mounting popular resistance to the regime had therefore to be violent. They were found during the first half of 1969, and immediately put into practice.

To move to the counter-offensive the regime had to seek direct confrontation with the armed organizations. To force them to a confrontation it had to discover their fixed bases. To discover these bases it had to utilize torture on a large scale. And to use torture as a routine weapon, and to draw maximum advantage from the information that it might extract, the regime had to recruit a team of meticulous assassins and torturers, able both to torture children in front of their mothers (there are rigorously confirmed cases of this) and to prepare ambushes and traps of every kind to annihilate the urban partisans. An institution highly characteristic of contemporary Brazil, the so-called Death Squadron, provided the regime with the new 'Rangers' it needed to wipe out 'subversion'. The monstrous crimes of the Death Squadron beggar description. Even the most reactionary sectors of the Brazilian ruling classes are forced to push their hypocrisy to the point of demanding 'energetic measures' against the Squadron, which they call a 'national disgrace' (one may find examples in the editorials of the arch-reactionary newspaper *O Estado de São Paulo*). But these worthy bourgeois are unfair, and above all ungrateful. For it is thanks to the Squadron that their state has pulled off the most successful coups in its counter-offensive.

The Squadron was not an *ad hoc* creation. It had a long history, as a kind of mafia organized within the police, aiming at the systematic extermination of 'irrecuperable delinquents'.

Taking up the Nazi example of the 'final solution', the Rio police launched an all-out attack on both the so-called 'outlaws' and on the unemployed reduced to begging. The former were massacred in the most hideous fashion, often after atrocious tortures (the police began by cutting out the 'delinquents' tongues to prevent them from crying out). The beggars were drowned in Guanabara bay. These atrocities, familiar to everyone in Brazil since they were denounced by the bourgeois press itself, caused little stir in public opinion, since they only involved 'outlaws' and beggars. However, in 1968 the Death Squadron began to widen its activities, not only in Rio city and state, but also in São Paulo and almost everywhere in Brazil. The Squadron executed hundreds of 'bandits', and took it on itself to advertise its work. It would telephone a newspaper or a police station to report that there was 'bacon' (police slang for a corpse) to be found in a certain place. The police apparatus thus spontaneously created the shock troops which the ruling classes needed to counter the urban guerrilla. Around August 1969 the Death Squadron turned its attention from the 'outlaws' and beggars, and began to hunt the 'subversives'. The most brutal of the assassins, the police officer Sergio Paranhos Fleury, murderer of Carlos Marighela, was placed at the head of this vanguard of Western civilization.

The second military measure was the large-scale use of torture. The Squadron needed information in order to organize its ambushes. The counter-revolutionary struggle in the city is by no means exclusively entrusted to these shock troops. Behind the Squadron there is the Army, and behind the Army the dictatorship's various secret services, directly subordinated to the President of the Republic. (Garrastazu was for long the chief of the SNI).

It is the Army secret service that has the task of extracting and coordinating information for the Squadron and the other forces engaged in the anti-guerrilla struggle. This coordination makes it possible to apply the anti-subversive tactics worked out by the general staff systematically: mass arrests of all suspects, 'scientific' torture, study of the information obtained, destruction operations.

We are not going to describe here the chief methods of torture practised in Brazil. In the last two years the number of persons tortured amounts to several thousand. International public opinion is constantly made aware of these 'special' methods of struggle against subversion. What we wish to stress here is the strictly political and military aspect of torture, its use as a normal and regular weapon of a social class, and more specifically, of a regime, the military-oligarchic regime. It is impossible to analyse all the aspects of this phenomenon without passing from political analysis into the realm of social psychopathology. To understand the conditions and causes that transform army officers into sexual criminals (the numerous dossiers on torture in Brazil are full of descriptions of sexual violence practised on prisoners of both sexes), that make them as brutal, cynical and pitiless as any member of the Death Squadron, concepts are needed which belong to the domain of collective mental illness. The testimony of one victim of Operation *Bandeirantes* in São Paulo outlined the internal organization of this vast torture apparatus:

'The unit that carried out Operation *Bandeirantes* . . . is divided into three groups; each group works one day out of three and is subdivided into sections each with a well defined role – interrogation, capture, investigation. . . . Each section has a leader drawn from one of the services taking part in the operation. The interrogation section (torturers) is generally directed by an army officer, Captain Guimaraes. Everyone involved in Operation *Bandeirantes* was called Guimaraes, to prevent any of the prisoners finding out their name'.

Another witness testifies to the generalization of torture and the significance it has acquired as a regular form of repression. 'Proof of the institutionalization of torture is found in the 'torture schools' where Army, Navy and Air Force are taught methods of torture, using both photographic and *live* illustrations. One of these courses was given by Lieutenant Haylton whose audience numbered over a hundred. Naturally there are always some pupils with weaker stomachs than the others, who are not cut out for this sort of work. One of the sergeants attending Lieutenant Haylton's course, seeing such a number of naked prisoners, some on the 'parrot's perch' (*pau de arara*), others writhing desperately around under electric shocks, could not stand the test and left the hall vomiting. Torture is today the chief weapon of political repression, and is used wherever there are investigations and interrogations. Torture is part of the very essence of political repression. It is one of its basic institutions, ... one of the very pillars of military rule.'[7]

Nothing needs to be added to this horrifying account of methods used against the armed organizations. They have been effective: all the serious blows that the revolutionaries have suffered were in one way or another connected with the discovery of their clandestine networks.

We can summarize the limitations of urban guerrilla: it is cut off from the masses by its clandestinity. The mobile strategic detachment in the country (*foco*) can retreat in space to progress in time, since rural guerrilla warfare is a war of attrition in which mobility gives the guerrilleros choice of terrain on which to fight. The urban guerrilla fighter on the other hand can only repeat indefinitely the same operation. Starting from a clandestine base of support, he attacks some objective only to return immediately to the point of departure. The role of time as a factor in the build-up of strength, which enables the rural guerrilla movement to shift the balance of forces bit by bit, and to become a peoples' army through the constant recruitment of sections of the peasant masses (a process which signals the transition from strategic defence to strategic equilibrium), has not the

[7] From a statement made by twelve prisoners from Linhares prison, Minas Gerais.

same effect in the case of the urban guerrilla. For as long as there is no permanent contact between the armed vanguard and the masses, there will be no progressive transformation of the vanguard detachment into a peoples' army. This is what is meant by saying that urban guerrilla action is not a mass struggle. The urban vanguard is thus in no way an 'insurrectional *foco*', i.e. a political-military organization of revolutionary cadres that develops into an insurrection *via* protracted war. Proselytism in the urban guerrilla movement is *individual* proselytism: the urban guerrilla movement recruits *new cadres*, it does not recruit *sections of the masses*.

One can now understand the spontaneist deviations so frequent in the Brazilian armed organizations, especially after two years of urban guerrilla action – a very peculiar spontaneism, since it is backed up by a rigorous, even 'militarist' conception of 'organizational life' and of professional militancy. Just because armed struggle in the city is limited (there is an abyss between urban guerrilla warfare, the vanguard struggle, and popular insurrection, the mass struggle; an abyss that cannot be bridged by the development into protracted war, contrary to what happens in the countryside), it is necessary to combine the military and the political struggle. One must rely right to the end on a 'war of interpenetration', sending detachments (in Lenin's sense) of the revolutionary army out everywhere. Revolutionary war in the city is a form of struggle on the border between war and politics, especially when military operations are confined to 'commando' actions. It is natural in such circumstances for differences to appear between those who consider the decisive factor in overcoming the limitations of urban guerrilla action to be organized political work amongst the mass of the people, and those who rely on the distant perspective of insurrection and on the future inauguration of rural guerrilla warfare, and who reject the 'politicization' of armed organizations in order to 'prevent the military organization becoming the armed wing of a party'.

Behind this attempt at mimicry which completely distorts the theory of the Cuban guerrilla, quite serious deviations are concealed.

## V. TERRORISM AND ARMED PROPAGANDA

The revolutionary organizations' use of terror as a tactic was a new feature of political struggle in Brazil, since apart from isolated cases, this form of violent action was previously unknown in our country. The first terrorist attacks (bombing of the US Consulate-General in São Paulo, of the oligarchy's newspaper *O Estado de São Paulo*, and of the headquarters of the Second Army in the same city) were accompanied by the first bank raids, and coincided with the upsurge of the mass movement (March–June 1968).

To analyse correctly the value of a given form of struggle, as much account must be taken of the *general principles* of revolutionary policy as of the specific requirements of a particular situation. In *What is to be Done* Lenin exposed the nature of terrorism as a particular form of spontaneism. Terrorism as a principle, i.e. terrorism as the principal form of political action, is incompatible with Marxism, since it cannot be the means for the liberation of the oppressed and exploited.

It would certainly be difficult to speak of 'terrorism as a principle' in Brazil. Terrorism exists, but it is the preserve of the organizations of the extreme right such as the CCC, which we have already mentioned. The armed organizations of the revolutionary left have nevertheless overestimated the 'mobilizing' value of terrorist attacks. Their rejection of the methods of the 'traditional left' often became, especially for those militants and groups that lacked a minimal Marxist-Leninist training, a sort of cult of action for action's sake, in which the most blind 'activism' was passed off as political 'theory'.

Under these conditions it became extremely difficult to know in what circumstances terrorism was an adequate form of struggle. For certain activists, a week without an attack seemed a week in which the revolution made no progress. Arguments of the kind that 'the workers are on the side of those who are throwing bombs' were used by the partisans of unlimited terror. In fact – and here the *class content* of the overestimation of terrorism shows itself – these militants let themselves be tempted by the free publicity they received in the bourgeois press ever greedy for news that increases the sale of its papers) and mistook the fuss made about their bombs by the class enemy for the support of the masses.

There are criteria however according to which terrorist actions should be evaluated. First of all it must be made clear to the mass of the people that the relation between ruling class violence and terrorist violence is one of cause and effect. Revolutionary violence is a response to specific acts of violence by the state. The attacks mounted by COLINA in Minas for instance which struck at union offices re-occupied by the agents of repression after the 1968 occupation were perfectly correct according to this criterion.

Other attacks did not fulfil the above criterion. One example, among many others, was the 'Sears bomb' in São Paulo (Sears Roebuck is the name of a chain of department stores belonging to a North American monopoly corporation). At the time of MacNamara's visit to Brazil (while he was still Secretary of Defence), the revolutionary organizations decided on violent protest against the presence in our country of one of the men most responsible for the genocide of the Vietnamese people. But what form should this take?

If it had been possible to kidnap MacNamara (as one year later it was possible to kidnap the American ambassador), or to mobilize the people against the visitor, the armed organizations would no doubt have obtained a major political success. However they were not in a position to do so. The POLOP opposition/MNR nevertheless took the decision to set off a bomb at the entrance of the Sears department store in São Paulo.

A few remarks are sufficient to show the major political errors behind this attack – about which the least that can be said is that it did not even attract public attention. Firstly its subjectivism: no one in Brazil, except the initiated few, knew that MacNamara owned shares in Sears Roebuck. A manifesto was admittedly left at the place of the attack, but it was only read by a few policemen. The bourgeois press only makes known *certain aspects* of the revolutionary struggle and these are generally the most sensational and the most ambiguous. One must consider here as well the failure to understand the feelings of the population and its level of consciousness. Sears, like all the big stores, sells its goods cheaper than the small shops. Closing it down for a few days meant upsetting the local housewives, without ever explaining to them the political meaning of the action.

A second criterion for evaluating terrorist actions applies to the character of the attack itself. Terrorism against the civil population, for example, is a characteristic feature of fascist violence, of the despair of the possessing classes, who will use any method of intimidation when they feel that their privileges are threatened. In September 1968, for example, at the time of the destruction of the Philosophy Faculty, the CCC, in the presence of the police, fired on an unarmed crowd. The armed organizations of the Brazilian left have always respected this second criterion. Every attack, without exception, has been directed either against public buildings at times when no one was inside, or against particular individuals marked out as agents of repression responsible for acts of violence against the people or against revolutionary militants. The armed organizations have moreover given advance warning on many occasions that the torturers would be punished.

But the most important criterion for evaluating the role of terrorism is the political one. Before throwing a bomb, one must decide what use it will be to the cause of the liberation of the exploited and oppressed. Here ultra-leftist errors are as dangerous as those of the right. The partisans of unlimited terror, for example, try to justify themselves by citing historical examples, such as the national liberation struggle in Algeria, and the methods of urban guerrilla used by the NLF in Saigon. They forget one 'small' detail. The NLF is at the stage of strategic counter-offensive. It has already liberated the greater part of the country and is fighting not only against internal reaction but also against a foreign army of occupation. The clandestine organizations of the Brazilian revolutionary left were to begin with almost unknown, even to the most advanced sections of the popular movement. They are now well-known but they have failed to develop a peoples' war, because there was no foreign army *directly* and therefore demonstrably present in Brazil.

In fact the fetishist attachments to certain forms of violence, which by their very nature are the acts of small groups cut off from the masses, encouraged the tendency to measure the progress of a revolutionary organization primarily by its capacity to harass the enemy police and military apparatus, and not by its capacity to enlist the participation of the masses in decisive struggles.

Overestimation of terrorism as a form of struggle only increases the uncertainties and difficulties of the armed organizations. The value of terrorism was indeed so overestimated that some elements on the Brazilian left failed to distinguish the different stages of revolutionary warfare (thus precluding an understanding of the role of each particular form of struggle at each specific stage of the war). It was argued, for example, that terrorism immobilized an important part of the enemy's armed forces in the city. But one small detail was forgotten. During the years 1968–69 the forces of the revolution were themselves concentrated in the city. (Even the militants commissioned with work 'in the strategic zone', i.e. in the countryside, were carrying on their activities in urban centres bordering on the rural zone. The ALN networks discovered by the police at the end of 1969 – in Riberao Preto, in São Paulo and Brasilia – are an example of this.)

In other words, the present stage of the Brazilian revolutionary war, at which rural guerrilla warfare had not even begun, was confused with a later stage at which it would be widespread enough to attract the main weight of the ruling classes' repressive apparatus. At that stage, it is true, any act of terrorism against the government's military and political centres in the cities, besides encouraging the masses, weakens the enemy's ability to fight the rural guerrilla by forcing him to divide his forces.

The political criterion for assessing terrorist actions – how does an action win the support of the masses? – raises the question of armed propaganda. In 1968 the main effect of terrorism was to concentrate the attention of the state on subversive activities. It was easy to confuse the impact of the publicity which the bombings received with a real building up of strength among the people. Many militants imagined that merely by exploding bombs they were bringing the Brazilian revolution nearer. It became essential however to ask whether throwing bombs in large cities in fact achieved this.

The partisans of unlimited terror had a reply to this question – armed propaganda. This expression is used to mean many things. The first, put into practice by, AP (Popular Action), is propaganda *for the necessity of armed struggle*. When the students shouted the slogan 'Only the armed people will overthrow the dictatorship', they carried out armed propaganda in this sense. This 'ideological' conception of revolutionary propaganda became known as 'unarmed armed propaganda'. For the armed organizations, armed propaganda meant primarily direct action. In this second sense of the expression, armed propaganda became the form that revolutionary warfare acquired in the city. Through it the clandestine organizations addressed themselves to the whole people. It enabled them to emerge from below ground, where they had been incapable of political work by themselves.

The most important distinction from a political point of view is between generalized armed propaganda and local armed propaganda. Which is the better tactic to adopt has become a major question among the armed organizations. The first kind is intended to have repercussions throughout the country as a whole. Kidnapping an ambassador, carrying out acts of revolutionary justice or the seizure of a radio station to broadcast a message to the people are all examples of generalized armed propaganda.

The armed organizations have no way of making their programmes heard at national level except by such means as seizing radio stations. On 1 May 1969 the radio station in São Bernardo was seized by a group of militants who broadcast messages and slogans, and a few weeks later the Radio Nacional was occupied by an ALN commando to broadcast a tape of one of Marighela's speeches. Because the military state has a monopoly on the means of communication any propaganda of this sort must be accompanied by arms. Acts of 'revolutionary justice' such as the execution of the US officer Captain Chandler, who after tours of duty in Vietnam and Bolivia had come to Brazil charged with the organization and training of ultra-right terrorist groups, may also serve as propaganda.

But this category 'revolutionary justice' must be used with care. The kidnapping of an ambassador may have many tactical justifications. Revolutionary justice is not one of them. It is torturers and not diplomats who deserve to be shot. To the extent that kidnappings succeed in their immediate aims such as freeing prisoners and victims of torture they deserve unconditional support. However, if there is to be revolutionary justice in kidnappings only those victims should be chosen whom one would be justified in shooting should the negotiations fail. One does not shoot hostages because they are hostages but because they are war criminals. If this principle is not scrupulously observed, one runs the risk either of shooting someone without justification (and thereby of vitiating the propaganda effect of the action) or of having to free the hostage before the demands have been met.

1970 saw a return to the tactic of kidnapping, in many cases for the liberation of prisoners. The June kidnapping of the West German ambassador Von Holleben was from this point of view a complete success: forty prisoners were freed. In March the Japanese consul, Okuchi, was kidnapped in São Paulo, and Bucher, the Swiss ambassador, was kidnapped from Rio in December. He was released unharmed in exchange for seventy prisoners.

Actions of this kind no doubt demoralize the regime, particularly since it has committed itself so openly to the 'crushing of subversion'. However, they pose the problem which arises in any debate on tactics: should one's main goal be to crush the enemy or to win the masses? It is essential for the success of kidnappings, bombings or other 'generalized' actions that they be carried out by small and highly disciplined groups. The mass of the people cannot participate. They are in many respects the passive recipients of the 'propaganda effect'.

It is no accident that the more militarist of the armed organizations have favoured such actions. They are not of course in themselves any more or less militarist than any other form of struggle. They become however a purely militarist tactic if they are practised to the exclusion of any other forms, particularly to the exclusion of propaganda at a local level. They can never be justified as an organization's normal method of struggle.

Localized armed propaganda is not aimed at the people as a whole. News of such actions does not have to be channelled through a press and broadcasting network which are predominantly under government control. Local propaganda is aimed at a particular factory, the people of a particular suburb, the peasants of a particular village. The size of the groups among which local actions are carried out is so small that communication can be direct. In the cities it most often takes the form of rapidly assembled factory meetings at which speeches are made and pamphlets distributed attacking the regime. Because the police will almost invariably intervene, it is necessary to protect such meetings with arms. Similar meetings can take place in the *favelas*. In the country such propaganda may take the form of reprisals against landlord's agents, burning records, sacking a company store, or slaughtering cattle and distributing the meat to starving peasants. Such actions must be chosen which will evoke a response in a particular factory or village, and slogans must appeal directly to workers' and peasants' most immediate needs and aspirations.

Certain organizations see armed propaganda not only as

a particular form of struggle, but as the main tactical objective. Consider the Tupamaros in Uruguay, where the urban percentage of the population is around seventy per cent and where forty per cent are concentrated in the capital, Montevideo. For this reason the National Liberation Movement (MLN – the official name of the Tupamaros) chose Montevideo as the main area of its activity. This ought to be called armed propaganda rather than urban guerrilla warfare. The MLN does not seek – at least in principle – direct confrontation with the ruling class's repressive apparatus, and consequently does not at the present stage envisage the military destruction of the enemy.

The MLN direct actions are of two types. Firstly, those whose object is the maintenance and reinforcement of the organization's clandestine infrastructure (bank raids, expropriations of arms, etc.). Secondly, what has been called generalized armed propaganda: occupation of radio stations (the MLN also has its own clandestine radio), seizure of prominent figures connected with the present regime and particularly hated by the population. They have kidnapped, among others, Pereyra Reverbel a major industrialist and director of the UTE, a state enterprise which controls electricity and telephones, and the banker Giampietro, seized during a bank workers' strike.

One of the Tupamaros's most spectacular actions was the exposure of the Financiera Monty, a financial institution which served as a façade for the activities of certain big Uruguayan capitalists, many of them directly connected with government. An MLN commando raided their main office, seized large sums of money and six account books which provided evidence of the fraudulent manoeuvres of the Financiera in which many major political figures were involved.

The MLN's limitation of its revolutionary practice to

armed propaganda can be explained by the specific features of Uruguayan society. Indeed the MLN has no strategy, and is not leading the workers in their everyday struggles. These limitations are compensated in Uruguay by two positive factors not found in Brazil. A high level of working-class organization and of popular movement in general, and a kind of 'revolutionary division of labour' which allows MLN to 'specialize' in armed propaganda (its monopoly here is guaranteed by the effectiveness of its actions), leaving other organizations the tasks of agitation, propaganda and organization within the popular movement.

The political error made by the partisans of unlimited terror does not arise from a tactical choice which presents 'armed propaganda' as a specific form of struggle, but from believing dogmatically that any action directed 'against the system' produces a propaganda effect, and from failing to understand that a struggle isolated from the broad masses is always a limited form of struggle. The danger does not lie in armed propaganda as such. On the contrary, this can be an important moment in the process of formation of the peoples' armed vanguard. The danger lies rather in the tendency to make armed propaganda a substitute for the mass struggle.

In the present phase of the revolutionary struggle therefore, localized armed propaganda should be the principle form and actions with national repercussions should be kept to a minimum and only attempted when certain political conditions have been met. In doing this the armed organizations may win themselves less international fame but they will forge far stronger links with the masses.

# Chapter 4

# The Perspective for Revolutionary Struggle

I. THE FIRST TWO YEARS
OF URBAN PARTISAN WARFARE

The ebb of the mass movement and the dictatorship's political and military counter-offensive have made armed struggle in the city a much harder task. The vanguard organizations' fighting detachments have had to join battle with the armed forces of the state at a time when the balance of forces was utterly unfavourable to them, and when the tactical preconditions for the transformation of urban partisan warfare into revolutionary civil war had not yet been realized.

This does not mean that the results of two years' armed struggle, and particularly the experience of 1969-70, have been solely negative. Whereas 1967 had been for the traditional left organizations the year of 'internal struggles', and 1968 had seen only the beginnings of direct action, 1969 was in contrast the year of the re-formation of the revolutionary movement around the fighting organizations. There has certainly been no uniform and linear process of 'left unification'. The new organizations have even suffered new splits. But under the pressure of the mounting violence of repression, and the inspiration of the fighting organizations, the popular forces have gradually moved towards unity. The same is true of the fighting organizations themselves. In this context, even those left tendencies and political organizations that still reject armed struggle – broadly speaking the democratic and nationalist bourgeois opposition, and the PCB – have been forced to define their position in relation to it. They continue to tail behind events, but they can no longer reject armed struggle *a priori*.

Despite their weakness, uncertainties and losses (especially human ones), the fighting organizations have become the hegemonic force in the Brazilian popular movement. What needs closer analysis is the extent to which the organizations engaged in armed resistance are *already* a vanguard *leading* the Brazilian people.

If we have criticized the Debrayist theory of the *foco* in the preceding chapters, or the theoretical conceptions with which those organizations that began direct action in 1968 tried to supersede it, we in no way intended to confine ourselves to a purely theoretical, and therefore abstract, critique of Debray's writings, or of the theories to be found in texts signed by Marighela and the ALN or by other fighting organizations (e.g. the VAR-Palmares). Several 'analyses' of that kind have already been produced by those more concerned to rationalize the lack of progress than to contribute to the clarification and solution of the *problems* of armed struggle in Brazil. Politics is not astronomy. However rigorous the method of analysis, however profound and correct the understanding of the course of events and the balance of forces, it is still necessary for anyone who undertakes this analysis to place himself unambiguously on the side of the forces whose task is to change reality. If this is lacking, then the analysis of what exists will always get the better of the effort to supersede it, and the moment of practice will be suppressed in the name of the objective – i.e. spontaneous – course of history. These considerations are all the more important insofar as we are concerned here with a discussion of programmes and tactics, the transformation of existing reality.

It is not enough to insist on 'the standpoint of the proletarian revolution and of the construction of socialism'. There are only too many opponents of armed struggle who claim to occupy the standpoint of the proletariat and of socialism. Only the actual situation in Brazil and the experience of the last two years can prove the *political* correctness of the slogan of armed struggle. Obviously, however stringent this analysis, it can never undermine all the arguments of those who do not *want* to fight. We will not bother to refute one after the other the sophisms of the right- and 'left'-wing 'Marxists', who are less concerned to contribute to the solution of the problems of revolutionary tactics than to justify their own passivity towards revolutionary warfare.

The PCB's position is a typical example of this. According to Luís Carlos Prestes, writing in *Voz Proletaria* about the kidnapping of the US ambassador in Rio, 'the dictatorship will not be overthrown by sensational actions without the participation of the masses'. We agree with the general secretary of the PCB. *By themselves*, 'sensational actions' will not overthrow the dictatorship. But can it be overthrown *without armed struggle*? Prestes is more discreet on this point. He says that 'Marxism–Leninism does not unconditionally reject any form of struggle', but he adds that 'violent actions have nothing to do with the process of revolution unless they contribute towards raising the level of consciousness and organization of the masses'. This is a really mediocre sophism. Everyone on the left aims at 'raising the level of consciousness and organization of the masses'. This kind of appeal only serves to evade the real question: in Brazil today, is it possible to organize the masses otherwise than by armed struggle against the dictatorship? Prestes does not even ask this question. Instead he merely repeats one of those magic formulae that apply equally to all situations and explain nothing. 'For revolutionary action, . . . it is firstly indispensable to win the masses in their millions.' This is undeniable, but how is it to be carried out? A reading of the PCB documents certainly provides no answer.

The same criticisms can be made of the 'extreme left'. According to the POC there is no such thing as revolutionary warfare in Brazil today, and neither Marighela's 'patriotic' vocabulary nor 'terrorist actions' in the city contribute towards advancing the class struggle. Other 'left'-wing organizations express similar opinions. We can let history be their judge.

However, the rejection of abstract and ahistorical attacks on armed struggle must be backed up by a critical and analytic attitude towards the present development of revolutionary warfare in Brazil. It is neither our intention to harp from the sidelines on what the armed organizations have not yet accomplished – everyone knows that they have not yet succeeded in mobilizing the 'masses in their millions' as Prestes recommends – nor to applaud blindly all those at present engaged in armed struggle. On the contrary, it is precisely because we consider the armed organizations to be the vanguard detachment of the Brazilian revolution that it is important for us to give a critical appraisal of their experience and their practice. To criticize those who still remain outside the real struggle would be a waste of time. The defeat of the various *focos* vindicated the tactics of the three major revolutionary organizations – the ALN, the VPR and COLINA – to start armed struggle where it was possible and where it would signify a real advance of the popular movement and of the most consistent sectors of the left, i.e. in the city, and more precisely in Brazil's three industrial metropoles: São Paulo, Rio de Janeiro and Belo Horizonte. By launching urban partisan warfare, these groups escaped the dilemmas of 'focism'. Yet this move was not without its own limitations. The fact that armed struggle in the city has been in progress for two years already is enough to show that it was no mere adventure and that it is much less isolated politically than its right- and 'left'-wing critics would like to believe. Nevertheless it is still true that partisan warfare in the city is far from generalized guerrilla warfare, and even further from a revolutionary civil war. Besides, the dictatorship mounted a terrible counter-offensive in 1969 which has so far lost nothing in efficiency or brutality. The progress made in 1969 towards the transformation of the armed groups into national organizations has now been put in question by the encirclement and destruction operation which the dictatorship has been carrying on in São Paulo and in Rio for almost a year. For this reason, before deciding how the revolutionary forces can increase in strength, one must first establish how they can maintain the strength they have already acquired.

At the beginning of 1969 the armed organizations were beginning to assess the experience of the first year of direct action. Once they had passed the initial stage of setting up a minimal clandestine structure, major political and strategic problems immediately arose. (We are referring here of course only to those organizations which had begun armed struggle during 1968: ALN, VPR, COLINA and, in a more discreet fashion, the 'Red Wing' of the PC do B.) The question whether revolutionary organization in the city should be limited to a military support structure for the rural guerrilla, or whether it should be built up as the political and military vanguard responsible both for armed struggle and for the leadership of the popular masses in the city, was now posed in practical terms.

The reasons for the distrust to be found in Debray's

writings of the city as the basis for guerrilla support are well known. If the group which sets up the guerrilla organization is not entirely self-sufficient but merely the *armed wing* of a party, it runs the very serious risk of being betrayed from the rear. This is what happened in Venezuela when the guerrillas were abandoned by the Communist Party. This distrust was further justified in Bolivia. The guerrilla column led by Guevara and the Peredo brothers was admittedly an independent force from the start and not an armed wing. However, they made the mistake of entrusting their urban rear-guard to another organization. Solemn though the promise of support made by Mario Monje and other leaders of the 'official' Bolivian parties of the left may have been, the weaknesses of this alliance were only too transparent. How could one believe that those who had failed to accept the responsibility of armed struggle on their own initiative would risk their lives to save a group of *guerrilleros* surrounded by the Rangers?

On the question of urban support networks, the Marighelists (who later became the main strength of the ALN) did not fail to draw the lessons of these mistakes. They argued that the tasks of guaranteeing military and political support from the town must be assumed by the guerrilla organization itself. They adopted, in short, the Peruvian model. In Peru the guerrillas did not start as the armed wing of a reformist party; nor were they based, as in Bolivia, on an artificial alliance with the 'official' left. (In that revolutionary division of labour the party supports the guerrilla so long as it brings success but washes its hands in case of defeat.) In Peru, neither the MIR (Revolutionary Left Movement) nor Bejar's ELN (National Liberation Army) left their rear-guards in the hands of 'tactical' allies sullied by years of opportunism, and one cannot explain the Peruvian hecatomb by appeal to these considerations.

Discussion of the nature of the urban support network however was for the Brazilian militants to some extent a diversion since there were no rural guerrillas to support. In fact the real problems centred round their role in mobilizing the urban masses. When the two vanguard organizations (Marighela's group and the POLOP opposition/MNR) moved to direct action, the bourgeoisie itself undertook to exacerbate the feelings of hundreds of thousands of communists and patriots. The newspapers made much noise over the bombs at the US consulate, in São Paulo and at the Second Army HQ and at the bank raids and arms thefts. The desire of most activists to participate in these actions was flatly contradictory to their very nature, which required rigorous clandestinity and the smallest possible number of participants. The great majority of revolutionaries had to be left out of these activities and, given the absence of a clear strategic conception of revolutionary war (in particular the activists' underestimation of the tasks of organization), this great majority remained in practice quite unmobilized and could only stand by admiring in silence the exploits of the small armed groups. To remedy this, small tasks were invented of little or no objective importance simply so as not to demobilize the mass of activists. Despite their lack of importance these tasks often carried serious risks. Sloganwriting or the distribution of leaflets often led to savage beatings and, because activists caught while engaged in these things were usually interrogated, it became necessary to reduce even this sphere of work.

For the armed organizations in the cities, the slogan that 'action builds organization' revealed its onesidedness in practice. The POLOP opposition/MNR under its new name of VPR started an internal struggle on these questions towards the end of 1968, which was to last for a whole year and which ended in the absolute hegemony of what we have called the 'militarist' tendency, characterized by the following positions: (1) rejection of systematic work in the mass movement; (2) rejection of the 'traditional' forms of agitation and propaganda; (3) tendency towards reducing organizational structure to armed groups alone; (4) adoption of the *foco* theory as presented in *Revolution in the Revolution?* The Leninist tendency held quite opposed positions, and was accused of seeking to return to the 'theory of the party' – a completely justified charge, if by 'party' one understands the fighting vanguard of the popular masses. This accusation really touched the root of the problem of the nature and tasks of the revolutionary vanguard in Brazil: whether or not the generalization of guerrilla warfare presupposes the existence of a national organization able to coordinate the popular struggle as a whole. The militarists replied in the negative and the Leninists in the affirmative. The former believed that guerrilla warfare could be indefinitely extended by the action of urban and rural 'small motors' alone; the latter insisted on the dialectical interdependence of the political and the military tasks of the revolution. This internal struggle was interrupted for a time by the police and military offensive that followed the Fifth Institutional Act of December 1968, and by the 'Fourth Infantry Regiment action' in January 1969. The latter episode deserves a close analysis. Besides providing a concrete example of partisan warfare in São Paulo, it spotlights the practical implications of the political and tactical debate within the armed organizations, and particularly the VPR.

By the time of the Fifth Act, the VPR was no longer a small isolated grouping. It had made links with important sections of the popular movement, sought to take a public position on all major national problems and took on responsibilities that went far beyond the limited perspectives of a small urban armed nucleus. The Fifth Institutional Act signalled both a deepening political crisis within the ruling classes and the regime's decision to move to the counter-offensive. It was obvious to all that this final liquidation of the façade of 'redemocratization' would only pay off for the ruling classes if they succeeded in 'crushing subversion'. In these circumstances, the correct response for the armed organizations would have been tactical withdrawal until the wave of repression had subsided. This tactic would not have been incompatible with carrying out a few rapid and effective armed actions in order to discredit the repressive apparatus and to show the urban masses that 'subversion' could not be abolished by decree. The application of such a tactic would have shown a correct understanding of the balance of forces between revolution and counter-revolution, and would have been a practical development of the strategy of protracted war.

But the VPR did exactly the reverse. While mass prison camps were being improvised in almost every city in the country, while all those vaguely suspected of 'communism' were being arrested, and torture was being used for the first time as the *principal* means of extracting information from the detainees, the VPR decided to attack the Fourth Infantry Regiment, stationed in the suburbs of São Paulo, near the workers' district of Osasco. The very fact that such a decision could have been taken in this conjucnture shows that the militarists had already prevailed within the organization. In fact, following a stormy conference, the urban military sector seized control of the central VPR command and prepared for the attack on the Fourth Infantry Regiment. The aim of this operation was purely logistic: to secure a few hundred FAL automatic rifles, sub-machine guns and grenades, as well as some heavier weapons such as machine guns, flamethrowers, etc. The existence of a VPR cell within the regiment seemed to justify the operation all the more so as the VPR leadership at this time had an unfortunate tendency to confuse the military possibility of an action with its political correctness. This cell was organized by Captain Lamarca, marksman and a specialist in anti-guerrilla warfare; he had just been made responsible for teaching bank officials to handle automatic weapons so as to defend themselves against 'terrorists'.

The attack on the Fourth Infantry Regiment was prepared in an almost suicidal fashion. Despite the vigorous protests of the Leninists, powerless since the internal crisis of December 1968, the VPR mobilized militants from all sectors of its organization, and particularly those working in the countryside, which on paper was considered the principal field of struggle. Prepared in such an irresponsible way, the project was bound to fail. In fact it was never even carried out. The militants of one cell were discovered painting a truck in army colours, and the whole of the dictatorship's repressive apparatus was put on the alert. The cell in the Fourth Infantry Regiment had just enough time to take flight, in a truck loaded with automatic weapons – which proves that the operation could have been carried out without committing to it almost the entire VPR strategic potential. The cost of this action was too heavy. The four militants arrested on the eve of the operation were savagely tortured and ended by disclosing everything. (One of them even went beyond the limit that separates weakness in the face of pain – which is always understandable – from collaboration with the enemy.) The vicious circle of capture – torture – confession – further captures, etc. rapidly endangered the very survival of the VPR, which found itself on the very edge of disintegration. The manhunt raged for two months, and enabled the regime to penetrate deep into the organization's clandestine structure. The São Paulo urban network was shattered, and by March the police could boast of having arrested around thirty VPR militants. However, in April the VPR was already reborn from its ashes, if no longer quite the same. Without understanding the profound reasons for the disaster that they themselves had prepared, the militarists took the occasion to purge the most prominent militants among the Leninists, while managing, thanks to their undeniable courage and tenacity, to reconstruct the organization's urban infrastructure. The VPR came out alive from the ordeal of January–March 1969, but it had squandered its strategic resources in operations of a purely tactical significance. It emerged decimated, but 'homogenous'. However, the problems brushed under the carpet with the purge of the Leninists were to reappear some months later, with the foundation of the VAR/Palmares.

The VPR disaster happened just when the changing political conjuncture considerably increased the importance of armed propaganda in the city. The violent repression of the student movement and the 'democratic' trade-union opposition (i.e. those trade-unionists who, while far removed from an independent working-class position, were not simply the regime's agents) severely limited the possibilities of mass struggle, as did the white terror of the CCC and MAC, which after organizing in 1968 the assassination of students and the punitive expeditions into 'left-wing' theatres, in 1969 turned their attentions towards the progressive sectors of the Catholic church. In Recife a sociologist priest, belonging to the group around Archbishop Dom Helder Câmara, was murdered after being savagely tortured. The dictatorship, delighted by this hideous act, refused to prosecute the assassins, saying that the affair must have been a *crime passionel*, since the murdered priest was a homosexual. The very weakness of the popular movement, whose most combative sectors were exhausted after the struggles of 1968, also tended to restrict popular resistance to the fighting organizations alone.

In these circumstances, a vanguard was needed that could lead the masses in a tactical withdrawal, while continuing to harass the regime's repressive apparatus in the urban zone and to advance both the political and military preparation of people's war in the countryside. But these very conditions also generated 'immediatist' tendencies within the armed organizations. Eager to respond to the dictatorship's crimes, whatever the cost, and wishing to show the masses that struggle was possible and that the criminals were vulnerable, the urban partisans took the risk of giving priority to direct confrontation with the repressive apparatus rather than to the development, necessarily slow, silent and marked by frequent retreats, of the strategic objectives of the Brazilian revolution. Forgetting that the annihilation of the enemy's armed forces required preserving its own, the revolutionary vanguard lost sight of the particular features of the actual situation, and over-exposed itself to the regime's counter-offensive. This was all the more true insofar as the development of armed propaganda and partisan operations in the city was matched by a parallel development of counter-revolutionary warfare.

This is why 1969 was the year of urban 'battles'. These are still not at an end, but their outcome so far has not been favourable to the revolutionary forces. In these battles, firstly in São Paulo, then in Belo Horizonte, Rio, and later in Pôrto Alegre and almost all the major cities, the revolutionary organizations joined battle with the forces of repression in conditions unforeseen by contemporary theorists of revolutionary warfare – including the technicians of counter-revolution.

Any historical parallels must be sought rather in the

European anti-fascist resistance, although the differences between the two situations are too obvious to need detailing here. Today, after two years of urban partisan warfare, the urban fighters show signs of exhaustion, although they have managed to preserve the minimal strength required to regain the initiative when the conjuncture is more favourable. The uneven development of the revolutionary organizations themselves explains the fact that they have been differently affected by the encirclement and destruction operation in the cities, and that certain groups have been literally decimated, while others, which managed to understand in time the tactical exigencies of the situation, suffered only superficial wounds.

II. THE MOST RECENT DEVELOPMENTS

There were many armed confrontations between the revolutionaries and the repressive forces during the autumn of 1969. Between 15 August and 4 November (according to the review *Veja*) there were six battles in São Paulo and one in Rio. The partisans lost six dead and five wounded while the police and army two dead and ten wounded. Up until August there was very little direct confrontation between the two sides. After the summer however the military apparatus began to 'seek out' their enemies and draw them into open battle.

In September 1969 armed struggle in Brazil gained international notoriety with the seizure of Burke Elbrick the US ambassador in Rio. Initially planned by the Guanabara Communist Opposition, the operation was given military support by the ALN, which then took over responsibility for it. The incident marks a major political milestone. Revolutionary violence became an instrument able to *explain* to the masses the very nature of the regime. The gorillas were forced to admit publicly that the Brazilian government considers the life of the US ambassador more important than the honour of the nation. Marighela himself stressed in his letter to the '15 patriots' freed in exchange for Burke Elbrick, that 'the dictatorship was obliged to comply, and be seen to comply, with all the revolutionaries' demands. It even had to broadcast the revolutionary manifesto denouncing the government's crimes and its treasonable policy towards the nation. All the means of information – radio, press and television, were momentarily freed from their stringent censorship and, for the first time since the 1964 military coup, permitted to tell the people the truth. Millions of Brazilians learnt that the military dictatorship tortures and murders political prisoners. On its side, the US government had to throw off its mask and publicly order the military junta to accept all the conditions imposed by the revolutionaries for the liberation of the North American ambassador'.

The regime's reprisals were severe. As soon as the ambassador was freed, it began a campaign of mass imprisonment and terror. There is unfortunately no means of measuring human suffering, but if there were the score would have been high. The Guanabara opposition and the ALN in particular paid the price for their bold initiatives.

The humiliation imposed on the dictatorship goaded it into frantic activity. The government cannot every day use thousands of its troops to arrest so many suspects; this extravagance is reserved for special occasions, and the kidnapping of the ambassador was one of these. But the social and political cost of obtaining information in this way is high. A close associate of the Brazilian Finance Minister admitted to Marcel Niedergang of *Le Monde* that 'the use of torture is very prejudicial to our economic progress and the improvement of our finances and financial system.... We believe that economic expansion will solve our social problems, but

## Perspective for Revolutionary Struggle 215

we still need three or four years of social stability.'[1] Thus the question facing the Brazilian ruling class is that of finding the socially optimal dose of torture that will guarantee 'social stability' for 'three or four years' at minimal expense.

The biggest success of the 1969 counter-guerrilla operations was the assassination of Carlos Marighela. A number of ALN militants were arrested in São Paulo after an unsuccessful action. The information extracted from them under torture enabled the police to prepare the ambush of 4 November, in which Marighela was murdered. There is no need here to stress the loss to the Brazilian revolution involved in the death of Marighela. He had become the symbol both of all that was best in Brazilian communism, and of the union between the old and the new generation of revolutionaries. He had been among the first to put up armed resistance to the military-oligarchic dictatorship, although his death also revealed the excessive vulnerability of the urban combat groups. The 'surprise effect' had long since ceased to work in the revolutionaries' favour.

The progress of urban partisan warfare all over Brazil ultimately attracted all those groups who in 1968 had accepted the slogan, 'Action builds organization'. But the increasing severity of the repression and the extension of counter-guerrilla operations tended to sharpen the lines between peaceful and armed struggle. Those organizations which, like the PC do B, Popular Action (left-wing Christians, self-styled Maoists) and the POC, proclaimed the abstract necessity for armed struggle while not developing any concrete practice to show how they intended to engage in it, remained isolated from the real political struggle. Without the means of resisting the dictatorship's encirclement and destruction

---

[1] *Le Monde*, 24 May 1970.

counter-offensive, each revolutionary organization was faced with the choice between passivity and suicide. Armed struggle must nevertheless be adequately prepared, and an organization should only engage battle when it commands the minimal resources needed to hold out for a while. The PCBR was to experience this truth in practice. Not possessing a clandestine structure adapted to the conditions of armed resistance, but feeling the need to begin direct action, even if only at the level of expropriations and with the limited aim of constructing the party's military organization, it took the opportunity offered it by the MAR militants who had escaped from the July urban actions and from the Angra dos Reis *foco*. The majority of the fugitives from the military prison Lemos de Brito (i.e. the best leaders of the Sailors' and Sergeants' movement before the 1964 coup) were again involved, along with the PCBR's military cadres, in a series of bank raids. On 17 December 1969 in Rio, disaster struck. An exchange of fire took place between the police and one of the cars being used to cover the action. The driver, a PCBR militant, surrendered to the police, while the gunner, the ex-sailor Aveline Capitane, resisted and took flight. Capitane succeeded in escaping, although wounded, and was sheltered in a hillside *favela*. The police now knew that the PCBR was involved in the raids. They obtained enough information to launch a vast annihilation operation. Within a few days, seven of the PCBR military organization's *aparelhos* were invaded by the army. There were many dead on both sides, among them the former vice-president of the Sailors' Association, Marco Antônio. At the beginning of 1970, the PCBR leadership itself fell into the hands of the army; the organization's leaders Mario Alves, and Apolônio de Carvalho ('old communists', Carvalho even having taken part in the French anti-fascist resistance) were arrested and brutally tortured. Mario Alves died as a result.

III. REGROUPMENT AROUND ARMED STRUGGLE:
THE QUESTION OF A NATIONAL ORGANIZATION

In 1969 the two main centres of revolutionary regroupment were the ALN and COLINA. The VPR, decimated by purges and by the disasters of January to March 1969, first had to rebuild its underground infrastructure. In July it fused with COLINA to form the VAR/Palmares. The creation of this new organization could have been a great step forward in the unification of the Brazilian revolution movement, but it turned out to be an ephemeral coexistence between two politically heterogenous tendencies. One of these, the VPR majority, wanted to confine the revolutionary organization to the armed nuclei alone. The contrary tendency, which formed the majority in COLINA, saw the urban and rural armed detachments as the embryonic form of the proletarian party, which was to be constructed in and through the development of armed struggle. In certain respects this polemic repeated on a larger scale that between militarists and Leninists within the VPR. As always happens, a compromise on overall strategic objectives broke down once it was necessary to draw practical and organizational conclusions from it. The questions that arose were whether it was already necessary to forge links with the urban masses, and whether or not the national unification of the revolutionary movement was a political precondition for generalized guerrilla warfare. The complete disagreement between the two tendencies on these issues led to a new step backwards in September 1969, scarcely two months after the unification: first the militarist tendency from the VPR (led by ex-captain Lamarca,) then the focist tendency from COLINA, broke with the VAR/Palmares, leaving this organization with the Leninist COLINA majority and the Leninist minority from the VPR. The dissident groups joined together in a new organization which once more took the name of VPR, and combined in its ranks both the partisans of an exclusively military urban struggle, and the orthodox Debrayists.

The VAR/Palmares lost the greater part of its military cadres, but it held to its more correct political positions. It also continued to attract those militants who broke with the small Marxist parties, which had failed to stand the test of the events of 1968–69: some of the 'dissidents', a fraction of the PC do B 'red wing'. The 'new VPR' on the other hand became a strictly military organization, which claimed to represent the most 'radical' current within the Brazilian left.

On all these questions the ALN stood between the VAR/Palmares, with its stress on the need for a Leninist party, and the VPR. The ALN upheld the necessity of 'mass work', though not of a revolutionary party. It benefited more than any other organization from the process of revolutionary regroupment. Before discussing the question of a national organization, and its dialectical relationship with the generalization of revolutionary warfare, the ALN's more rapid rate of growth demands a few words of explanation.

'In 1968 ... we were only a revolutionary group in São Paulo with almost no resources, and our ties to the rest of the country were almost non-existent ... Since then our forces ... became ever larger. Our contact and revolutionary support area broadened, we were evolving gradually from a revolutionary group into an organization with branches throughout the country.'[2] This transformation of 'revolutionary group' into 'national organization' is not unique to the ALN. But the ALN has been better able than others to combine a correct line on the absorption of small independent revolutionary groups with a correct line on alliances.

[2] Carlos Marighela, 'The role played by revolutionary action in organization', in *Marighella*, op. cit.

The fragmentation of the Brazilian revolutionary movement raises these two different, but mutually dependent, types of task: the construction of a national revolutionary *organization*, and the construction of a *front* against the dictatorship and imperialism. The former is built up by organizing militants around a common maximum programme; the latter by organizing groups or parties around a common minimum programme. In principle a national organization (i.e. a party) organizes a social class, or a socially and ideologically defined sector of a class, while a front organizes several social classes or sectors (e.g. the 'workers' united front' organizes different sections of the working class, and in particular different ideological tendencies – revolutionary and reformist). In Brazil this problem presents special features. It is not that the general laws of political organization and struggle are different in Brazil. In the last instance, the political fate of the Brazilian fighting organizations will be determined by the social classes whose historic interests they claim to represent. But the concrete tasks that confront revolutionary organizations at a particular moment cannot be mechanically deduced from the general objective interests of this or that social class. As we previously emphasized, the armed resistance and mass struggles of 1968 expressed the undifferentiated aspirations and demands of all sections of the population oppressed by the dictatorship. The urban partisans did not function as the vanguard of the working class as such, nor of the middle classes and still less of the peasantry, but of the most advanced sectors of the popular movement as a whole.

If the Brazilian working class were as organized as the Argentinian, and could therefore play the role of the vanguard in the struggle against the dictatorship and imperialism, the question of the party and the front could be presented in more classical terms. However the concrete movement of history pays no attention to classicism. The principal task in 1968 was to generalize armed struggle, given the undifferentiated present role of the various popular classes, and the fragmentation of the revolutionary movement. To claim *a priori* that the *first* task is either to 'construct' the proletarian party, or to organize the 'masses in their millions' around democratic demands, is to fall into opportunism, either of the 'left' (viz. the amateur ideologues of the POC, the 'Maoist' spiritualists of Popular Action, etc.), or of the right (the PCB, the so-called 'Maoist' PC do B, etc.). This was the specific situation in which the ALN was able both to build itself into a national organization and to make tactical alliances with other revolutionary groups too heterogenous to permit organizational integration. The VAR/Palmares, on the other hand, reacting to the experiences of July–September 1969, has since then tended to swing too far in the direction of 'classicism', tending to apply Lenin's formulae too mechanically to Brazilian conditions. It failed to understand why the July 1969 unification had been an error, based on a confusion between the sufficient conditions for an alliance and the sufficient conditions for integration. Premature integration may be more damaging to the cause of revolutionary unity than continued fragmentation. The attempt to form a single organization where the conditions only exist for an alliance may lead to internal conflicts which destroy not only the too hastily sought unity but also the possibility of alliance which had been deemed insufficient. The ALN has certainly not found some sort of magic formula able to indicate in every specific instance with whom it is possible to integrate and with whom to limit the relationship to one of alliance. Even a correct method has its limitations, and the ALN's flexible policy on alliances carries certain risks.

The double problem of a national revolutionary organization (revolutionary party/peoples' army) and an anti-imperialist front is still far from being resolved. We will now analyse the nature of the tasks on which the construction of a national organization depends, and leave the problem of the anti-imperialist front until we study the programme of the Brazilian revolution.

Despite the assertions of the dogmatic Debrayists of the 'new VPR', the preparation of people's war in the countryside, far from conflicting with the task of building a national organization, is in fact an essential part of it. Without a coordinated revolutionary struggle (i.e. military and political), it will be impossible either to generalize guerrilla warfare or to unify proletarian struggle. It is certainly true that a unified political and military leadership is not formed at one blow, but by the continuous process through which armed struggle develops into guerrilla warfare. However, this unity is a problem that must be solved; it is not enough to assert that it will be solved in the course of struggle, for no struggle ever develops unless suitable forms of organization are found at each stage.

The 'orthodox Debrayists' evidently see the construction of a national organization as only a subtle ruse to re-establish the primacy of 'the' party over 'the' guerrilla, and the 'left' opportunists' incessant chatter about 'constructing the proletarian party' through 'ideological' struggle, only reinforces their distrust of all 'traditional forms of organization'. We shall now try to show what specific practical problems are involved in the relationship between the development of guerrilla warfare and the construction of the revolutionary party, in the particular conditions of class struggle in Brazil.

Revolutionary warfare in the countryside will be chiefly conducted by mobile strategic detachments. The mobility of the guerrilla detachment is the military *sine qua non* of its existence and development. This alone enables it to operate continuously, as an embryonic army, whereas simple peasant partisan warfare is invariably localized and, like urban partisan warfare, can only play a tactical role. It is their continuous presence as small-scale armies that enables the strategic detachments or *focos* to carry out the strategic operation of guerrilla warfare. But precisely because they must devote themselves to this operation, the strategic detachments cannot direct the overall struggle. This will appear still more clearly when we remember that guerrilla warfare must progress through three phases.

In the first – preparatory – phase, armed struggle is chiefly urban partisan warfare; the generalization of guerrilla struggle by means of vanguard operations and localized peasant warfare is still in the future. The principal force of both the vanguard and the revolutionary movement as a whole is concentrated in the urban zones. The transition to the second stage requires the construction of a national organization (as well as the consolidation of urban partisan warfare), the construction of the rural guerrilla infrastructure (which involves setting up strategic detachments or *focos* as well as localized peasant guerrilla) and a certain degree of unification of the different popular forces. The existence of a centralized national organization with an overall view of the possibilities of struggle and the particular characteristics of each region, able to channel and direct the masses' revolutionary energies according to a global strategic plan, is a precondition not only for the coordination of political struggle, agitation and propaganda, but also for the preparation of people's war in the countryside.

In a second phase, which Debray's writings all assume is already attained, people's war in the countryside is launched and takes root. The strategic detachments struggle to survive and to entrench themselves in their zones of operation. At this stage the action of the vanguard rural detachments takes precedence, since the progress of the revolutionary forces as a whole depends on their progress. This is what is meant by saying that these detachments have a *strategic* role. But the principal struggle is not the only one. At this stage, which certain fighting organizations have for some months been trying to inaugurate – albeit very inadequately – the role of the national organization is to coordinate and direct not only urban struggles but also all rural struggles outside the strategic detachments' zones of operation. The VAR/Palmares grasped the interdependence of the principal and the overall struggle very well in insisting in its programme that 'revolutionaries must fight a war of position at the political level, but not at the military level'. The conception behind this is completely sound, although the formulation is not quite correct, since in a war of total interpenetration (in the city) the positions to be won are not only political ones. The revolutionaries' task at this stage is not only to exert an ideological and organizational influence over the workers' and students' movements (legal or illegal), which could answer to the description of 'positional warfare at the political level', but also to carry on partisan warfare, not exactly behind the enemy's lines – since there are no spatial lines at this stage – but by infiltrating everywhere and by applying the principle of total interpenetration. (The importance of clandestine work among NCOs and sailors cannot be overestimated.)

In a third phase, still too distant to speak of except hypothetically, the guerrilla detachments are transformed into a revolutionary people's army. This already controls one or more regions of the country politically, through a revolutionary party, and the popular masses are directly engaged in armed struggle, which thus ceases to be predominantly guerrilla warfare and becomes a revolutionary *civil* war in the precise sense of the term. Marxism is of course not a divinatory art, but a scientific theory and a method of analysis, and so it is almost ridiculous to claim to know now whether or not the urban proletariat will be able to seize power through insurrection before the people's army encircles the cities from the countryside. This kind of exercise, which even otherwise highly serious militants indulge in, only reveals a certain dogmatism which abandons the firm ground of concrete analysis of concrete situations for the murky waters of speculative reason. For it is impossible to predict *a priori* at what stage US imperialism might intervene to internationalize the revolutionary war. This is a very probable contingency, but, even without direct imperialist intervention, the Brazilian revolutionary war is bound to be a protracted one. What must be avoided at all costs is any form of mechanical and one-sided conception which would tend to substitute for 'neglect of the peasantry', a neglect of the proletariat, even assuming that the proletariat has to wait on the peasantry for its liberation. As Lenin said, 'the Bolsheviks must send detachments of their army everywhere'.

This is why the abstract antitheses of *Revolution in the Revolution?* must be rejected. There is no need to choose between the party and the guerrilla, between the city and the countryside, between military and political struggle. The problem is to decide on the forms in which these elements must be combined in the overall process of revolutionary struggle. The problem of *leadership*, which so preoccupies Debray, can only be solved within this process as it develops. As long as armed struggle is limited to urban partisan warfare, overall revolutionary leadership will coincide with that of the national organization (or organizations). This leadership may be situated in the city or in the countryside, but cannot be at the head of any guerrilla *foco* because no *focos* are yet possible. With the general extension of guerrilla warfare – which implies the formation of strategic detachments in the countryside – a certain separation will develop between the command of each of these detachments (which will have full political and military power in its own area) and the central leadership of the national organization, which continues to coordinate the overall struggle of rural and urban workers in all regions where there is no strategic detachment. If Debray sees dangers in this model, and possible antagonisms between the guerrilla command and the leadership of the 'party', this is because he mistakenly generalizes from highly specific experiences and situations, where certain communist parties initiated rural guerrilla actions with purely tactical and reformist perspectives, and subsequently abandoned them to their own fate. In this final stage of revolutionary civil war, where two antagonistic states confront one another, representing antagonistic social classes, and where it is possible and even probable that certain metropoles (such as São Paulo and Rio) will be directly occupied by imperialist armies (as Saigon, Vientiane and Phnom Penh are today) overall leadership of the revolutionary war will belong to the revolutionary people's army, while the political leadership will be carried on by the party – or front – of the popular classes. At that stage the only clandestine urban organizations will be those operating behind enemy lines. We are still far from this position, and it would be wrong to exclude *a priori* the hypothesis of a less painful collapse of the Brazilian bourgeois state.

IV. THE MINIMUM PROGRAMME

There is no question on which Marxism runs a greater risk of degenerating into scholastics than that of the revolutionary programme. This cannot however just be sidestepped on the pretext of avoiding pointless discussion.

Any revolutionary programme must specify, firstly, the class nature of the revolution, secondly, the tasks which the revolutionary classes must carry out, and thirdly, tactics, in the general sense of 'what is to be done' and how it is to be done. Three main programmatic lines can be distinguished within the Brazilian left.

The first maintains the national and democratic character of the revolution and includes the national bourgeoisie in the revolutionary class bloc. This tendency considers the main tasks of the Brazilian revolution at the present stage to be the national development of capitalism and the democratic transformation of relations of production in the countryside. Anti-imperialist struggle does not in this view involve anti-capitalist struggle. The two antagonistic contradictions that the revolution must resolve are that between the nation and imperialism, and that between the peasantry as a whole (including the rural bourgeoisie) and the latifundist oligarchy. According to one theorist of this tendency, 'it is only by subordinating the contradiction between the national bourgeoisie and the workers ... that we can subsist as a nation.'[3]

The second line affirms the popular character of the revolution, and includes the urban and rural middle classes in the revolutionary class bloc. For this tendency the main tasks of the present stage of the revolution are the liquidation of monopoly capitalism, the nationalization of key sectors of the economy, the democratic transformation of relations of production in the countryside, and the liquidation of the bourgeois state apparatus. The associated bourgeoisie and

---

[3] Nelson Werneck Sodré, *Introdução a revolução brasileira* (Editora Civilização Brasileira, Rio de Janeiro, 1963), p. 181.

the big national bourgeoisie are considered the counter-revolutionary classes. The urban and rural middle bourgeoisie are to be neutralized, while the intermediate sectors of the population, and the traditional urban and rural petty bourgeoisie, must be won over. The requirement of neutralizing or even winning over anti-imperialist and democratic sectors of the bourgeoisie must not interfere with that of destroying the bourgeois state apparatus. Anti-imperialist struggle therefore also involves anti-capitalist struggle, though the two must not be confused. The dominant role of the people, that is all the exploited and oppressed, applies for each stage of the revolution.

The third programmatic line proclaims the immediate proletarian and socialist character of the revolution, and only includes the peasantry and petty-bourgeoisie in the revolutionary class bloc insofar as they identify themselves politically with the proletariat. The basic task of the present stage of the Brazilian revolution is therefore the suppression of capitalist relations of production by means of proletarian dictatorship. The anti-imperialist struggle is only revolutionary insofar as it is a necessary concomitant of anti-capitalist struggle. The proletarian and socialist programme must be relied on to mobilize the masses through all stages of the revolution. The working class must ally itself not with the peasantry as a whole, but only with the agricultural proletariat and the poor peasantry. The traditional petty bourgeoisie and middle classes are only allies of the proletariat insofar as they are in the process of being proletarianized.

The polemic on the Brazilian left over the revolutionary programme is conducted mainly between these three positions. The partisans of national-democratic revolution claim that Brazil has not yet fully accomplished its capitalist development. The task of the revolution for them is therefore to sweep aside the two major obstacles to full development: international monopoly capital and the landed oligarchy. The partisans of immediate socialist revolution on the other hand maintain that Brazil is essentially capitalist, and that the major task of the revolution is to lead the workers in a struggle against the class dictatorship of the bourgeoisie as such.

Politically these two positions correspond with right wing and left wing opportunism. In concrete terms they mean the avoidance of the main question in Brazil today: how is one best to struggle against the dictatorship here and now? Asserting the historically progressive role of the national bourgeoisie reflects the need to subordinate the contradiction between labour and capital in the name of an alliance of all national forces (from which even the 'progressive latifundists' are not excluded). To reject the leading role of the urban and rural workers in the fight and the dictatorship and imperialism means in practice that one tails behind the spontaneous course of events.

The ultra-leftists succeed in avoiding the main issue by failing to distinguish between the struggle against the *present* dictatorship and the struggle against the class dictatorship of the bourgeoisie. The only difference as far as they are concerned between the military oligarchy and previous bourgeois regimes is one of greater 'unpopularity' and greater 'exposure'. The 1964 coup and the liquidation of the bourgeois republic are for them minor details. They are only concerned with the class dictatorship of the bourgeoisie which is everywhere the same and everywhere amenable to the same tactic: ideological struggle. This is not mere chance. By 'forgetting' the specific character of the present dictatorship they are unable to understand the difference between Brazil and Sweden, for instance, where the bourgeoisie is also the ruling class. In practice they restrict themselves to forms of struggle which by themselves are ineffective against a violent and oppressive dictatorship.

Setting these deviations aside, what will the motive force of the revolution be? There may well be democratic transformation of the relations of production in the countryside (as the Peruvian and Bolivian experience show), and this may up to a point have an anti-imperialist content, even though the revolutionary people (proletariat and peasantry) are not in power. But these partial accomplishments of the revolution's democratic and national tasks cannot go beyond the limits of the bourgeoisie's own class interests, especially where the bourgeoisie keeps direct control of the state apparatus.

It is quite clear that if the bourgeoisie maintains its hegemony through the national-democratic stage of the revolution, then not only will this stage not be achieved (since the bourgeoisie is historically incapable of carrying it through), but it will be divorced from the socialist stage. In other words there will not be a continuous development in which the revolution retains its democratic character while going beyond the democratic stage in the direction of socialism. For this uninterrupted development of the revolution through to socialism is only possible when there are motive forces which impel it beyond the bourgeois limits of the national-democratic stage. Marighela's remarks made in this connection in 1966, when he was still a member of the PCB leadership, are apposite here. 'The contradiction between bourgeoisie and proletariat has acquired a new dimension. This means that it is impossible to struggle against imperialism and the latifundia while continuing to cradle illusions about the leadership of the Brazilian bourgeoisie, or while abstaining from class struggle against the bourgeoisie.' The thesis of the interdependence of the anti-imperialist and anti-capitalist struggles could not be better formulated, yet

Marighela avoids falling into the ultra-leftist confusion of identifying the two struggles, which makes it impossible to win the urban and rural middle classes for the revolution. Marighela adds: 'The basic point is that the leading role of the Brazilian bourgeoisie in the revolution is not historically inevitable. ... The proletariat can exercise its hegemony in the revolution right from the start, and can struggle determinedly for this hegemony. ... This possibility does not modify the anti-feudal and anti-imperialist, national and democratic character of the revolution. It rather enables this revolution to be carried through.'[4]

Marighela makes the decisive point that the need for proletarian hegemony in the democratic revolution. Against the bourgeois materialism that has become the dominant ideology of the PCB, he returns to the Leninist thesis of the hegemonic role of the proletariat, not only at the socialist stage of the revolution but also at the present stage. His message to the 'fifteen patriots' freed in September 1969 in exchange for the US ambassador show his sensitivity to the permanent character of the Brazilian revolution. 'Our revolution is a struggle for national liberation, for the overthrow of the oligarchy that stifles us, and to attain the full economic and social development of the nation by the path of socialism.' However, there is no point in talking of socialism unless one is prepared to start from the present aspirations of the masses, and to struggle against the people's immediate enemies. 'Our path must be that of revolutionary strategy, which means overthrowing the present dictatorship. This will not be achieved through elections, nor by following the peaceful road hoping one day to arrive somehow at armed struggle. ... The dictatorship over our country will only

---

[4] Carlos Marighela, *A crise Brasileira*, 1966, p. 24.

come to an end by force.'[5] This is a completely adequate criticism of right and 'left' opportunism. Both the line of tailing behind the bourgeoisie because the revolution still has bourgeois tasks ahead, and the line of denying that there is yet such a thing as revolutionary war in Brazil,[6] show the same inability to rise to the concrete revolutionary tasks confronting the Brazilian people today. The attitude of the Brazilian opportunists (whether of the right or 'left') today is similar to that of the opportunists of the Second International, who were prepared to 'fight for socialism' but not for the immediate goal of ending an imperialist war. The rightists in Brazil pay lip service to Lenin while following Plekhanov; the ultra-leftists pay lip-service to Mao, Trotsky and Guevara only to follow Kautsky. Both these deviations must be avoided in articulating a minimum programme. What must not be forgotten however is the fundamental need to win the masses. Since any programme by its very nature lays out the goals of the struggle and not its starting point, it must be complemented with tactical slogans which will appeal directly to the masses. For it is only through their immediate aspirations and demands that the broad mass of the people can be mobilized.

The first such demand is for an end to the dictatorship and a return to democracy. As the first chapter showed, the present regime is no longer able to pretend that it is in any way democratic. In 1967 when the organizations of the left were torn by internal struggle and when the PCB, in alliance with the republican bourgeoisie, linked 'democracy' with the development of national capitalism, it was perfectly correct

---

[5] ibid., p. 25.
[6] Two texts by POC expounding this view are to be found in *Informe Nacional*, no. 15 (September 1969) and in *Document Rouge*, no. 3, under the title *'Lutte armée et lutte de classe en Amérique Latine'*.

to expose the emptiness of this demand. Once the revolutionary organizations and the people's movement as a whole took up the struggle against the regime, however, it was forced to respond with an unparalleled degree of repressive violence. In these conditions the call for liberty and democracy acquired a fundamental importance. The failure to realize this simple point makes it quite impossible to understand one of the most basic demands of the whole population. The return to democracy becomes, of course, a purely abstract slogan if it is allowed to obscure the question of which class can guarantee and deepen the exercise of democratic liberties. Nevertheless in the struggle against the present dictatorship the demand for democracy can be used to mobilize not only the peasantry, the proletariat and other exploited groups but the nationalist and anti-oligarchic sections of the bourgeoisie.

A correct minimum programme must involve firstly, the expulsion of imperialism and the liquidation of monopoly capital; secondly, the transformation of the relations of production in the countryside and thirdly, the establishment of a workers' democracy. Precisely which key sectors of the economy would be nationalized it is pointless to say in advance. The steel industry, the motor and machine tool industry, the petro-chemical industry and mining would certainly be among the first. A quantitative criteria would also be used by which businesses with more than a hundred workers would be nationalized. The banking system would be nationalized and a state monopoly established in foreign trade. The major point, however, is that workers' control of production should accompany these transformations if state socialism of the bureaucratic kind is not to develop in Brazil. The replacement of capitalist relations of production by socialist ones will mean firstly that the profit motive will cease to be the fundamental motor of the economy and will be replaced by the need to satisfy social goals, and secondly that workers' democracy will guarantee the true socialization of the means of production and not its socialization by state institutions.

The basic demands which must be articulated by all revolutionary groups in attempting to mobilize the mass of workers are as follows:

(1) Strike for higher wages to combat inflation and meet increases in productivity. Under the present regime any strike which attempted to win back gains lost in inflation would not merely be a strike for economic demands but would, like the 1968 strikes, have important political repercussions.

(2) Demand independent unions. This demand would be democratic to the extent that it involves ridding the unions of government and military personnel, guaranteeing free bargaining and preventing government intervention. It would also involve the right of all workers to vote in union elections as well as the freeing of all unionists now in gaol. The demand for freedom within the unions would be a nationalist demand insofar as it involved the expulsion of AFL-CIO representatives and an end to their 'training' of Brazilian unionists.

(3) Demand the nationalization of foreign businesses, such as utilities (electricity, telephones) and extractive industries. Accompanying this there should be the demand for strict controls on the repatriation of profits.

The main enemies of the peasantry as a whole are the latifundists and the owners of 'modern' large-scale farms. The demands of the peasants are therefore not capitalist as such but rather anti-oligarchic. They want land. The agricultural proletariat want an improvement in their living standards and working conditions. Their condition is getting constantly worse and they are ready to fight. The peasants' demands could be satisfied by different class forces. An agrarian reform carried out by the national bourgeoisie would be perfectly possible in a suitably transformed military state. But this would grant the ruling class a respite and would have entirely different political consequences from an agrarian revolution carried out by the armed people under the leadership of the proletariat and its revolutionary party.

Such a revolution could not be accomplished at once by decree. During the construction of socialism there would be at least three distinct agrarian sectors. Firstly there would be a collectivized sector comprising the largest units. These would take the form either of self-managed cooperatives or of state farms. Secondly, there would be a private sector which would result from the distribution of land to landless peasants. The size of this sector would depend on the relationship between different social classes after the revolution, but it would have to be limited as far as possible to land whose crops did not involve the heavy use of capital equipment and which could not benefit from economies of scale. This sector would also extend wherever immediate collectivization was politically or economically impossible. Thirdly, there would be a market sector of small and medium sized farms. The state would have to control the development of this sector not only by fiscal and monetary means but also by equalizing profits (through the expropriation of differential rent to prevent the development of capitalist production).

Organizational work in the country at the present stage of the struggle should focus on the expropriation of unproductive latifundia and land owned by foreigners living abroad. The federal government would have no difficulty in liquidating the latifundists merely by forcing them to pay their taxes. The land that became available should be turned over to poor peasants for subsistence agriculture or to the state to be run as co-operatives. Together with this demand there are other ways, already mentioned, of mobilizing the peasantry in struggle. Speaking on Havana radio before he was killed by the Brazilian police last year, Câmara Ferreira said: 'The struggle must be taken into the countryside. Cattle must be killed and the meat distributed to the people. Sharecroppers must refuse to pay the latifundists the required third or half of their production, and labourers must sabotage the production of all latifundists who refuse to grant wage increases.'

Among the growing concentrations of agricultural workers revolutionary work should concentrate on the demand for equal treatment. The main objective should be a minimum salary applicable throughout the country as a whole, and the establishment of rural unions. The government has in some cases begun to set these up and where it has, in São Paulo and Paraná, revolutionary work can be conducted within them. Where there are no unions they must be organized.

The final requirement of the minimum programme is for the hegemony of the proletariat in the town and in the country. By the proletariat we mean the class of wage-earners whose core is the industrial working class. By the dictatorship of the proletariat we mean the political hegemony of this class and not the control of the state apparatus by the workers' party. The one does indeed imply the other but only in principle. There can be no such thing as workers' democracy unless the unions are independent of the state and unless there is freedom for all tendencies within socialism. During the construction of socialism the main task of the revolutionary Marxist party is not administering the state or running the economy but rather fighting as an *avantgarde* for the construction of a communist society. It is not only the relationship between the working class and the other oppressed classes but also the relationship between the

Marxist tendencies and the bureaucratic tendencies in the revolutionary movement which will decide eventually what type of regime will replace the present dictatorship and lead the transition to socialism.

## V. PERSPECTIVES FOR THE REVOLUTION

The unifying theme of this book has been that armed struggle in Brazil is not the adventure of a handful of radicals. The dangers of adventurism, however, must be repeatedly stressed, for there is a risk that the armed organizations will be wiped out before guerrilla warfare can be generalized. The 'surround-and-destroy' mission is at its height, and to underestimate the strength of the government at this stage could lead to disasters like Cuzco, Nacahuasu, and Caparáo. The army and the police have failed in their declared aim to 'crush subversion' but they have scored tactical successes. The government's response to the kidnapping of the Japanese consul should be cited as an example of what such tactical successes can involve. The casualties suffered by the VPR as a result of the massive search by the police and the army were not justified by the political gains of the kidnapping. Moreover the police learnt from those arrested the existence of an important VPR training camp in the Vale de Ribeira in the Southern part of São Paulo state. In this poor region, relatively hilly and wooded, where immigrants of Japanese origin cultivate bananas and a local variety of tea, the VPR had several military cadres working and had built up a clandestine support network. All indications show however that this was not intended as a *foco* but simply as a training zone. It should not need pointing out that given the present military initiative of the enemy it was a mistake to concentrate weapons and valuable cadres in a region less than three hundred kilometres from São Paulo.

The region was encircled in mid-April and bombarded with napalm. Some VPR militants were captured though the majority managed to break the encirclement.

The rapidity and ferocity of the armed forces' intervention shows yet again that present conditions in Brazil do not permit the survival of isolated bases of 'red power' in the countryside and that consequently the formation of mobile strategic detachments is more than ever dependent on the overall situation of class struggle and revolutionary war. Secondly the claim that a *foco* will serve as a tactical instrument inspiring the urban masses to struggle has also been disproved. These positive lessons were drawn from the disaster and the failure of the Vale da Ribeira experiment has paradoxically strengthened the urban guerrilla. Nevertheless if the guerrillas now solidly entrenched (the ALN, the VPR, the VAR/Palmares and others less prominent) are to survive and broaden the struggle certain conditions must be met.

Unless an upsurge of the mass movement comes to relieve the revolutionary fighters, unless there is considerable progress in the reorganization of the popular forces on a national scale, unless the vanguard organizations understand that the military initiative of the counter-revolution is not an isolated event but depends on the balance of forces between the dictatorship and the people; unless in short the revolutionary forces respond tactically in the present situation according to the slogan 'retreat in breadth to advance in depth' then there is a real danger that armed struggle begun in 1968 may end with the death of a whole generation of revolutionaries.

Any change in the present situation will depend on three things: Firstly, whether the regime's increasingly nationalist stance is a sign of a genuine change of policy or not; secondly, on whether or not there will be an upsurge of the mass movement as there was in 1968 and thirdly, on the revolutionary movement itself.

Both military and political work must be developed in the cities. The struggle must be carried on both clandestinely and among the masses, mobilizing them around the tactical slogans against the dictatorship for democracy and socialism. Work in the countryside must aim at the widespread construction of peasant cells and the eventual generalization of guerrilla warfare. The transition to armed actions in the country should only be made when the clandestine infrastructure is secure and support has been won among the peasants.

Finally, the revolutionary left must become united since it is only its fragmentation which prevents it from posing a real threat to the established order. To accomplish this, the small organizations which have resulted from the numerous splits of the last few years must reorganize around the strongest and most consistent. Next the different fighting organizations must unite around a minimum anti-oligarchic and anti-imperialist programme. The extent to which this will be socialist and the extent to which Marxist-Leninists win hegemony will depend on the development of workers' struggles and the concrete role which Marxist-Leninist *fighters* play in this unification. Lastly there must be the formation of a vast anti-imperialist and anti-oligarchic front, organizing all the democrats and socialists – all those really opposed to the regime – even if they are not fighting for socialism but only against the regime.

The revolutionaries must continue with all these tasks. It is not only the liberation of the Brazilian people that is at stake. The struggle in Brazil is part of a world-wide struggle against imperialism. Victory is not inevitable because it is not inevitable that socialism will triumph.

# Appendix
# Parties and Organizations

AL *Aliança Liberal* (Liberal Alliance). Pact formed for 1930 election led by Vargas and leaders from southern states. Joined by PDP in opposition to the Paulist Republicans.

ALN *Ação Libertadora Nacional* (Action for National Liberation). Started in late 1967 as the São Paulo Communist grouping, led by Carlos Marighela, an ex-member of the PCB's Executive Committee. In 1967 Marighela broke openly with the PCB on the question of the peaceful road. The party refused to send a delegate to the OLAS conference in Havana in August where the slogan of armed struggle was launched. Marighela went himself and broadcast to Brazilians a call to arms over Havana radio. On his return he resigned from the PCB taking with him militants who were to form ALN. In February 1968 they called for the launching of armed struggle in the cities and carried out the kidnapping of the US Ambassador in September 1969 and the Swiss Ambassador in December 1970. Marighela was killed by police in November 1969 and his successor Câmara Ferreira was killed in October 1970. Nevertheless the ALN together with the VPR/VAR remains the strongest and most active of the clandestine organizations. However, it too contains a political tendency (committed to national liberation) and a militarist tendency. In 1970 it drew close to the new VPR.

ANL *Aliança Nacional Libertadora*, see **PCB**.

AP *Ação Popular* (Popular Action). Leftist Catholic movement active in North East.

ARENA *Aliança Nacional Renovadora* (Alliance for National

Renewal). Government party under the military dictatorship.

**CGT** *Comando Geral dos Trabalhadores* (General Workers' Executive). Union set up by Goulart in 1962 to circumvent the CNTI.

**CNTI** *Confederacão Nacional dos Trabalhadores* (National Confederation of Industrial Workers). The official union organization controlling all legal unions. Under direction of Ministry of Labour.

**COLINA** *Comando da Libertação Nacional* (National Liberation Commando). Armed organization formed in 1967 from Minas and Rio groups within POLOP. It was around COLINA that VAR-Palmares was formed in July 1969.

**CTB** *Confederação dos Trabalhadores Brasileiros* (Confederation of Brazilian Workers). Set up by the PCB in 1945 as an independent union body. Banned in 1947.

**MDB** *Movimento Democratico Brasileiro* (Brazilian Democratic Movement). The opposition party under the military dictatorship.

**MNR** *Movimento Nacionalista Revolucionario* (Revolutionary Nationalist Movement). A movement which never really came into existence. The revolutionary nationalist were a group composed mainly of ex-soldiers and sailors expelled from the forces after the 1964 coup. They took their inspiration from Brizola and the Jacobin left. In an issue of *O Panfleto* (Brizola's old newspaper) for May 1966 they published a manifesto calling for armed opposition to the dictatorship and for national liberation. They used their underground military organization to launch the Caparao foco which was surrounded and crushed. Plans to launch the MNR foundered and the 'survivors' went to join armed organizations in the cities. In São Paulo they merged with the POLOF opposition and in Rio de Janeiro (Guanabara state) they formed MAR or MR-26.

**MR-8** *Movimento Revolucionario-8* (Revolutionary Movement of the Eighth). A dissident group from the PCB centred in Rio Grande do Sul and Paraná which took up armed struggle in October 1968. They attempted to set up a foco but their network was penetrated by the police. They survived and worked with the ALN.

**MR-26** (or **MAR**) *Movimento Revolucionario-26* (Revolutionary Movement of the 26th). So called after the Cuban organization which commemorated in its name Castro's attack on the Moncada barracks on 26 July 1953, also known as *Movimento Armada Revolucionario*. A group formed by Rio veterans of MNR attempted to organize a foco in Angra dos Reis but were surrounded. They merged with the PCBR in 1969 and were active in Rio in 1970.

**PCB** *Partido Communista Brasileiro* (Brazilian Communist Party). Founded 1922. After the collapse of the São Paulo uprising in July 1924 Luís Carlos Prestes led a guerrilla band into the countryside to 'keep the revolution alive in the interior'. Committed to the peaceful road in 1935 the PCB organized the *Aliança Nacional Libertadora* (ANL: National Liberation Alliance), a popular front. It was disbanded in May when it posed a direct threat to Vargas. In November the militant wing of the party organized revolts in the garrisons of Natal and Recife. The risings were uncoordinated and so easily crushed that Vargas's provocation was suspected. A state of siege was declared and the left leadership imprisoned. Prestes escaped but was captured in May 1936 and sentenced to forty-six years prison. The PCB emerged again in April 1945 with Prestes, amnestied, at its head. It supported Vargas's campaign and itself won fifteen seats in the Congressional elections of December, but after mounting a campaign of opposition to the Dutra regime it was again outlawed in May 1947. Communists were purged from government offices. During the fifties and early sixties the PCB continued to work in the unions. In July 1962 the Communist dominated CGT organized strikes in support of Goulart. The PCB also carried out work among peasants in the North East in competition with the Catholic church and the peasant leagues of Francisco Julião. Despite widescale mobilization of support for Goulart in March 1964 the PCB was quite unprepared for the 1964 coup. Its leadership was suppressed by the military regime and its political decomposition began in the years immediately afterwards.

**PCBR** *Partido Communista Brasileiro Revolucionario* (Brazilian Revolutionary Communist Party). Broke away from the PC do B on the question of methods of work, under the leadership of Jacob Gorender and Mario Alves. At the start of armed struggle the PCBR denounced it as an 'infantile disorder' but it took to arms itself in 1969 when its organization in Rio merged with militants in MR-26. It has also engaged in work among the agricultural workers in the North East.

**PC do B** *Partido Communista do Brasil* (Communist Party of Brazil). Formed in 1962 when a pro-Chinese faction led by Joaõ Amazonas and Mauricio Grabois broke away from the PCB on the question of the party programme. The PC do B rejected Prestes's united front policy and called for revolutionary organization among the peasantry. Militants from this group themselves split off in 1966 to form the PCR (*Partido Communista Revolucionario*) which has engaged in work among the sugar cane workers in the North East. The ALA (Red Wing) broke in 1966 as well and took up armed struggle, but its organization was smashed by the police in 1969. Some survivors joined VAR-Palmares, some the VPR and some the ALN.

**PDP** *Partido Democratica Paulista* (São Paulo Democratic Party). Allied with Vargas in 1930 election. Joined with PRP in 1932.

**POC** *Partido Operario Communista* (Communist Workers' Party). Formed in 1967. Combined cadres from POLOP in Rio Grande do Sul and PCB dissidents. For a long time it represented an ultra-leftist tendency favouring ideological struggle particularly among students. In Spring 1970 a majority was formally recognized for armed struggle, and POC moved close to VAR-Palmares.

**POLOP** *Política Operária* (Workers' Politics). Formed in 1961 to re-group the left outside the PCB. Active among workers and students, it was committed to a minimum programme and building up of strength among the working class. At the São Paulo Congress in September 1967 the party split on the question of armed struggle. The majority dismissed it and argued rather for the construction of a revolutionary party. The minority was for armed action. This latter group was divided on a regional basis: in São Paulo they became known as the POLOP opposition and merged later with survivors from the MNR to form the VPR. In Minas Gerais those for armed struggle were in the majority. They joined later in the year with POLOP members from Rio de Janeiro (Guanabara state) to form COLINA.

**PRP** *Partido Republicano Paulista* (São Paulo Republican Party). Opponents of Vargas in 1930 election. Allied with PDP in Constitutionalist rebellion 1932.

**PSD** *Partido Social-Democratico* (Social Democratic Party). Established 1945. Getulist, with backing of rural oligarchy.

**PTB** *Partido Trabalhista Brasileiro* (Brazilian Labour Party). Established 1945 to organize labour movement.

**UDN** *União Democratico Nacional* (National Democratic Union). Established 1945. Anti-Getulist coalition of middle class and political bosses.

**UNE** *União Nacional dos Estudantes* (National Union of Students).

**VAR-Palmares** *Vanguarda Armada Revolucionaria-Palmares* (Armed Revolutionary Vanguard-Palmares). Named after the black slave republic of Palmares in the seventeenth century. In July 1969 remnants from the VPR and other organizations which had been penetrated by the police earlier in the year regrouped around COLINA. VAR-Palmares split again in September 1969 into a Leninist group (from COLINA mainly and from the old POLOP opposition) which kept the name of VAR and in 1970 began to work with the militant wing of POC, and a militarist group under Captain Lamarca (mainly 'focists' from COLINA, and MNR veterans) which took the name of VPR again. After kidnapping the Japanese Consul from São Paulo in March 1970 the leadership was arrested. A VPR training camp was discovered in the Vale de Ribeira in May, encircled and napalmed. The majority escaped from the country to return to urban work where they kidnapped the German Ambassador and exchanged him for forty of their militants. In July 1970 Lamarca signed a join communique with Ferreira of the ALN. Later in December the VPR (and ALN) kidnapped the Swiss ambassador and exchanged him for seventy prisoners.

VPR *Vanguardia Popular Revolucionaria* (Revolutionary People's Vanguard). In March 1968 the POLOP opposition from São Paulo began armed actions with ex-soldiers and sailors from the MNR. The armed organization which emerged took the name of VPR in December 1968. Because of its origins the VPR was severely split between Leninists and militarists. Its organization was smashed by the police campaign of December 1968/January 1969, but its survivors joined VAR-Palmares in July 1969.

# Index

AL (Liberal Alliance), 13, 21-3, 239
ALA (Red Wing), 242
Aleixo, Pedro, 82
ALN (National Liberation Action), 83, 163 and n, 181, 195-6, 202, 204-6, 213-20, 237, 239-42
ALN-MR 8, 148
Alvarado, Juan Velasco, 112
Alves, Marcio Moreira, 79
Alves, Mario, 216, 242
Amazonas state, 91, 131, 173
Amazonas, João, 242
Américo, José, 25, 37
Angra dos Reis forests, 174-5, 241
ANL (Alliance for National Liberation), 13, 24, 241
Antônio, Marco, 216
AP (Popular Action), 138-41, 196, 220, 239
Aragão, General Moniz, 81-2
Aranha, Oswaldo, 25, 37
ARENA (National Alliance for Renovation), 15, 66n, 74, 78, 79, 84, 239-40
Arismendi, Rodney, 159
armed propaganda, 191-200, 211-212; generalized, 196; local, 196, 198, 200
army, the, 13, 15, 20-2, 26, 30, 33-8, 45, 47, 49-55, 57-61, 64-6, 74-8, 80-6, 89, 97-102, 104-14, 117-8, 120, 136, 143-7, 164-6, 175-6, 182, 187-9, 191, 201, 207, 213-4, 216, 233, 236
Arraes, Miguel, 52

Bahia, 137
Barrientos, René, 112
Barros, Adhemar de, 33, 37, 41, 54, 66, 108
Bejar, Hector, 172, 206
Belo Horizonte, 11, 18, 27, 33, 117, 143, 204, 212
Blanco, Hugo, 172
Bonaparte, Louis, 153
Borges, Mauro, 54, 58
bourgeoisie, 20-4, 39-42, 44, 46, 51, 58-9, 61, 64, 72-5, 77-9, 89, 96, 100-5, 107-8, 111-12, 115-17, 120, 136, 152, 170-1, 183, 185, 193, 207, 226, 228-34; associated with imperialism, 34, 103-6, 226-227; big, 62, 64-5, 68, 94, 116, 140, 227; big coffee, 86-8; democratic, 78, 183, 227; industrial, 86, 96, 106, 136; liberal, 28; national, 37, 64, 78, 139, 202, 226, 232-4; new national, 105; republican, 59, 61, 79, 231; rural, 93, 226, 227; urban, 25, 227
bourgeois democracy, 19, 28, 62, 65, 226-7
bourgeois press, 72, 164, 187, 193
Brazilian Rural Society, 53
Brasilia, 14, 42, 50, 82, 142-4, 148, 150-1, 195
Brazilian Socialist Party, 31
Brizola, Leonel, 45, 47-54, 115, 138-140, 156, 240
Bucher (Swiss Ambassador), 197, 239, 244

Buzaid, Alfredo, 85

Câmara, Archbishop Dom Helder, 211
Campos, Milton, 67
Campos, Roberto, 62-3, 73, 76, 102, 106
Caparáo mountains, 157-8, 169, 174, 236
Capitane, Aveline, 216
Cardoso, Adaúto, 55, 74
Cardozo, General Espírito Santo, 38
Castelo Branco, General Humberto de Alencar, 15, 51, 54-5, 57-62, 64-7, 72-4, 76, 93-5, 100, 102
Castro, Fidel, 64, 241
Castro, Josué de, 137
catholic church, the, 75, 153, 211, 239, 241
CCC (Communist Pursuit Commando), 145-7, 191, 193, 211
cessionism, 96, 99-102
CGT (General Workers Executive), 15, 48-9, 52-3, 55, 115-16, 240, 241
Chandler, Captain, 197
CNTI (National Confederation of Industrial Workers), 15, 28, 48, 240
coffee, 13, 19-21, 25, 32-4, 39, 87-8, 137
'Cohen plan', 25-6 and n
COLINA (National Liberation Commando), 81, 192, 204-5, 217, 240, 243; see also VAR/Palmares
Colonos, 69, 134
Communism, 41, 54
Congress, 14-16, 24-6, 45, 48-54, 57-61, 66-8, 73-4, 78-9, 83, 93, 101, 107, 140-1
Côno Sur, 157
Conselheiro, Antonio, 135 and n
Contra o arrôcho ('against the freeze'), 117, 122
Costa, General Zenóbio, da, 38
Costa e Silva, General, 15-16, 54-5, 57, 60, 65-6, 71-7, 79, 81-4, 90, 105
Counter-revolution, 51, 108, 155, 156, 158, 185-9, 201, 205, 211-15; armed, 139
Communist Party, see PCB
Communist Party of Brazil see PC do B
Cruzada Democratica, 36-8, 41
CTB (Confederation of Brazilian Workers), 32, 240
Cuba, 44, 47, 155, 158, 159; revolution, 47, 49, 167-8, 170
Cuzco, 236

Dantas, San Tiago, 48, 52
Death Squadron, 186-8
Debray, Régis, 112, 145, 155, 161, 167-8, 171-2, 175-6, 177, 202, 205-6, 222, 225
'Denationalization', 99-105
devaluation, 20, 44, 117
Dutra, General Enrico Gaspar, 14, 29, 32-3, 241

Eisenhower administration, 37, 43
Elbrick, Burke (American Ambassador), 9, 83, 148, 174, 203, 213-214, 230, 239
elections, 14, 23, 29, 31-2, 64, 65-6, 230; congressional, 13-15, 24, 29, 32, 66, 241; gubernatorial, 15, 58, 60, 65, 68; municipal, 78; presidential, 13, 15, 21, 25, 30, 32-4, 37, 41-4, 51, 54, 58-9, 61, 65, 83
Espírito Santo state, 137
Estado Nova, 14, 19, 22, 26-9 and n, 31, 34, 40

factory committees, 121
favelados, 18, 134-5, 150-2, 198, 216
Ferreira, Câmara, 235, 239, 243
Filho, General Café, 14, 41, 53
Firmino, João, 137
Fleury, Sergio Paranhos, 187
foco, 155, 157-8, 166, 171-9, 184, 189, 202, 204, 208, 222, 237, 240; Angra dos Reis, 216; Caparáo, 157-8, 240; guerrilla, 156, 164, 168-9, 171-2, 174, 180, 184, 224-225; 'insurrectional', 157, 184;

## Index

military, 168; preparation of, 172, 174–7; rural, 156, 158, 168, 180–181
foreign investment, 31, 34, 42–3, 45–6, 51, 101, 234; North American, 48, 64, 101, 130
Frei, Eduardo, 106
*Frente Ampla*, 15, 74–6, 160
Furtado, Celso, 15, 50, 90

Garrastazu Medici, 83–5, 90, 113, 152, 187
getulism, 22, 30–1, 41, 46, 75, 114, 116; anti- 39, 243; *see* Vargas
Goiás state, 58, 60, 131, 173
Gomes, Eduardo, 14, 26
Gorender, Jacob, 160, 242
Goulart, João, 14–15, 19, 26, 37–8, 41–55, 57, 59, 61, 69, 71, 108, 114–16, 240, 241
Grabois, Mauricio, 242
Guanabara state, 49, 53, 59, 80, 148n, 186, 240
Guanabara Communist Opposition, 213–14
guerrilla warfare, 123, 135, 155, 169, 179, 221–2, 225, 236, 238; rural, 165–80, 183, 189, 191, 195, 205, 207; urban, 16, 80, 110, 159, 180–200, 206, 209, 237
Guevara, Che, 78, 120, 155, 161, 168–71, 181–3, 206, 231
Guimaraes, Captain, 180

IBRA (Brazilian Institute for Agrarian Reform), 95
imperialism, 35–6, 39–43, 45, 50, 55, 63, 83, 86, 96, 98–9, 103–4, 109, 111, 113, 124–5, 136, 143, 148, 219, 225–6, 229–30, 232, 238; North American, 71, 109, 113, 116, 224; *see* monopoly capitalism
import substitution, 96, 99
industrialization, 23, 25–7, 31, 33–4, 39, 42, 60, 89, 97, 114
inflation, 14, 36–8, 39–40, 43, 46, 50, 62–4, 100, 116, 124, 233
*Integralistas*, 24, 26
'Interventors', 27

Julião, Francisco, 46, 137–8, 241

Kautsky, Karl, 231
Kennedy, John F., 47
Kruel, General Amaury, 55
Kubitschek, Juscelino, 14, 19, 41–7, 58–9, 62, 100

Lacerda, Carlos, 38–9, 41, 44, 53, 54, 59, 74–5
Lafer, Horácio, 34
Lamarca, Captain, 215, 217, 243
Lampião (Virgulino Ferreira da Silva), 135 and n
Latifundists, 23–4, 31–3, 36, 39–40, 48–9, 53, 54, 62, 68–70, 86, 89–95, 114, 116, 126–30, 132n, 132–3, 136, 138, 182, 226, 228–9, 233–5; super-, 131–2
Leal, Estillac, 36
Lenin, 109, 123, 169, 179, 190, 191, 220, 224, 230, 231
Lima, General Albuquerque, 82–4, 110–11
Lira Tavares, Marshal, 81, 82
loans, imperialist, 88–9; US, 27, 50
Lopes, General Machado, 45
Lott, General Henrique, 14, 41, 43
Luis, Edson, 142
Luiz, Washington, 13, 21

MAC (Anti-Communist Movement), 146, 211
MacNamara, Robert, 192–3
Mao tse Tung, 231
MAR, *see* MR-26
Maranhão state, 60
marginals, the, 150–4
Maria, José, 135–6
Marighela, Carlos, 159–60, 162–4 and n, 187, 196, 202, 204, 207, 214–15, 218n, 229–30 and n, 239
Marx, 80
Mato Grosso state, 92n, 131, 173
'Matos, Colonel Meira, 74
MASERT, 138
Medici, *see* Garrastazu
MDB (Brazilian Democratic Movement), 15, 65n, 66, 79, 83, 240

Melo, Souza, 82
Meneghetti, Ildo, 54
middle class, 18–24, 35–8, 45–6, 52, 58, 62, 75–6, 113, 219, 227, 243
Military Club, 36
military coups, 14–15, 30, 47, 55
Minas Gerais state, 19–20, 22, 28–9, 53–4, 59, 67, 80–1, 118–20, 137–8, 148n, 157n, 161–2, 164, 182, 189n, 192, 240, 243
mining, 17, 18–19, 98, 232
MNR (Revolutionary Nationalist Movement), 157–8, 162, 174, 240–241, 243–4; survivors, 161, 174; *see also* POLOP opposition/MNR
Monje, Mario, 206
monopoly capitalism, 226, 232; foreign, 71, 104, 113; international, 34, 45–6, 71, 86, 88–9, 91, 96–8, 100–6, 109, 228; North American, 62–3, 91, 100–1, 192; state, 96, 100, 104–5, 108
Monteiro, General Góes, 17, 30
Mota, Admiral, 53
*Movimento de Educação de Base* (Movement for Basic Education), 49
MR-8 (Revolutionary Movement of 8 October), 172–4, 240–1
MR-26 (Revolutionary Movement of 26 July, or MAR, Revolutionary Action Movement), 172–4, 216, 241–2

Nacahuasu, 236
Natal, 13, 24, 241
nationalization, 15, 24, 27, 47, 102–3, 115, 232–3; of foreign companies, 233; of oil, 35
Neto, Delfim, 108
Neves da Fontoura, 38
Neves, Tancredo, 15, 48
Niedergang, Marcel, 214
Niteroi, 173

Okuchi (Japanese Consul), 197, 236, 243
Onganía, Carlos, 117
Osasco, 115, 119–21, 143, 209

Ovando, General Alfredo Candía, 112

Pacecho, Gregorio, 117
PAEG, the (Plan of Government Economic Action), 71
Pais de Almeida, 43
Paraíba state, 22, 92n
Paraná state, 22n, 134–5, 172, 173, 235, 240–1
partisan warfare, 205, 208; peasant, 222; localized, 222; urban, 200, 205, 212, 219, 222–4
*Paulistas*, 25, 239
PCB (Brazilian Communist Party), 13–14, 21, 24, 30–3, 46, 48–52, 74–5, 102, 114–16, 139–42, 163n, 172, 202, 203, 220, 229–31, 239–42
PCBR (Brazilian Revolutionary Communist Party), 159–60, 175, 216, 241–2
PC do B (Communist Party of Brazil, pro-Chinese), 205, 218, 242
PCR (Revolutionary Communist Party), 242
PDC (Christian Democrats), 59
PDP (São Paulo Democratic Party), 13, 239, 243
peasant cells, 177, 238
Peasant Leagues, 46, 49, 52, 137–8, 171–2, 182, 241; congress of, 138
peasants, 18, 20, 22, 46, 60, 69, 89, 91–4, 97, 115, 126–39, 148, 150–3, 170–2, 175–84, 189, 198, 219, 224, 226–9, 232–4, 238, 241; 'Galiléia', 139; movements, 50, 62, 69, 77, 92, 94, 95, 146, 182; struggles, 22, 53, 135–9, 181
Pedro II, Emperor, 13
Pele, 152
People's army, 167, 189, 221, 223–234
People's war, 176–8, 194, 221
Peredo brothers, 206
Perón, Juan, 30, 38, 40, 117
Pernambuco state, 46, 52
petty bourgeoise, 54, 96, 227; rural, 126; urban, 33, 108, 143–4
Pinto, Margalhães, 54, 76

*Plano de Metas*, 71
plebiscite, 15, 26, 49, 52; constitutional, 50
Plekhanov, Georgy, 231
POC (Communist Workers Party), 149, 204, 215, 220, 231, 242
police, 16, 25, 37, 59, 68, 72, 67, 78, 80, 110n, 118, 141, 144–7, 162–4, 173–5, 180, 182, 185–7, 193–4, 198, 213, 215–16, 236, 239–44; military, 142; secret, 27; terrorism and, 26, 191–200
POLOP (Worker's Politics), 141–2, 158–62, 240–4
POLOP opposition/MNR, 163–6, 172, 175–7, 193, 207, 243
Popular Mobilization Front, 139
population, 11, 17–18, 32, 90, 97, 99, 126–32; rural, 129, 150; urban, 129, 150
POR (Revolutionary Workers Party), 142
Portela, General, 82
Pôrto Alegre, 11, 212
Prestes, Julio, 13, 21
Prestes, Luís Carlos, 13, 21, 24, 50, 203, 204, 241
Prestes de Paula, Antonio, 174
proletariat, 117, 120, 153, 178, 227–229, 230–2, 234–5; agricultural, 136, 181–2, 227, 233; dictatorship of the, 227, 235; urban, 422
propaganda, 72, 120, 121, 125, 137, 143, 208, 222; *see also* armed propaganda
PRP (São Paulo Republican Party), 13, 243
PSD (Social Democratic Party), 14, 30–4, 41, 43–4, 47, 48, 50, 54, 59, 66, 243
PSP (Social Progressive Party), 37, 41, 59, 66; of São Paulo, 33
PTB (Brazilian Labour Party), 14, 30–4, 36, 41, 42–4, 45–7, 59, 66, 114–16, 243

Quadros, Jânio, 14, 19, 37–8, 43–6, 58, 62

Rademaker, Admiral, 82, 84
Recife, 11, 13, 18, 24, 211, 241
reform, agrarian, 15, 47–52, 68, 89, 93–5, 135–6, 234; land, 15, 54, 68–70, 95, 233–4
revolts, Sailor's, 15, 53, 119, 174, 216; Sergeants', 14, 51, 53, 110, 174, 216
Revolutionary Nationalists, 156
Ribeiro da Costa, 60
Rio Grande do Sul state, 18, 22, 37, 45, 47–9, 53–4, 133, 138, 148n, 156, 240, 242

Sailor's revolt, *see* revolts
Salgado, Plinio, 14, 108
Salinas, Siles, 112
Salles Oliveira, Armando de, 25
Salvador, 11, 18
Santa Catarina state, 22n, 135
Santo Domingo, 74
São Bernardo, 196
Schilling, Paulo, 84, 99n, 100, 132n, 133 and n, 138
Sergeants' revolt, *see* revolts
Silva, José Gomes da, 69
SNI (National Information Service), 68, 80, 83, 187
strikes, 13–15, 32, 37, 47, 50, 68, 72, 117–20, 122, 233; general, 48–53
students, 15, 49, 75, 78, 80–1, 119, 139–50, 196, 211, 243; demonstrations, 29; movement, 15, 49, 78, 81, 139–50, 160, 211
SUDENE (North East Development Scheme), 14
sugar, 17, 25, 94, 125n, 130
suffrage, 14–15, 24, 32, 52, 59–61, 65, 68, 83, 115
SUPRA (Superintendency of Agrarian Reform), 69
Supreme Revolutionary Council, 54

*Tenente* rebellions, 13, 20–3, 25
terrorism, 191–200
Terry, Belaunde, 112
*trabalhismo*, 29 and n, 37, 40, 114
trade unions, 19, 23–4, 28, 31–2, 39,

trade unions—*cont.*
   43–4, 46–8, 107, 116–21, 123, 140, 192, 211, 233, 235, 240–1; peasant, 182; rural, 235
Trotsky, 231
trotskyists, 138, 158
Tupamaros (MLN), 199–200

UDN (National Democratic Union) 14, 30–5, 37–8, 41, 43–6, 54, 59, 66, 243
UEE (state students' union), 145
UNE (National Union of Students), 49, 78, 81, 140, 147, 243
US government, 'aid', 92, 143, 148; economic relations with Brazil, 64; Eisenhower administration, 43; Kennedy administration, 44; loans, 27, 50; political relations with Brazil, 14, 30, 36, 44, 214

Vale de Ribeira, 237, 243
Vargas, Getúlio, 13–14, 19, 21–41, 44–5, 49, 114, 136, 239, 241–3
VAR-Palmares, 202, 211, 217–18, 220, 237, 240–4; *see also* COLINA and VPR
*volante*, 134–5, 177; *see also* working class, agricultural
Von Holleben (German Ambassador), 197, 243
VPR (Revolutionary People's Vanguard), 81, 204–5, 208–11, 217–18, 236–7, 242; 'new', 218, 221, 239; *see also* VAR/Palmares

Wages, 36, 38, 43, 46, 50, 62–3, 116–17, 119, 121, 124, 235
wheat, 18, 44, 87, 93, 99
working class, 19, 22, 24, 26–32, 37–40, 43, 46, 48–9, 52, 65, 75, 96, 115–25, 141, 143, 149, 152–4, 160, 168, 181–2, 192, 198, 219, 223, 226, 228, 233, 235, 238, 242; agricultural, 94, 128, 134, 173, 177, 182, 227, 233, 235, 242, see *also volante*; democracy and, 232–233; industrial, 33, 97, 151; militants and, 50; rural, 23, 200; urban, 59, 138, 182, 226, 228